NICHOLAS I
PATRIARCH
OF CONSTANTINOPLE

MISCELLANEOUS WRITINGS

GREEK TEXT AND ENGLISH TRANSLATION

by

L. G. WESTERINK

Dumbarton Oaks
Center for Byzantine Studies
Trustees for Harvard University
Washington, District of Columbia
1981

Manufactured in the United States of America by
Sheridan Books, Inc., 450 Fame Avenue, Hanover, PA 17331 | (717) 632-3535

LIBRARY OF CONGRESS CATALOGING IN PUBLICATION DATA
Nicholas I, Patriarch of Constantinople : miscellaneous writings
Greek text and English translation by L. G. Westerink
(Dumbarton Oaks texts ; 6) (Corpus Fontium Historiae Byzantinae ; 20)
Greek text with English translation.
Includes bibliographical references and index.

ISBN 978-0-88402-089-9 (first clothbound: alkaline paper)
ISBN 978-0-88402-447-7 (first paperbound: alkaline paper)
LCCN: 80-70736

*In accordance with the rules adopted by the
International Commission
for the Edition of Sources of Byzantine History,
the text and translation of this volume have been verified
by Cyril Mango.*

EU GPSR Authorised Representative
LOGOS EUROPE, 9 rue Nicolas Poussin, 17000, La Rochelle, France
E-mail: Contact@logoseurope.eu

PREFACE

The present volume is a supplement to *Nicholas I, Patriarch of Constantinople: Letters,* DOT, II (Washington, D. C., 1973). It includes everything else known to be extant: decrees and other documents, a few letters that have been preserved otherwise than by regular manuscript tradition, a sermon, extracts from a treatise on the tetragamy, and finally five hymns, for which, however, Nicholas' authorship is doubtful, and in two cases even extremely unlikely.

For the biographical introduction customary in the CFHB, the reader is referred to the *Letters,* pp. xv–xxvii.

The collations of the numerous manuscripts used were mostly done from microfilms made available to me by the Institut de Recherche et d'Histoire des Textes and the Institut Français d'Etudes Byzantines. For this, as well as for other help and guidance generously offered, I have to thank Mme Gilberte Astruc, R. P. Joseph Paramelle, and R. P. Jean Darrouzès. In dealing with the *Tome of Union,* M. Jean Gouillard's edition of the *Synodicon Orthodoxiae* has been most useful.

A special word of thanks is due to Dr. Enrica Follieri and Msgr. Paul Canart for helpful information in the field of hymnology, and to Prof. Krikor Maksoudian for kindly allowing me to reproduce his translation of the Letter to the Catholicus and for verifying the Armenian text. Prof. Cyril Mango, the CFHB revisor, contributed many valuable hints and corrections; finally, Dr. Timothy Miller's care in preparing the typescript for the press and Miss Julia Warner's and Mrs. Nancy Bowen's painstaking revision of the proofs should be gratefully acknowledged.

TABLE OF CONTENTS

CRITICAL INTRODUCTION

I. QUESTIONS OF AUTHORSHIP

The question of authorship arises with regard to two categories of texts included in this volume: the documents and the hymns.

Apart from the Letter to Andronicus Ducas (Op. **193**), which may be a deliberate forgery, there is no reason to doubt the authenticity of any of the prose works. This does not exclude, however, the possibility that some were not written by Nicholas, but for him by one or more secretaries. I incline to the view that Nicholas preferred to compose himself all his important documents (in particular, the *Tome of Union*). The correspondence reminds us that we have to do with a man who was for many years imperial secretary before he became patriarch; one who writes (or dictates) with great ease and speed, who is obviously aware of his gift for literary composition, and who might have resented leaving so important and agreeable a task to others less qualified. From the point of view of style the small collection is sufficiently homogeneous to support this assumption.

The case of the hymns is entirely different. Three of them are attributed explicitly, and independently, to a patriarch Nicholas. The fact that no distinctive name is added does not necessarily mean that the first is meant: the canonical decisions of Nicholas III appear in a great many manuscripts as the work of the Patriarch Nicholas without any kind of specification. For the *Stichera to Peter and Paul* (Op. **205**), only Nicholas I and perhaps Nicholas II (Chrysoberges, 979–91) qualify as possible authors because of the age of the manuscript (X cent.); the third, Grammaticus, who did write verse (of a sort) is too late (1084–1111) to be considered. Since nothing is known of any literary activity by Chrysoberges, Nicholas Mysticus is the most likely candidate. If he did write the *stichera,* the statistical probability is that he is also the author of the two canons on the *Theotokos* and Gregory the Illuminator, since only a small minority of the patriarchs of Constantinople engaged in writing hymns. Here the matter

ends. I fail to notice any striking resemblance in style and manner between the poems themselves, or between the poems on the one hand and Nicholas' prose on the other.

The first canon (Op. **203**) shows the acrostic *Nikolaou* in the *theotokia*. The same acrostic is used by several other hymnographers named Nicholas. It appears in two canons of Nicholas Kataskepenos, a monk of the Kataskepe monastery in the early twelfth century,[1] included in the *Theotokarion* of Nikodemos Naxios the Hagiorite;[2] in some *stichera* edited by G. Schirò;[3] in *stichera* for the Little Vespers of the Sunday of Orthodoxy, for Adoration of the Cross, and for Palm Sunday in the printed Triodion;[4] and in a canon to St. Theodore the Stratelates by Nicholas Malaxos, *protopapas* of Nauplia in the sixteenth century, known only through the printed Menaea.[5] It is found also in two more canons, which I have added as an appendix (Opera **206** and **207**), not because there is any positive information to connect them with the Patriarch, but to enable the reader to judge for himself. The canon to St. Nicholas (Op. **206**) is attributed to the Patriarch by A. Papadopulos-Kerameus,[6] but without any manuscript authority; it has the tearful repetitiousness of the "Canons of Compunction" produced by Nicholas Kataskepenos. Opus **207**, a canon for Akathistos Saturday, is more impressive as a poem, but as its oldest (and practically only known) manuscript is of the year 1379, any other Nicholas has as much claim to it as the Patriarch.

Two further items have been excluded from this edition. The first is the short text Κανόνες περὶ γάμων καὶ πολυγάμων, published as a work of Nicholas by Konstantinides,[7] who observes himself, however, that it is a summary of the *Tome of Union*. In this form it has nothing to do with Nicholas.

The other is a canonical letter attributed to Photius in the overwhelming majority of the manuscripts (*Photiou Epistolai,* ed. I. Valetta [London, 1864], Ep. 84; PG, 102, cols. 792–93), but claimed for "the Patriarch Nicholas the Ancient" in two codices: *Moscow Gr. 316 Vlad.,* XII

[1] Beck, 639; MS *Athos, Panteleimon 392.*

[2] (Venice, 1883), 79–81; 98–100.

[3] *Bolletino della Badia greca di Grottaferrata,* n.s., 3 (1949), 150, 202, and 219.

[4] *Triodion,* 223, 349, 630.

[5] Feb. 8; no manuscripts known. On Malaxos, see Beck, 797–98.

[6] A. Papadopulos-Kerameus, Ἱεροσολυμιτικὴ Βιβλιοθήκη, II (Saint Petersburg, 1894), 477.

[7] 126–27.

cent., fols. 125ᵛ–126ᵛ and *Ambrosianus E 94 sup.*, XVI cent., fols. 220ʳ–221ʳ (the latter apparently derived from the former). At first sight it might seem that there is a case for this attribution, especially since the letter in question, the last of a group of five canonical letters, is missing from one of the oldest manuscripts, *Marc. App. gr. III 2*. One could, therefore, assume that a letter of Nicholas was added to those of Photius because of the similarity in subject matter and that the heading with the author's name was lost subsequently, which could easily happen since the rest of the group has no titles. Such a hypothesis, however, is not borne out by the manuscript readings. In the first place, the *Marcianus* does not represent a separate branch of the tradition but is closely related to *Laurentianus 5,22*, which contains all the five letters; secondly, the "Nicholas" manuscripts do not offer an independent text either but share certain errors with a part of the "Photius" group.[8] We must, therefore, conclude that this letter, after having become detached from its group, was attributed to Nicholas because of his well-known legislation on marriages.

II. THE MANUSCRIPT TRADITION

Opus **191**. Ranklist of Metropolitan and Archiepiscopal Sees

The Preface (**191A**) is followed in some manuscripts by a complete *taktikon* including also the suffragan sees, in others by a list of metropolitan and archiepiscopal sees only, as announced in the title of the Preface. No manuscript containing the Preface, however, has preserved the *Notitia* in its authentic form; it always appears in various stages of updating.

Complete *Notitiae* appear in:

Q = *Munich Gr. 380,* XII cent., pp. 528–33.

n = *Marcianus gr. 169,* XV cent., fols. 306ᵛ–312ᵛ.

a = *Andros, Hagias 88,* XIII cent., fols. 404ᵛ–408ʳ. Grumel, 133 and 134, erroneously states that the manuscript is incomplete.

[8] Especially *Photiou Epistolai,* ed. I. Valettas (London, 1864), 412, lines 1–4: Εἰ μὲν ἠγνόει . . ., ὁ τοιοῦτος οὐ παντελῶς μέν ἐστιν <u>ὑπεύθυνος οὐδὲ ἑκουσίῳ ἁλώσιμος ἁμαρτήματι,</u> οὐκ ἀνεύθυνος δὲ παντελῶς ἀπολύεται, ὅτιπερ ἔδει τοῦτον ἐξερευνῆσαι. Thus (with minor variants) *Vat. gr. 829, Laur. 5,40, Vat. Regin. gr. 57,* and the editions, while the Moscow and Milan manuscripts, with *Monac. gr. 380, Laur. 5,22, Sinai 1117,* and *Vat. gr. 828,* have ἀνεύθυνος οὐδὲ ἑκουσίου ἀλλότριος ἁμαρτήματος instead of ὑπεύθυνος – ἁμαρτήματι.

Meteoron, Metamorphoseos 589, XVI cent., fols. 285^{v}–297^{r}, and *Athens 1430,* XVII cent., fols. 212^{r}–218^{v}, seem both to derive from a.
Lists of metropolitan and archiepiscopal sees only are found in:
l = *Laurentianus 5,2,* XIV cent., fols. 384^{v}–385^{r}.
Vaticanus gr. 1455II, a. 1299, fols. 222^{v}–223^{r}.
Basel, University A.III.6, XVI cent., fols. 303^{v}–304^{r}.

The edition of Bonefidius (p. 118), on which those of Leunclavius (pp. 243–44), Rhalles-Potles (V, p. 474), Migne (PG, 119, cols. 817D–820A), and Parthey (pp. 321–22) depend, derives either from l or from the Basel manuscript.

A *Notitia* apparently belonging to the patriarchate of Nicholas, but without the Preface, is extant in:
i = *Jerusalem, Taphou 39,* s. XIII, fols. 170^{v}–186^{r}.

The text was published by Gelzer, 550–59, from *Istanbul, Metochion 522, a.* 1663/67, fols. 154^{r}–167^{v}, a good copy of the Jerusalem manuscript.

After considerable hesitation, I have decided to include only (for completeness' sake) the lists of metropoles and archbishoprics, omitting the list of suffragan sees, though, as Gelzer observes, this is a necessary and contemporary complement to the former. The reasons for this decision are, first, that historical geography requires a great deal of special knowledge, and, second, that a separate edition of one *Notitia* is practically useless, all the more so now that a collected edition of the *Notitiae* is being prepared by Fr. Jean Darrouzès (to appear in the CFHB).

Opus **192**. Sermon on the Capture of Thessalonica

The text has been preserved in one manuscript as an appendix to Cameniates' report on the sack of Thessalonica.

v = *Vaticanus gr. 172,* XV cent., fols. 91^{r}–96^{r}. Its main part (fols. 1–138: Cameniates, Nicholas, Anagnostes) may have been written not long after the conquest of Thessalonica by the Turks in 1420, described by Anagnostes; the second part (fols. 139–83) is dated 1439.

v is damaged in places; its only transcript, *Vatic. Barber. gr. 241,* was unfortunately taken when the damage had already been done. The gaps have therefore to be filled conjecturally.

The text was published first by Tsaras, 236–46. Before this, a short extract (44–61) had already been printed by A. Mai, *Spicilegium Romanum,* X (Rome, 1844), p. xxvi; corrections to this by I. Sakkelion, in Δελτίον τῆς Ἱστορικῆς καὶ Ἐθνολογικῆς Ἑταιρείας, 3 (1890), 109.

Opera **193, 194 I, 195, 196**. Documents from the *Vita Euthymii*

The only manuscript, *Berlin Gr. fol. 55,* XI cent., was published by C. de Boor, *Vita Euthymii, ein Anecdoton zur Geschichte Leos des Weisen* (Berlin, 1888). It was lost in World War II, but in the meantime de Boor's readings had been carefully checked by N. Veis, in Πρακτικὰ τῆς Ἀκαδημίας Ἀθηνῶν, 19 (1944), 105–36. The readings of both de Boor and Veis are reported in the new edition of the *Vita Euthymii* by P. Karlin-Hayter.

Opus **194 II**. First Abdication II

The longer version of the First Abdication is extant in two forms: without the preamble as part of the Deposition of the Metropolitans, Opus **197** lines 84–96 (on manuscripts and editions see below); and with the preamble, separately in some canonical manuscripts, of which I know the following:

p = *Parisinus Coislin gr. 211,* XII cent., fol. 350ᵛ.
Munich Gr. 277, end XV cent., fols. 331ᵛ–332ʳ.
z = *Patmos 366,* XIV cent., fol. 342.
Athens 1474, XVI cent., fol. 73ᵛ.
Moscow Gr. 336 Vlad., a. 1687, fol. 75ᵛ.

The text was published from the Munich copy by Sp. P. Lampros in *BZ,* 1 (1892), 553.

Opus **197**. Deposition of the Metropolitans

k = *Kosinitsa 1,* copied in 1686 from an "extremely old canonical manuscript of the Pammakaristos" by John the Great Sakellarios of the Great Church at Byzantium (see *Arethae scripta minora,* I, p. viii). The manuscript has been missing since World War I; its place is taken by A. Papadopulos-Kerameus' edition, in *Varia Graeca sacra* (Saint Petersburg, 1909), 255–59.

j = *Istanbul, Metochion 2, a.* 1680, fols. 16ʳ⁻ᵛ. Written by the same hand as k, according to A. Papadopulos-Kerameus, Ἱεροσολυμιτικὴ Βιβλιοθήκη, 4 (Saint Petersburg, 1899), 2–7.

Moscow Gr. 336 Vlad., a. 1687, fols. 31ᵛ–32ᵛ, and *Vaticanus Gr. 2408,* XIX cent., fols. 321ʳ–323ʳ, written by Stavraki Aristarchi Bey, are transcripts of the preceding.

Two later editions (Karlin-Hayter, "Appendix," with an English translation; *Arethae scripta minora,* II, 115–21) depend entirely on Papadopulos-Kerameus. I. Oudot, *Patriarchatus Constantinopolitani acta selecta,* I (Vatican City, 1941), 2–11, has used the Vatican manuscript besides.

Opus **198**. Letter to John the Catholicus

The text is that of the Tbilisi edition; the translation is K. Maksoudian's (217–19), with slight modifications.

Editions of the Armenian: (Jerusalem, 1843), 192–94; M. Emin (Moscow, 1853), 144–46; E. V. Zagarejšvili (Tbilisi, 1965), 189–93 (with Georgian translation). French translation: M. J. Saint-Martin, *Histoire d'Arménie par le patriarche Jean VI (dit Jean Catholicos)* (Paris, 1841), 263–66.

Opus **199**. Tract on the Tetragamy

Only extracts are preserved by Arethas, who says that he quotes verbatim (Op. 14, *Arethae scripta minora,* I, 129, 6).

The only manuscript is:

m = *Moscow Gr. 441 Vlad.,* end XVI cent., fols. 65^r–81^v (66^r–81^r).

Editions of Arethas' pamphlet: Karlin-Hayter, "Documents," 387–487; *Arethae scripta minora,* I, 122–77.

Opus **200**. Tome of Union

The original document consisted of three sections: B (the text), D (acclamations, not extant in their original form), and E (anathemas and prayer). To these were later added: A, an argument dating from the reign of Constantine VII (945–59) and C, an appendix to the text, inserted in the reign of Basil II and Constantine VIII, *ca.* 996.

In none of our manuscripts do all these five elements appear jointly; this is the case only in the editions.[9] The versions including the argument (sections A and B or A, B, and C) belong to the canonical and historical tradition and, accordingly, omit the acclamations and the anathemas; those intended (originally) for the purposes of liturgy omit the purely secular argument and thus contain either sections B, D, and E or B, C, D, and E, the acclamations (section D) being periodically adapted to the situation of the moment. When the destination of the texts changes, i.e., when they pass into a canonical collection, the acclamations are sometimes reduced to an incipit or to a statement to the effect that they have been left out [D]. Some good manuscripts contain only sections B or B and C.

In spite of some dropping and adding, and consequent mixing of groups, there is usually a clear correspondence between classification by content and by variants. On the whole, the tradition shows a fairly distinct pattern. While there are plenty of variants proper to one manuscript or one

[9] On *Patmos 366,* however, see *infra,* p. xv.

particular branch, there is nearly always a substantial majority for what we may confidently assume to be the true reading.[10] Consequently, readings limited to certain families must be considered as conjunctive errors. The picture is different in the Argument: here we have an equal division between two families, each of which shows some deliberate changes in details.

I. Manuscripts including the Argument

(1) Manuscripts containing sections A and B:

H = *Escorial X.II.10,* XIII cent., fols. 374^{r}–76^{v}.
Vaticanus gr. 1148A, XIII cent., fols. 12^{r}–14^{r}.
Sinai 1117, XIV cent., fols. 323^{v}–324^{v}.
Athos, Iviron 381, XV cent., fols. 155^{v}–158^{v}.
Andros, Panachrantou 7, XIII cent., fols. 60^{r}–62^{v}. In this manuscript the argument has been drastically abridged, apparently in order to eliminate anything anti-Nicholaän.

(2) Manuscripts containing sections A, B, and C.

L = *Lesbos, Leimonos 7, a.* 1421, fols. 328^{v}–330^{r}.
Baroccianus gr. 149, a. 1425, fols. 4^{v}–7^{v}.
Vienna, Hist. gr. 34, a. 1430, fols. 311^{v}–313^{v}.
Parisinus gr. 1388, XV cent., fols. 245^{v}–249^{r}.
Wolfenbüttel 713 (*Helmstedt 663*), end XV cent., fols. 53^{r}–56^{r}.

Two manuscripts differ from this pattern:

Patmos 366, XIV cent., fols. 350^{v}–352^{r}; it contains sections A, B, C, [D], and E, but from different sources: in section A, it sides with the L group, in B with the H group, in C through E with the F group (*infra,* p. xviii).

Z = *Athens 1429,* XII cent., fol. 27^{r-v}; this manuscript breaks off at section B line 70 through loss of one or more leaves. It holds an intermediate place between groups H and L, which may be due either to independent changes in those two groups, in which case Z can be used as the arbiter, or to conflation in the text of Z itself. Because of the rather frequent common errors of HZ in section B, I have assumed the latter and based the text of the argument on L.

[10] Some exceptions: section B lines 6, 16, 30, 61, 67, and 101.

II. Manuscripts containing sections B, D, and E

(1) The oldest and most important copy:

J = *Jerusalem, Staurou 2,* X cent., fols. 265ᵛ–268ᵛ. Acclamations I, patriarchate of Tryphon (927–31).

(2) W = *Escorial X.III.2,* XIII–XIV cent., fols. 68ʳ–70ᵛ. Acclamations II, reign of John I Tzimisces (969–76).

Vienna, Hist. gr. 7, XII–XIII cent., fols. 198ᵛ–201ʳ, while presenting the same text of the acclamations, yet also includes the Appendix (of *ca.* 996) and often parts company with W, obviously as a result of conflation.

(3) A group of seven manuscripts headed by V, with Acclamations III, pertaining to the patriarchate of Nicholas II (979–91):

V = *Athos, Vatopedi 585,* XII cent., pp. 114–21.
Athens 1377, XII cent., fols. 321ʳ–323ᵛ.
Vienna, Jur. gr. 9, XIII cent., fols. 307ʳ–310ᵛ.
Vaticanus gr. 827, XIII cent., fols. 239ʳ–241ᵛ and fol. 245ʳ⁻ᵛ (= fol. 240ʳ⁻ᵛ = B lines 71–135; D III lines 1–12).
Parisinus gr. 364, XIV cent., fols. 53ᵛ–56ʳ.
Parisinus gr. 1321, XVI cent., fols. 452ʳ–453ᵛ.
Parisinus Coislin gr. 39, XVII cent., fols. 275ʳ–276ʳ, a direct copy of the preceding.

(4) Two closely related manuscripts representing the liturgical practice of the Antiochene patriarchate in the middle of the eleventh century, though their version of the Tome, which omits the appendix, is at least half a century older:

G = *Vaticanus Barber. gr. 578,* XI–XII cent., fols. 230ʳ–233ʳ. Acclamations V, Antioch, reign of Constantine IX and Zoe (1042–50).

U = *Oxford, Holkham gr. 6,* XI cent., fols. 1ʳ–22ᵛ. Acclamations VI, Antioch, reign of Constantine IX and Theodora (1050–55). Musical notation. Between fols. 1 and 6 some of the original leaves were lost at an early time and replaced from a text of the F group (= section B lines 7–53).

III. Manuscripts containing sections B, C, D, and E

(1) N = *Laurentianus 9,8,* XII cent., fols. 201ʳ–204ᵛ. Acclamations IV, reign of Constantine VIII (1025–28).

(2) A group of five (three plus two) manuscripts, of which the Acclamations date from the second, resp. third quarter of the eleventh century:

P = *Parisinus Coislin gr. 34,* XII cent., fols. 39r–41r. Acclamations VII, reign of Constantine IX, after the death of Zoe (1050–55).

Cambridge, Univ. Ee.4.29, twin of the preceding.

Q = *Munich Gr. 380,* XII cent., pp. 37–40, closely related; same acclamations, updated to 1118/34 in the margin.

Athos, Iviron 520, XV cent., fols. 59v–64v, though it contains only sections B and C (plus the words Πολλὰ τὰ ἔτη τῶν βασιλέων), is linked to Q by some conjunctive errors.

R = *Vallicellianus F 22,* XV cent., fols. 382r–388r. Acclamations VIII, reign of Romanus IV (1068–71).

Y = *Marcianus, App. gr. III 5,* XVI cent., fols. 269r–271r; same acclamations.

(3) O = *Vaticanus gr. 2198,* XII cent., pp. 125–28. Acclamations IX, last quarter of XI cent.

(4) X = *Vienna, Hist. gr. 70,* XIV cent., fols. 87r–90r, sections B lines 1–61, C, D, X, E lines 21–29). Acclamations X (1102/11).

(5) K = *Athos, Koutloumous 42,* XII cent., fol. 335r–v (most of section D and all of section E missing through loss of a leaf). Acclamations XI, Antioch, same time as preceding.

(6) S = *Vaticanus gr. 829,* XIII–XIV cent., fols. 186v–189v. Acclamations XII, patriarchate of Leo Stypes (1134–43).

Three manuscripts seem to be descendants of S:

Vaticanus gr. 430, XVI cent., fols. 213r–218r.

Parisinus Suppl. gr. 407, a. 1592, fols. 122r–125v, a transcript of the preceding.

Angelicus gr. 115 (*B.1.12*), XVI cent., fols. 242v–245v.

IV. Manuscripts containing sections B, C, [D], and E

In this group, the acclamations have been replaced by the formula καὶ μετὰ τὴν εὐφημίαν τῶν τότε κρατούντων (or κρατησάντων) ἐξεφωνήθη (καὶ) ταῦτα. It has a common ancestor with the S group.

The following manuscripts belong to it:

F = *Laurentianus 5,40,* XIV cent., fols. 315v–318v.

Parisinus Suppl. gr. 484, XIV cent., fols. 23r–24v.

Athos, Dionysiou 120, XIV cent., fols. 703v–705r (the text from section B line 61 [τέταρτον] to the end of section C is omitted because it was already included in Balsamon's commentary on Basil, canon 4).

Moscow Gr. 322 Vlad., XV cent., fols. 11^{v}–14^{v}.
Istanbul, Metochion 2, a. 1680, fols. 50^{r}–51^{r}.

In *Oxford, Holkham gr. 6* (cf. U *supra,* p. xvi), fols. 2–5, containing section B lines 7–53 and inserted to replace the lost original leaves, also belong to this group.

Two manuscripts join the group in sections C through E only:
Moscow Gr. 336 Vlad., which is very unstemmatic in section B;
Patmos 366, on which see *supra* p. xv.

V. Manuscripts containing sections B and C only

There is one group of excellent quality, which includes:
M = *Marcianus App. gr. III 2,* XII cent., fols. 114^{r}–116^{v}.
Ambrosianus B 107 sup., XII–XIII cent., fols. 120^{v}–122^{v}.
British Museum, Addit. 28822, XIII cent., fols. 2^{v}–5^{r}.
Parisinus gr. 1370, a. 1297, fols. 58^{v}–60^{r}.

The same sections are found also in:
Vaticanus gr. 1167, XIII cent., fols. 24^{v}–26^{v}, which, however, does not share the (rare) distinctive readings of this group or those of any other, and has few errors of its own. It may represent an earlier stage of the same text.

On *Athos, Iviron 520* see *supra* p. xviii.

VI. The T Group

One group, while forming a stemmatic unit, varies in content:
T = *Vaticanus Regin. 57, a.* 1359, fols. 397^{v}–399^{r}, contains sections B and C.

The same sections, plus the final prayer, are found in *Vaticanus gr. 1455II, a.* 1299, fols. 317^{r}–319^{r}.

Only sections B and E lines 21–29 in:
Moscow Gr. 320 Vlad., XII cent., fols. 241^{r}–242^{r}.
Parisinus gr. 1369, XIV cent., fols. 206^{v}–208^{v}.

Two manuscripts containing only section B form a separate branch of the group:
Athens 1371, XII–XIII cent., fols. 358^{r}–359^{v}.
Athos, Vatopedi 227, a. 1232, fols. 342^{v}–345^{v}.

Abridged versions

Because of the abundance of good complete manuscripts, several of which are quite old, there is no need to take account of abridged texts (usually containing only the strictly canonical part of section B), such as

those in these manuscripts: *Moscow Gr. 318 Vlad.,* fol. 228; *Palatinus gr. 233,* fols. 20^{v}–22^{r}; *Vaticanus gr. 1409,* fol. 230; *Parisinus gr. 1335,* fols. 35^{v}–36^{v}; *Sinai 441,* fols. 260^{r}–261^{v}; *Escorial Ψ.II.20,* fols. 97^{r}–98^{r}; and in the canonists: Balsamon, PG, 138, cols. 597B–601A (= sections B line 60–C line 9); Blastares, PG, 144, cols. 1157A–60A (summary of sections A and B).

Editions

Leunclavius, I, 104–8 (omits section E lines 21–29); Mansi, XVIII A, cols. 336B–341A; Zachariae von Lingenthal, III, 228–32; Zepos, I, 193–96; Rhalles-Potles, V, 4–9.

The concluding prayer (section E lines 21–29) was first published in P. Lambeck, *Commentariorum de augustissima Bibliotheca caesarea vindobonensi liber,* VIII (Vienna, 1679), 446–47; then again by A. Mai, *Spicilegium Romanum,* VII (Rome, 1842), 480.

In the present edition, groups are represented by the leading manuscript, which as a rule is cited only if supported by all, or most, of the others of its class. Similarly, readings of isolated manuscripts (G, U, W, N, O, X, K) have usually been ignored unless shared by other witnesses. Only J is reported in full.

Opus **201**. Decree on Patriarchal Letters

Manuscripts collated (there are no doubt many more.):

Type 1:

S = *Vaticanus gr. 829,* XIII–XIV cent., fols. 190^{v}–191^{r}.

Vaticanus gr. 430, XVI cent., fols. 220^{v}–221^{v}, a copy of S.

Vaticanus gr. 1150, fols. 40^{v}–41^{r}, same text as S, with some additional mistakes.

Q = *Munich Gr. 380,* XII cent., pp. 524–25.

n = *Marcianus gr. 169,* XV cent., fols. 306^{r-v}.

Type 2:

s = *Sinai 1117,* XIV cent., fol. 355^{r-v}.

Vaticanus gr. 1137, fol. 49^{r-v}, text as in s, with some additional errors.

d = *Athos, Dionysiou 120,* XIV cent., fols. 678^{v}–679^{r} and 707^{r-v}. (Essentially the same text in both places.)

Athens 1474, fols. 72^{v}–73^{r}.

Istanbul, Metochion 2, a. 1680, fol. 50^{r}.

Moscow Gr. 336 Vlad., a. 1687, fol. 73^{r-v}.

Type 3:

w = *Wolfenbüttel 713, Helmstedt 663,* end XV cent., fol. 174^{v}.

In the opening sentence there is a corruption, the second πάθος being an echo of the first, which has replaced the correct word; πάχος in S is not a very successful conjecture; in w the phrase has been rewritten to make sense of it.

The editions derive from w: Leunclavius, I, 249; Rhalles-Potles, V, 1–2; PG, 119, col. 825B–D.

Opus **202**. Decree on the Great Habit

b = *Vienna, Phil. gr. 330,* XIV cent., fol. 132^{v}.

t = *Jerusalem, Taphou 181,* end XIII cent., fol. 61^{r}.

h = *Athos, Panteleimon 152,* XV cent., fol. 307.

Jerusalem, Saba 366, XIII cent., fol. 23^{r-v}.

Edition from t by A. Papadopulos-Kerameus, Ἱεροσολυμιτικὴ Βιβλιοθήκη, I (Saint Petersburg, 1891), 271; repeated by Konstantinides, 125.

Opus **203**. Canon on the Lament of the Mother of God

Π = *Parisinus gr. 400,* XIV cent., fols. 12^{r}–15^{v}.

Edition: J. Pitra, *Spicilegium Solesmense,* IV (Rome, 1858), 492–95.

Opus **204**. Canon to St. Gregory the Illuminator

Λ = *Athos, Laura Γ 16,* XI cent., fols. 217^{v}–220^{v}.

Θ = *Messina Gr. 135,* XIII cent., fols. 78^{r}–81^{v}.

Δ = *Parisinus gr. 1580,* XV cent., fols. 82^{r}–84^{v}. This manuscript, though the latest, is on the whole the best.

Edition: Ada Debiasi Gonzato, *Analecta hymnica graeca,* I (Rome, 1966), 380–86 (from Θ).

Opus **205**. Stichera to Peter and Paul

Σ = *Sinai 596,* X cent., fols. 2^{v}–3^{r}.

The *stichera* on Peter's Chains in *Athos, Laura Γ 74,* XI cent., fol. 40^{r} (inc. Ὁ τοὺς πεπεδημένους), joined to these two stanzas as a third by L. Sophronios, in Ἐκκλησιαστικὸς Φάρος, 46 (1947), 75, follow a different metrical pattern and belong to a different liturgical date.

Opus **206**. Canon to St. Nicholas

Ξ = *Jerusalem, Saba 362,* XIII cent., fols. 133^r–134^r.

Γ = *Grottaferrata Δα XXIV,* XIII–XIV cent., fols. 22^r–24^v.

Φ = *Vaticanus gr. 1853, a.* 1173, fols. 92^v–96^v.

The Vatican manuscript is carelessly written and badly spelled. (Φ) indicates its support of the reading cited, but with a minor (usually orthographical) difference.

This canon has been published in *Analecta hymnica Graeca,* ed. I. Schirò. IV, *Canones Decembri,* ed. A. Kominis (Rome, 1976), 164–78; cf. 803–4. The text is based on Γ, with the following additional manuscripts collated: *Parisinus Suppl. gr. 32,* fols. 107^v–108^v; *Parisinus gr. 928,* pp. 245–249; *Athos, Konstamonitou 31,* fols. 207–211; *Meteoron, Metam. 473,* fols. 35–38^v.

Opus **207**. Canon of Thanksgiving to the Mother of God

Ψ = *Vaticanus gr. 786, a.* 1379, fols. 263^r–268^r (ends at line 188).

Athos, Laura 1994 (*Katholikon 27*), XIX cent., after the *Akathistos.* I have not seen this manuscript, which may be a copy of the edition.

ε = Nikodemos Naxios, *Theotokarion* (Venice, 1883), 123–24. The original of Nikodemos' text, which, besides being complete, differs not inconsiderably from Ψ, has not yet been found.

As a general rule, purely orthographical variants have been ignored throughout.

LIST OF ABBREVIATIONS

ACO	*Acta Conciliorum Oecumenicorum,* ed. E. Schwartz, 4 vols. (Berlin, 1914–40)
Arethae scripta minora	*Arethae scripta minora,* ed. L. G. Westerink, 2 vols. (Leipzig, 1968–72)
Beck	H.-G. Beck, *Kirche und theologische Literatur im byzantinischen Reich* (Munich, 1959)
Bonefidius	E. Bonefidius, *Juris orientalis libri III* (Paris, 1573)
BZ	*Byzantinische Zeitschrift*
CFHB	Corpus Fontium Historiae Byzantinae
Christ-Paranikas	W. Christ and M. Paranikas, *Anthologia graeca carminum Christianorum* (Leipzig, 1871; repr. Hildesheim, 1963)
Darrouzès	J. Darrouzès, *Epistoliers byzantins du X*[e] *siècle* (Paris, 1960)
DOT	Dumbarton Oaks Texts
Gelzer	H. Gelzer, *Ungedruckte und ungenügend veröffentlichte Texte der* Notitiae episcopatuum, Abhandlungen, Akademie der Wissenschaften, München, Philosophisch-historische Klasse, XXI, 3 (Munich, 1901), 529–641
Grumel	V. Grumel, *Les regestes des actes du patriarcat de Constantinople,* I, fasc. 1, 2nd ed. (Paris, 1972); I, fasc. 2 (Socii Assumptionistae Chalcedonenses, 1936)
Jenkins	R. J. H. Jenkins, *Studies on Byzantine History of the Ninth and Tenth Centuries* (London, 1970)
Karlin-Hayter, "Appendix"	P. Karlin-Hayter, "Vita Euthymii, Appendix," *Byzantion,* 25–27 (1957), 747–78
Karlin-Hayter, "Documents"	P. Karlin-Hayter, "New Arethas Documents IV," *Byzantion,* 32 (1962), 387–487
Karlin-Hayter, "Le synode"	P. Karlin-Hayter, "Le synode à Constantinople de 886 à 912 et le rôle de Nicolas le Mystique dans l'affaire de la tétragamie," *Jahrbuch der Österreichischen Byzantinistik,* 19 (1970), 59–101
Konstantinides	I. Ch. Konstantinides, Νικόλαος Α', ὁ Μυστικός (Athens, 1967)
Letters	*Nicholas I, Patriarch of Constantinople, Letters,* ed. R. J. H. Jenkins and L. G. Westerink (Washington, D. C., 1973)

Leunclavius	J. Leunclavius, *Juris graeco-romani tam canonici quam civilis tomi duo* (Frankfurt, 1596)
Maksoudian	K. Maksoudian, *Yovhannes Drasxanakertc'i, History of Armenia, Translation and Commentary* (University Microfilms International, Ann Arbor, 1973)
Mansi	J. D. Mansi, *Sacrorum conciliorum nova et amplissima collectio*, 31 vols. (Florence-Venice, 1759–98)
Parthey	G. Parthey, *Hieroclis Synecdemus et notitiae graecae episcopatuum* (Berlin, 1866; repr. Amsterdam, 1967)
PG	Patrologiae cursus completus, Series graeca, ed. J.-P. Migne
Rhalles-Potles	G. A. Rhalles and M. Potles, Σύνταγμα τῶν Θείων καὶ ἱερῶν κανόνων, 6 vols. (Athens, 1852–59)
REB	*Revue des Etudes Byzantines*
Synod. Orthod.	"Le Synodikon de l'Orthodoxie," ed. J. Gouillard, *Travaux et Mémoires*, 2(1967), 1–316
Triodion	*Triodion* (Rome, 1879)
Tsaras	G. Tsaras, Νικολάου Πατριάρχου ὁμιλία εἰς τὴν ἅλωσιν τῆς Θεσσαλονίκης, in *Μακεδονικά*, 1 (1940), 236–46
Vita Euthymii	*Vita Euthymii*, ed. P. Karlin-Hayter (Brussels, 1970)
Zachariae von Lingenthal	K. E. Zachariae von Lingenthal, *Jus graecoromanum*, 7 vols. (Leipzig, 1856–84)
Zepos	J. and P. Zepos, *Jus graeco-romanum*, 8 vols. (Athens, 1931)

LIST OF SIGNS

F = Laurentianus 5,40, s. XIV (200BCE)

G = Vaticanus Barberinianus gr. 578, s. XI–XII (200 BDE)

H = Escorial X.II.10, s. XIII (200AB)

J = Jerusalem, Staurou 2, s. X (200BDE)

K = Athos, Koutloumous 42, s. XII (200D)

L = Lesbos, Leimonos 7, a. 1421 (200ABC)

M = Marcianus App. gr. III 2, s. XII (200BC)

N = Laurentianus 9,8, s. XII (200BCDE)

O = Vaticanus gr. 2198, s. XII (200BCDE)

P = Parisinus Coislinianus gr. 34, s. XII (200BCDE)

Q = Munich Gr. 380, s. XII (191A, 200D, 201)

R = Vallicellianus F 22, s. XV (200D)

S = Vaticanus gr. 829, s. XIII–XIV (200BCDE, 201)

T = Vaticanus Reginensis gr. 57, a. 1359 (200BC)

U = Oxford, Holkham gr. 6, s. XI (200BDE)
V = Athos Vatopedi 585, s. XII (200BDE)
W = Escorial X.III.2, s. XIII–XIV (200D)
X = Vienna, Hist. gr. 70, s. XIV (200D)
Y = Marcianus App. gr. III 5, s. XVI med. (200D)
Z = Athens 1429, s. XII (200AB)

a = Andros, Hagias 88, s. XIII (191A)
b = Vienna, Phil. gr. 330, s. XIV (202)
c = Berlin Gr. f. 55, s. XI (193, 194I, 195, 196)
d = Athos, Dionysiou 120, s. XIV (201)
h = Athos, Panteleimon 152, s. XV (202)
i = Jerusalem, Taphou 39, s. XIII (191B)
j = Istanbul, Metochion 2, a. 1680 (194II, 197)
k = Kosinitsa 1, a. 1686 (194II, 197)
l = Laurentianus 5,2, s. XIV (191A)
m = Moscow Gr. 441 Vlad., s. XVI ex. (199)
n = Marcianus gr. 169, s. XV (191A, 201)
p = Parisinus Coislinianus gr. 211, s. XII (194II)
s = Sinai 1117, s. XIV (201)
t = Jerusalem, Taphou 181, s. XIII ex. (202)
v = Vaticanus gr. 172, s. XV (192)
w = Wolfenbüttel 713, Helmstedt 663, s. XV ex. (201)
z = Patmos 366, s. XIV (194II)

Γ = Grottaferrata Δα XXIV, s. XIII–XIV (206)
Δ = Parisinus gr. 1580, s. XV (204)
Θ = Messina Gr. 135, s. XIII (204)
Λ = Athos, Laura Γ 16, s. XI (204)
Ξ = Jerusalem, Saba 362, s. XIII in. (206)
Π = Parisinus gr. 400, s. XIV (203)
Σ = Sinai 596, s. X (205)
Φ = Vaticanus gr. 1853, a. 1173 (206)
Ψ = Vaticanus gr. 786, a. 1379 (207)

ε = Nikodemos Naxios, Θεοτοκάριον (Venice, 1883) (207)

⟨ ⟩ = addenda
[ ] = supplenda in lacuna codicis
*** = lacuna statuenda
† † = corrupta
α̣ = puncto notantur litterae incertae

TEXT and TRANSLATION

191. Ranklist of Metropolitan and Archiepiscopal Sees

A. Preface

Νικολάου πατριάρχου τοῦ παλαιοῦ περὶ τῆς κατὰ τὴν καθέδραν τάξεως τῶν μητροπολιτῶν καὶ ἀρχιεπισκόπων, καθὼς ἐν τῷ χαρτοφυλακείῳ νῦν ἀναγράφονται

Ἔδει τὰς πόλεις αἳ τῷ τῆς ἀρχιερωσύνης τετίμηνται ἀξιώματι καὶ αἷς ἱεροὶ ποιμένες παρὰ τῆς πατριαρχικῆς προχειρίζονται δεξιᾶς ἐνταυθοῖ διαγράφεσθαι, ὥσπερ τινὶ οἰκουμένῃ βραχείᾳ συνεχομένας καὶ τῷ βουλομένῳ ἀταλαιπώρως προφαινομένας. Τῇ γὰρ ἀναιμάκτῳ ἀνηκούσας ἀρχῇ ἀξιόχρεων ταύτας τῷ ἰδίῳ σηκῷ κατατάττεσθαι, ὡσαύτως τε καὶ πᾶσι τοῖς ἄλλοις τὴν ἐπ' αὐταῖς ἐξουσίαν καὶ τὴν τάξιν αὐτῶν εὐσύνοπτον εἶναι καὶ εὐεπίγνωστον.

Σὺν ταῖς πρὸς ἀνίσχοντα δὲ ἥλιον καὶ αἱ πρὸς δυόμενον διαγράφονται. Ἐκ παλαιοῦ γὰρ αὗται οὔπω μέχρι τῆς δεῦρο ταῖς ἄλλαις συνετετάχατο· ὧν οἱ τὴν ἐφορείαν πεπιστευμένοι, ἡνίκα καθέδρας καιρὸς ἐκάλει, παρὰ τῶν ὁμοταγῶν διωθοῦντο καὶ ἀντώθουν τούτους (φεῦ τῆς ὕβρεως) τῷ ἴσῳ μέτρῳ τῆς ἐπιπλήξεως.

Ἀλλ' ὅ γε φιλόχριστος καὶ πανευσεβὴς ἡμῶν βασιλεὺς προὐκάθητο μὲν ἅμα ἡμῖν ἐν τῷ σεβασμίῳ ναῷ τῆς ἁγίας Εἰρήνης, ἡνίκα τὴν τῶν ἀοιδίμων πατριαρχῶν μνήμην ἐπιτελοῦμεν, συμπαρῆσαν δὲ καὶ μητροπολῖται θεοφιλεῖς· μεθ' ὧν τὸ ἑκάστου θρόνου αἰδέσιμον

---

191 A: Q 525 n 306ᵛ a 404ᵛ 1 384ᵛ ‖ 1 Νικολάου — παλαιοῦ a: τοῦ αὐτοῦ (= Ν. π. τ. π.) Qn τοῦ ἁγιωτάτου πατριάρχου κυροῦ (om. nomine) 1 ‖ 3 νῦν ἀναγράφονται Qna: ἐπαναγράφονται 1 ‖ 7 προσφαινομένας 1 ‖ 9 ὡς αὐτῇ a ‖ 11 αἱ om. a ‖ 11–12 καταγράφονται 1 ‖ 12 αὗται a: αὐτοὺς Qn αὐτὰς 1 ‖ τῆς al: τοῦ Qn ‖ 13 συνετάχατο Qn: συντετάχαμεν 1 ‖ 13–14 καιρὸς καθέδρας colloc. a ‖ 16 καὶ om. 1 ‖ βασιλεὺς ἡμῶν colloc. 1 ‖ 16–17 προὐκάθητο] πρὸς a ‖ 18 τὴν Qna: τε 1 ‖ ἐπετελοῦμεν 1 ‖ συμπαρῆσαν Qna: σὺν τούτῳ 1 ‖ δὲ al: τὲ Qn

191. Ranklist of Metropolitan and Archiepiscopal Sees

A. Preface

The Patriarch Nicholas the Ancient on the Order of Seating of the Metropolitans and Archbishops, as Listed now in the Archives

It was found necessary to list here the cities that are honored with the dignity of archpriesthood and for which shepherds are ordained by the patriarch's hand, arranged as in a concise description of the world and readily accessible to anyone interested. For inasmuch as they belong to the realm that is not sullied with blood, it is fitting that each should be assigned its own place in the fold and that the authority to which they are subject and their order should be easy to survey and to ascertain for all others as well.

With the cities of the East, those of the West are also included. From of old and until the present time they were not listed with the others; but those charged with their supervision, when the time to be seated came, would be thrust aside by their equals and would thrust them aside in their turn (oh outrage!), returning like punishment for like.

However, when our Christ-loving and most pious Emperor presided jointly with us in the venerable Church of St. Irene, at the time we celebrated the memory of the illustrious patriarchs, in the presence also of metropolitans loved by God, we considered together with them the esteem

συνδιασκεψάμενοι πρόσφορον πᾶσι χώραν ἀπεκληρώσαμεν, καθὰ καὶ ἡ παροῦσα τάξις ἡ τῷ ἡμετέρῳ τῆς προτροπῆς λόγῳ περιεσκεμμένως γραφεῖσα δηλοῖ.

Ἄτοπον γὰρ ἐδόκει τοὺς τοῦ βήματος πρωτείων ἀντιποιεῖσθαι, καὶ δόξης ἕνεκα, ἥτις ἐστὶν ἀδοξία, εἰπεῖν δὲ μᾶλλον αἰσχύνη, τὸ τῆς ἀρχιερωσύνης τίμιον τοῦ λοιποῦ καθυβρίζεσθαι, μόνης τῆς ἀθανάτου δόξης φροντίζειν ὀφειλόντων ἡμῶν, ἣ μαρασμὸν οὐ προσίεται, ἀλλ' εἰς ἀεὶ ἐπανθεῖ καὶ τοὺς ἐραστὰς δόξῃ ἀκηράτῳ κατακοσμεῖ καὶ ἀποσεμνύνει.

B. The Ranklist

Τάξις τῶν ὑποκειμένων μητροπόλεων τῷ ἀποστολικῷ καὶ πατριαρχικῷ θρόνῳ τῆς θεοφυλάκτου καὶ βασιλίδος Κωνσταντινουπόλεως· αὕτη ἡ τάξις ἐκ συνοδικῆς διασκέψεως τὸ ἀκριβὲς εἰλήφει, καθὼς σήμερον ἐν τῷ ἱερῷ χαρτοφυλακείῳ ἀναγέγραπται

α' ἡ Καισάρεια
β' ἡ Ἔφεσος
γ' ἡ Ἡράκλεια
δ' ἡ Ἄγκυρα
ε' ἡ Κύζικος
ς' ἡ Σάρδις
ζ' ἡ Νικομήδεια
η' ἡ Νίκαια
θ' ἡ Καλχηδών
ι' ἡ Σίδη
ια' ἡ Σεβάστεια
ιβ' ἡ Ἀμάσεια
ιγ' ἡ Σικελία
ιδ' τὰ Τύανα
ιε' ἡ Γάγγρα
ις' ἡ Θεσσαλονίκη
ιζ' ἡ Κλαυδιούπολις
ιη' ἡ Νεοκαισάρεια
ιθ' ἡ Πισσινοῦς
κ' τὰ Μύρα
κα' ἡ Σταυρούπολις ἤτοι Καρία
κβ' ἡ Λαοδίκεια
κγ' τὰ Σύναδα
κδ' τὸ Ἰκόνιον
κε' ἡ Ἀντιόχεια
κς' ἡ Πέργη ἤτοι Σύλαιον
κζ' ἡ Κόρινθος
κη' αἱ Ἀθῆναι
κθ' ἡ Μωκησός
λ' ἡ Σελεύκεια
λα' ἡ Καλαβρία
λβ' αἱ Πάτραι
λγ' ἡ Τραπεζοῦς
λδ' ἡ Λάρισσα
λε' ἡ Ναύπακτος
λς' ἡ Φιλιππούπολις
λζ' ἡ Τραϊανούπολις
λη' ἡ Ῥόδος

---

20 χώρα Q χώρας n ‖ 27 εἰς om. I

191 B: i 170ᵛ–171ᵛ ‖ 21 θεσσαλονικαία i ‖ 31 σύλεον i ‖ 34 μώκησος i

due to each see and assigned its appropriate place to each, as set forth in the present Order of Precedence, carefully drawn up at our behest.

It appeared incongruous, indeed, that those of chancel should rival for precedence and that for the sake of honor, which is really dishonor or rather infamy, the dignity of the archpriesthood should still further be disgraced, when we ought to heed only the immortal glory which cannot wither but blossoms forever and bestows upon its lovers the grace and dignity of unfading renown.

B. The Ranklist

Order of precedence of the metropoles subject to the jurisdiction of the Apostolic and Patriarchal See of the God-guarded Imperial City of Constantinople. This order of precedence has, by a synodical examination, received its accurate form, in which it is at present registered in the Sacred Archives.

1 Caesarea
2 Ephesus
3 Heraclea
4 Ancyra
5 Cyzicus
6 Sardes
7 Nicomedia
8 Nicaea
9 Chalcedon
10 Side
11 Sebastea
12 Amasea
13 Sicily
14 Tyana
15 Gangra
16 Thessalonica
17 Claudiopolis
18 Neocaesarea
19 Pessinus
20 Myra
21 Stauropolis or Caria
22 Laodicea
23 Synada
24 Iconium
25 Antioch
26 Perge or Sylaeum
27 Corinth
28 Athens
29 Mocesus
30 Seleucia
31 Calabria
32 Patras
33 Trapezus
34 Larissa
35 Naupactus
36 Philippopolis
37 Traianopolis
38 Rhodes

λθ′ ἡ Φιλίππου
μ′ ἡ Ἀδριανούπολις
μα′ ἡ Ἱεράπολις
μβ′ τὸ Δυρράχιον
μγ′ ἡ Σμύρνα
μδ′ ἡ Κατάνη
με′ τὸ Ἀμώριον
μς′ ἡ Κάμαχος
μζ′ τὸ Κοτυάειον
μη′ ἡ Ἁγία Σευερίνα
μθ′ ἡ Μιτυλήνη
ν′ αἱ Νέαι Πάτραι
να′ τὰ Εὐχάϊτα

Τάξις τῶν ἀρχιεπισκοπῶν αἳ τῷ τῆς βασιλίδος θρόνῳ ὑπόκεινται

α′ ἡ Βιζύη
β′ ἡ Πομπηϊούπολις
γ′ ἡ Λεοντόπολις
δ′ ἡ Μαρώνεια
ε′ ἡ Ἀπάμεια
ς′ τὰ Γέρμια
ζ′ ἡ Ἀρκαδιούπολις
η′ τὸ Πάριον
θ′ ἡ Μίλητος
ι′ ἡ Προκόννησος
ια′ ἡ Σηλυβρία
ιβ′ ἡ Μήθυμνα
ιγ′ τὸ Ῥούσιον
ιδ′ τὰ Κύψελα
ιε′ ἡ Ὑδροῦς
ις′ ἡ Νίκη
ιζ′ ἡ Νεάπολις
ιη′ ἡ Σέλγη
ιθ′ ἡ Χερσών
κ′ ἡ Μεσήνη
κα′ ἡ Γαρέλλα
κβ′ ἡ Βρύσις
κγ′ ἡ Δερκούς
κδ′ αἱ Σέρραι
κε′ ἡ Καραβιζύη
κς′ ἡ Ἄμαστρις
κζ′ ἡ Λῆμνος
κη′ ἡ Λευκάς
κθ′ ἡ Νακώλεια
λ′ ἡ Μίσθεια
λα′ ἡ Κολώνεια
λβ′ αἱ Χῶναι
λγ′ αἱ Θῆβαι
λδ′ ἡ Σωτηριούπολις
λε′ ἡ Πηδαχθόη
λς′ ἡ Γέρμη
λζ′ ἡ Βόσπορος
λη′ ἡ Κοτραδία
λθ′ ὁ Ῥοΐνων
μ′ ἡ Κάρπαθος
μα′ ἡ Αἶνος
μβ′ ἡ Μεσημβρία
μγ′ τὸ Ῥύζαιον
μδ′ ἡ Γοτθία
με′ ἡ Σογδία
μς′ οἱ Φοῦλλοι
μζ′ ἡ Σεβαστόπολις
μη′ ἡ Αἴγινα
μθ′ ἡ Κέρκυρα

---

52 κατυάειον i ‖ 57 τῷ Gelzer: τῶν i ‖ post 70 exciderunt ἡ Κῖος et ἡ Ἄπρως (Gelzer) ‖ 73 ἱδρούς i ‖ 83 καραβιζὴν i ‖ 84 μάστρις i ‖ 87 νακόλεια i ‖ 96 κοτρωδία i ‖ 106 αἴγεια i

191 B

39 Philippi
40 Adrianople
41 Hierapolis
42 Dyrrhachium
43 Smyrna
44 Catana
45 Amorium
46 Camachus
47 Cotyaëum
48 Hagia Severina
49 Mitylene
50 New Patras
51 Euchaita

Order of precedence of the archbishoprics subject to the jurisdiction of the See of the Imperial City

1 Bizye
2 Pompeiopolis
3 Leontopolis
4 Maronia
5 Apamea
6 Germia
7 Arcadiopolis
8 Parium
9 Miletus
10 Proconnesus
11 Selymbria
12 Methymna
13 Rousion
14 Cypsela
15 Otranto
16 Nike
17 Neapolis
18 Selge
19 Cherson
20 Messene
21 Garella
22 Brysis
23 Derkos
24 Serres
25 Karabizye
26 Amastris
27 Lemnos
28 Leucas
29 Nacolea
30 Misthia
31 Colonia
32 Chonae
33 Thebes
34 Soteriopolis
35 Pedachthoe
36 Germe
37 Bosporus
38 Cotradia
39 Roïnon
40 Carpathus
41 Aenus
42 Mesembria
43 Rhyzaion
44 Gothia
45 Sogdia
46 Phoulloi
47 Sebastopol
48 Aegina
49 Corfu

192

Νικολάου πατριάρχου ὁμιλία εἰς τὴν ἅλωσιν τῆς Θεσσαλονίκης, ῥηθεῖσα ἐν τῷ ἄμβωνι τῆς μεγάλης ἐκκλησίας μετὰ τὴν εἴσοδον

Μικρῷ πρότερον ὑμῖν εἶπον, ἀγαπητοί, αἴτιον τοῦ μὴ τῆς θείας ἀπολαύειν εὐμενείας τὸν περιούσιον καὶ ἠγαπημένον λαὸν τὰ ἐμὰ πταίσματα· οὕτω λέγω καὶ νῦν. Ἡ γὰρ ἐμὴ τεταπεινωμένη καὶ πρὸς τὸν ὕψιστον μὴ ἀναβαίνειν οἵα τε οὖσα δέησις καταστρέφει μου τὴν ψυχὴν εἰς ἀνήνυτον.

Οὕτω φρονῶ καὶ οὕτως ἔχω περὶ ἐμαυτοῦ, πλὴν τῆς αὐτῆς φύσεως καὶ ὑμεῖς, καὶ πάντας ὑφ' ἁμαρτίαν κεῖσθαι ἀνάγκη. Καὶ σκοπήσατε τὸ οἰκεῖον ἐπιμελῶς συνειδός, καὶ εἴ τι τοιοῦτον ἐν ὑμῖν οἷον φέρει κατάγνωσιν, ὃ διΐστησι τῆς πρὸς θεὸν οἰκειότητος καὶ τὴν κραυγὴν ἡμῶν, ἐπειδὰν κράζωμεν, εἰς ἀέρα ποιεῖ διαλύεσθαι. Σκοπῶμεν δὲ εἰ μὴ διδόαμεν ἔλεγχον τῆς τοιαύτης συνειδήσεως, ὁπότε θεία ἐπὶ κεφαλῆς ὁρᾶται νέμεσις καὶ ταύτην οὐχ οἷοί τέ ἐσμεν παραιτήσασθαι, ὥσπερ τοὺς Χριστῷ ἀνατεθειμένους ἀκούομεν πρότερον, οἳ ἀληθῶς τῷ παναγίῳ ἐπικεκλημένοι ὀνόματι αὐτίκα τῇ δεήσει φιλανθρωπίας ἐτύγχανον.

Ἀλλὰ γὰρ εἴ τι τοιοῦτον, ὃ καταισχύνει καὶ κακοὺς ἐλέγχει καὶ παρρησίας οὐ μεταδίδωσι, μεταβαλώμεθα, μεταθώμεθα τὴν προαίρεσιν, καὶ σπουδάσωμεν μὴ κλήσει μόνον ἀνατεθεῖσθαι τῷ ὑπὲρ ἡμῶν παρασχόντι τὸ αἷμα, πολὺ δὲ πρότερον τῇ τῶν πράξεων οἰκειότητι· τοιοῦτοι γὰρ οἱ πάλαι καὶ διὰ τοῦτο τῆς πρὸς αὐτὸν ἠξιοῦντο παρρησίας. Οἴμοι, ὅτι πάντες ἠχρειωμένοι γεγόναμεν καὶ ὡς ἐπιλελησμένοι παρὰ θεοῦ, καὶ οὐκ ἔστιν οὐδεὶς οὗ θαυμάζει τὸ πρόσωπον, οὐδ' ὃς ἐπὶ καιροῦ ταῖς περιστάσεσιν εἰλημμέν[ου, ὑπ' ἐνθέ]ου γνώμης ἅμα καὶ φιλανθρώπου κινούμ[ενος], στῆναι καὶ προσφθέγξασθαι ἱκανός, «Εἰ μὲν ἀφεῖς αὐτοῖς, ἄφες, εἰ δὲ μή, κἀμὲ ἐξάλειψον,» καὶ τὴν θείαν ἀποστροφὴν εἰς οἰκτιρμοὺς διαλύσασθαι.

192: 5: Tit. 2:14; cf. Exod. 19:5; Deut. 14:2. ‖ 16–17: cf. Is. 43:7. ‖ 24: Ps. 13:3; 52:3. ‖ 25: Gen. 19:21. ‖ 28: Exod. 32:32.

192: v 91[r]–96[r] ‖ 2 μεγά v ‖ 8 ψυχὴν] fort. εὐχὴν ‖ 13 κράζωμεν Wk: -ομεν v κράξωμεν Tsaras ‖ 20 μεταβαλώμεθα Wk: -λλ- v ‖ 26 lac. 9 litt., ex. gr. supplevi: εἰλημμένος καὶ τῆς ἐκείνου Tsaras ‖ 27 lac. 4 litt., suppl. Tsaras

192

Sermon of Nicholas the Patriarch, on the Capture of Thessalonica, Pronounced from the Pulpit of the Great Church after the Entrance

A while ago I told you, dearly beloved, that the reason why God's peculiar and beloved people does not enjoy the Divine Favor, are my transgressions; and this I repeat now. My worthless prayer, which cannot rise to the Most High, condemns my intent to futility.

Thus I think and thus I feel about myself; you, however, are of the same nature, and inevitably you are all subject to sin. Examine your own consciences carefully, whether there is anything in you such as deserves reproof, anything that severs you from God's friendship and causes our cries, when we cry out, to dissolve into air. Let us consider whether we do not give evidence of a conscience thus burdened, when Divine Retribution is seen coming down upon our heads and we are unable to deprecate it, as we hear it was deprecated in former times by those dedicated to the service of Christ, who rightfully bore his All-holy name and obtained mercy as soon as they prayed for it.

Well then, if there is anything of this kind, of which we are ashamed, by which we stand convicted as wrongdoers, and which prevents us from approaching God with confidence, let us change ourselves, let us shift the direction of our minds, and let us endeavor to be dedicated to Him Who gave His Blood for us, not only in name, but much rather by being like Him in our actions; such were the faithful of olden times, and this is why they were deemed worthy of coming to Him with confidence. Alas that we all should have become unprofitable and forgotten, it seems, by God, so that there is none whose person He regards, nor who at a time fraught with vicissitudes is capable of standing up, moved both by ⟨piety⟩ and loving-kindness, and saying to Him, "If Thou wilt forgive them, forgive, and if not, blot me out, too," and thus dissolving the Divine Wrath into compassion.

192

Καὶ οὔπω ἐκεῖνό φημι, ὅτι πάντες ἐσμὲν ἔνοχοι, καὶ εἰ μὴ ἐφ' ἡμᾶς ὁ θεῖος ὀφθαλμὸς ἐχρηστεύετο, πάντες ἂν ἀπολώλειμεν. Πόθεν γὰρ αἱ προλαβοῦσαι τῆς γῆς ἀφορίαι; Πόθεν ὄμβρων ἐπικλύσεις ἀήθεις καὶ τὸ πρᾶον καὶ ἱλαρὸν ἀποθέμεναι τῆς ποιότητος; Πόθεν νῦν δυσσεβὴς ἔφοδος ἐξ Ἀσσυρίων σύμμικτος καὶ Αἰγυπτίων ἀνθρωπίων, ἣ γεννάδας αὐτούς (φεῦ τῶν ἐμῶν κακῶν) καθ' ἡμῶν ἐκστρατεύσασα δείκνυσιν ἀντὶ παρειμένων καὶ μικροῦ καὶ αὐτῆς ἐρήμων δορᾶς, ὡς οἱ ἀκριβῶς ἀπαγγέλλουσιν ἐκείνους εἰδότες; Πόθεν ταῦτα καὶ δι' ἣν αἰτίαν οὕτω περιστοιχιζόμεθα τοῖς κακοῖς; Ἆρ' οὖν [οὐχ ὅτι πταίον]τες ἐξ ἴσου παρὰ θεοῦ λελογίσμ[εθα]; Οὐχ ὅτι παρὰ φαῦλον ἡμᾶς ἥγηται καὶ πρὸς τὴν χείρονα μοῖραν ἀπέκρινε καὶ μεμισημένοι ἀντὶ ἠγαπημένων γεγόναμεν; Εἰ γάρ τις ἦν ἀψευδὴς θεράπων θεοῦ, ἐφ' ᾧ θεραπευόμενος ἀναπέπαυτο, πάντως ἂν ἐξ ἧς εἶπον παρρησίας κινούμενος ἀπέστρεψε τὰ δεινά, τῆς διὰ τοὺς πταίσαντας ἀναστελλομένης ὀργῆς τῇ ἀρετῇ τοῦ θεράποντος· νυνὶ δὲ ἐφ' ἡμᾶς ἐξεχύθη ἄκρατος ἡ ὀργή, καὶ ὁ παρρησιαζόμενος ἢ ἀναστέλλων οὐδείς.

Ἐκενώθησαν πόλεις οἰκητόρων, ἄνδρες ἴσα βοσκήμασι κατεσφάγησαν, γυναῖκες διασπώμεναι τῶν ὁμοζύγων βιαίως ἐλεεινὸν θέαμα τοῖς ἀσελγεστάτοις ἐνασχημονούμεναι πρόκεινται. Τίς δώσει τοῖς ἐμοῖς ὀφθαλμοῖς δακρύων πηγάς, καὶ κλαύσομαι ταῦτά τε καὶ τὰ τούτων ἐλεεινότερα πάθη; Ἐβεβηλ[ώθησαν ναοί, παρ]θένοι ἀφιερωμέναι ο̣[ὐρανίῳ νυ]μφῶνι πρὸς ὕβριν ἀπήχθη[σαν], θυσιαστήρια τοῦ θεοῦ τῇ τῶν ἀκαθάρτων ἐχράνθη ἀκαθαρσίᾳ, μονάζοντας καὶ ἱερεῖς ξίφος καὶ δουλεία μερίζεται· οἴμοι, τῶν ἐμῶν κακῶν τὸ βαρύτατον, τὰ πολύαθλα τῶν ἁγίων λείψανα παίζεται τοῖς βεβήλοις καὶ καταικίζεται καὶ μετὰ θάνατον δευτέρους ἄθλους ὑφίστανται.

Ποῦ μοι, Δημήτριε μάρτυς, ἡ ἀήττητος συμμαχία; Πῶς τὴν σὴν πόλιν ὑπερεῖδες πορθουμένην; Πῶς ὑπὸ σοὶ πολιούχῳ ἡ ἐχθροῖς ἄβατος, ἀφ' οὗ χρόνου ταύτην ἥλιος ἐθεάσατο, τοσούτων κακῶν εἰς

44–45: Ps. 68:25; 78:6; cf. 74:9. ‖ 48–49: Ier. 8:23.

---

31 ἀπωλώλειμεν Tsaras ‖ 33 ποιότητος corr. Tsaras: πιότητος v ‖ 34 ἀσυρίων v ‖ 34–35 ἀνθρωπείων v ‖ 35 ἣ Tsaras: ἡ v ‖ 36 ἀντὶ Wk (cf. 41): ἁμαρτία (sequente puncto) v ‖ 37 ἀπαγγέλλουσιν corr. Tsaras: ἀπεγγέλλουσιν v ‖ 38–39 lac. 10 litt., ex. gr. supplevi: Ἆρ' οὐκ ὡς ἀσεβοῦντες Tsaras ‖ 39 lac. 4 litt.: λελογίσμεθα καὶ Tsaras (sed ante οὐχ signi interrogandi vestigium) ‖ φαῦλον corr. Wk: φαύλων v ‖ 43 τοῦ πταίσαντος v, corr. Wk (διὰ del. Tsaras) ‖ 50 lac. 12 litt., supplevi (cf. 114): ἐβεβηλώθησαν παρθένοι Mai ‖ 51 lac. 11 litt., suppl. Mai; an potius ἀ[κηλιδώτῳ νυ]μφῶνι? ‖ lac. 4 litt., suppl. Sakkelion

192

I have not even yet mentioned that we are all accountable and that, if the Divine Eye did not look kindly upon us, we would all have perished. What, indeed, was the cause of the recent crop failures? What of the unwonted downpour of rains, which had lost their mild and beneficent quality? What of the impious invasion at this moment of a mixed rabble of Assyrians and Egyptians, who in their campaign against us (oh for my miseries!) appear like heroes, instead of the paralyzed and almost skinless weaklings they are, according to the reports of those who know them well? What is the cause of all this, and for what reason are we thus beset by evils? Is it not because in God's eyes we are reckoned equally guilty? Is it not because He scorns us and has relegated us to the side of the rejected and because we have become hated instead of loved? If there were a single sincere servant of God, on whose service He could rely, surely God would have been moved by that confident prayer of which I spoke, and would have averted these disasters, the wrath against the sinners being checked by the servant's virtue; as it is, the wrath has been poured out on us unmixed, and there is no one to intercede or to ward it off.

Cities have been depopulated; men slaughtered like sheep; women, wrenched from their spouses by main force, are pitifully exposed to the shameless looks of a licentious foe. Oh that my eyes were fountains of tears to weep over these things and others even more pitiable! Churches have been desecrated; virgins, hallowed for the heavenly bride-chamber, have been carried off to be raped; altars of God have been soiled by the filth of the impure; monks and priests are divided between the sword and slavery. Alas for the heaviest of my woes: the relics of the saints, after all their struggles, are now mocked and mangled by the profane, and even after death they suffer a second martyrdom.

Where, Martyr Demetrius, is your invincible succor now? How could you allow your city to be sacked? Inaccessible to enemies under your patronage from the time the sun saw it first, how could it experience

192

πεῖραν ἐγένετο; Πῶς τῆς τῶν δυσσεβούντων ὀφρύος ἠνέσχου κατορχουμένων τῆς ἱερᾶς προστασίας; Πῶς ὑπέμεινες ταῦτα καὶ διεκαρτέρησας; Ἢ πάντως ἂν εἶπες ἡμῖν, εἴπερ ἄξιοι [ἦμεν τῆς σῆς φω]νῆς· ἀκούομεν δὲ ὅμως [. . . . . ,] ἐκ τοῦ οἰκείου συνειδό[τος λα]μβάνοντες τὴν ἀπόκρισιν.

Τίς οὖν ἡ ἀπόκρισις; «Ὅτι πολλῇ κεκρατημένον λύπῃ τὸν δεσπότην ὁρῶ τὸν κοινόν, ἐφ' οἷς τὸ δεσπόζειν ἡ ἁμαρτία λαμβάνει καὶ ἡ ἐλευθερία ἣν μεγάλοις ἡμῖν ἐχαρίσατο πόνοις, σταυρῷ καὶ θανάτῳ, καταπεφρόνηται, μᾶλλον ἐθελόντων ὑπὸ τὸν ἄτιμον ἐκείνης ὑποβεβλῆσθαι ζυγὸν ἢ τῆς δεδομένης ἀντιποιεῖσθαι τιμῆς. Ὅτι ἐπὶ τούτοις αὐτὸν σφοδρότερον καθορῶν ὀδυνώμενον ἢ ὅτε συνεῖχον ὀδύναι ἡνίκα τὰ πανάγια μέλη τὰς τρήσεις ὑπέμενον, κατηφείας εἰμὶ πλήρης καὶ τῆς δεσποτικῆς ὅλως ἐγενόμην ἀλγηδόνος. Καὶ διὰ τοῦτο τῆς ἐμῆς πορθουμένης ἠλόγησα πόλεως, οὐδ' ἐπεστράφην πρὸς τὸ θράσος τῶν δυσμενῶν, οὐδ' ἀντισχόμην τῶν οἰκείων τῆς σωτηρίας, οὐ[δὲ τὴν κατ' ἐμοῦ ὕ]βριν καὶ τῶν συνθεραπόντ[ων γινομένην] διεγνώκειν· ἐπεὶ καὶ πολλά[κις τις βα]σιλεῖ παρεστὼς καὶ τοῦτον θεώμενος ὀξείαις ἀλγηδόσι βαλλόμενον, εἰ καὶ παῖδες αὐτῷ θνῄσκειν φίλτατοι κινδυνεύουσιν, εἰ καὶ τῶν κτημάτων τὰ τιμιώτερα πυρπολοῖτο, εἰ καί τινες ὑβρισταὶ χεῖρας ἐπάγοιεν, τούτων οὐδενὸς ποιεῖται τὴν ἐπιστροφήν, μόνης δὲ τῆς τοῦ βασιλέως γίνεται συνοχῆς καὶ ἐπὶ ταύτην ὅλως σπαράσσεται τὴν καρδίαν, καὶ τῶν ἰδίως λυπούντων τὴν αἴσθησιν οὐ προσίεται.»

Ταῦτα ἐγὼ ἐνηχοῦμαι· ταῦτα καὶ ὑμεῖς, μὴ μόνον τῆς ἐμῆς γλώσσης, ἀλλὰ καὶ ὑφ' ἑαυτοῦ ἕκαστος ἐνηχείσθω. Ἐπεὶ πῶς ἂν ἄλλως ὁ πολλαῖς μυριάσιν ἐθνῶν πολλάκις ἐπαρκέσας μόνος καὶ ἀντικαταστὰς καὶ καταισχύνας καὶ τρεψάμενος καὶ τὴν οἰκείαν ἑστίαν περισωσάμενος, [νῦν ἀθρόον ἀφ]ηρημένος τὴν δύναμιν [καὶ τοὺς αὐτοῦ ο]ἰκειοτάτους ἀρνησάμενος [παντελῶς, ο]ὐκ ἐπεδείξατο τὴν συνήθη [κηδεμ]ονίαν; Ἀλλὰ τοῦτό ἐστιν ὅπερ εἶπον· σφοδραῖς ὁ σωτὴρ ἡμῶν

59–60 κατορχουμένων corr. Sakkelion: κατορχουμένω v ‖ 60 ὑπέμεινας Tsaras ‖ 61 ἢ v ‖ lac. 12 litt., supplevi (accentus dispiciuntur): ἦμεν ἐλεημοσύνης Tsaras ‖ 62 lac. 11 litt., suppleas ἅπερ ἂν ἔλεγες (πάντα τὰ φαῦλα Tsaras) ‖ lac. 5 litt., suppl. Tsaras ‖ 71 scr. ὅλος? ‖ 73 scr. ἀντεσχόμην? ‖ 74 lac. 13 litt., ex. gr. supplevi: οὐδ' ἀντέτεινα ὕβριν Tsaras ‖ lac. 10 litt., ex. gr. supplevi: συνθεραπόντων οὐδέν τι Tsaras ‖ 75 lac. 10 litt., supplevi: πολλάκις τῷ ἐμῷ βασιλεῖ Tsaras ‖ 79 ἐπὶ corr. Tsaras: ἐπει (sic) v ‖ 80 scr. ταύτῃ? ‖ scr. ὅλος? ‖ 86 lac. 12 litt., ex. gr. supplevi: εὑρεθήσεται ἐστερημένος Tsaras ‖ 86–87 lac. 10 litt., suppl. Tsaras ‖ 87 lac. 8 litt., ex. gr. supplevi: πάντῃ οὐκ Tsaras ‖ 88 lac. 5 litt. et ωνίαν v, supplevi: κοινωνίαν Tsaras

192 evils so great? How could you bear the pride of the impious deriding your holy protection? How did you endure and tolerate this? You would certainly have told us, if we deserved ⟨to hear your voice⟩; but we, nevertheless, understand ⟨what you have to say,⟩ finding the answer in our own consciences.

What, then, is the answer? "It happened because I see our common Lord overcome with deep grief that sin is getting the upper hand and that the freedom which He bestowed on us at the cost of great pains, of the cross, and of death is despised, and we prefer to bear the shameful yoke of sin rather than to claim the honor granted to us; because, seeing Him smarting more grievously on account of this than when pain tortured Him in the piercing of His holy limbs, I am filled with sadness and became wholly immersed in the suffering of my Master; and for this reason I paid no heed when my city was wrecked, nor did I attend to the insolence of the enemies or fight to protect my friends, or even notice the indignities done ⟨to myself⟩ and to my fellow servants. Often, indeed, when ⟨a man⟩ is standing by the side of his king and sees him struck by sharp pains, even though his dearest children are in danger of death, even though his most precious possessions are on fire, even though assailants lay their hands on him, he does not heed any of these things; he is only aware of his king's anguish, and because of it his heart is all rent with pain and he shuts out the perception of what hurts him personally."

This is what I hear, and what I want you to hear also, not only from my mouth, but each of you from yourselves. How else could it be that one who on many occasions was all by himself a match for many thousands of heathens, who withstood them and put them to shame and to flight and saved his own homestead—how could it be that he ⟨suddenly⟩ lost his power, altogether forsook his nearest and dearest, and failed to display his wonted care? The reason is the one I said: our Saviour and God, Who

192

καὶ θεὸς ὁ τῶν τοῦ πατρὸς ἑαυτὸν κενώσας κόλπων, ὁ ἀγαπήσας ἡμᾶς καὶ συμφυεῖς ἐξ ἀφράστου ποιήσας ἀγάπης, κεντεῖται καὶ δριμείαις ὀδύναις, ὅτι τοσοῦτον ἀγαπήσας οὐκ ἔχει ποθοῦντας, ὅτι τιμήσας ἀσυγκρίτως οὐ μόνον οὐχ ὁρᾷ τιμῶντας, ἀλλὰ καὶ τὸ ὑβρίζειν παρ' οὐδὲν ποιουμένους.

Καὶ μή τινι δόξῃ βαρὺ τὸ λεγόμενον· παντὸς γάρ ἐστιν ἀληθέστερον μᾶλλον. Ἢ γὰρ οὐχ ὕβρις, ὅταν τῶν νόμων τοῦ δεσπότου καταφρονοῦντες τῷ νόμῳ τῆς ἁμαρτίας πειθώμεθα, καὶ πρὸς μὲν τὰ προστάγματα τούτου κωφεύωμεν, πρὸς δὲ τὰ ἐκείνης ἕτοιμοι πειθαρχεῖν εὑρισκώμεθα; Ἢ τί πράττομεν, ὅταν μισῶμεν, ὅταν φθονῶμεν, ὅταν συκοφαντῶμεν καὶ ταῖς κα̣[τ' ἀλλήλων ἐν]τρυφῶμεν λοιδορίαις, ὅταν [τὸ συμπα]θὲς πρὸς τοὺς συμπαθείας ἐ̣π̣ι̣[δεο]μένους οὐ μόνον οὐκ ἐπιδεικνύωμεν, ἀλλὰ καὶ τὸ δάκρυον τούτων ἡδονὴν ἰδίαν καὶ εὐπορίαν ποιώμεθα; Ταῦτα οὐχ ὑβρίζει, ταῦτα οὐ λυπεῖ, ταῦτα τὸν δεσπότην οὐκ ὀδυνᾷ πλέον τῶν ποτὲ διαπειράντων αὐτὸν ἥλων; Ἐγὼ τοῦτο καὶ ὑπολαμβάνω καὶ πείθομαι. Εἰ γάρ τις νομοθέτης οἰκεῖον νόμον ἀθετούμενον ἐπιγνούς, ὕβριν ἑαυτοῦ τὸ πρᾶγμα ποιεῖται καὶ λύπην καὶ ἄλγος, καίτοι οὐ πόνοις ἰδίοις οὐδὲ πάθεσιν οὐδ' ἄχρι τοῦ τι παθεῖν τὸν νόμον σπουδάσας, ἀλλ' ἀπὸ δίφρου μόνον δικαιῶν ⟨καὶ⟩ θεμιστεύων, τί χρὴ λογίζεσθαι περὶ τοῦ καμάτῳ τοσούτῳ καὶ πάθεσι τὸν νόμον ἡμῖν γεγραφότος; Καὶ παραλείπω τὸ μέσον θεοῦ καὶ ἀνθρώπων.

Διὰ ταῦτα δορυάλωτος ἡ πόλις, [ἧς τὸ κλέος] πανταχοῦ διεφοίτα, δι[ὰ ταῦτα ἡ δ]υστυχὴς Θεσσαλονίκη ἔργον π̣[. . . χ]ειρὸς πολεμίας, διὰ τοῦτο τοῦ λαοῦ τὴν σφαγήν, τῶν γυναίων τὴν ὕβριν, τῶν μοναζόντων καὶ ἱερέων τὴν ἀπώλειαν, τὴν βεβήλωσιν τῶν ἁγίων ὑπέμεινεν ὁ μάρτυς καὶ τὴν ἄμυναν οὐκ ἐπεδείξατο· διὰ ταῦτα καὶ τὰ λοιπὰ ἐκαρτέρησεν, ὅσα τοῖς εἰδόσι τραγῳδεῖν πάθη διὰ παντὸς ἀπόχρη τοῦ βίου πρὸς τραγῳδίαν.

89: cf. Ioann. 1:18; Phil. 2:7. ‖ 96: Rom. 7:21; 25.

---

94 δόξῃ corr. Wk: δόξει v ‖ 99 κα (α dub.) et lac. 11 litt., supplevi: κεναῖς ἐντρυφῶμεν Tsaras ‖ 100 lac. 7 litt., suppl. Tsaras ‖ ἐπι (dub.) et lac. 2 litt., supplevi: ὡπλισμένους Tsaras ‖ 101 ἐπιδεικνύωμεν corr. Tsaras: ἐπιδεικνύομεν v ‖ 102 εὐπορίαν Wk: ἀπορίαν v ‖ 103 ἥλον (sic) v ‖ 106 καίτοι Tsaras: καίτι v ‖ 107 καὶ add. Wk ‖ 111 lac. 12 litt., ex. gr. supplevi: ἐγένετο καὶ Tsaras ‖ 112 lac. 8 litt., διὰ τοῦτο ἡ δυστυχὴς suppl. Tsaras ‖ π (potius quam ω) et lac. 4 litt.: ὠμῆς χειρὸς Tsaras, fort. πάσα χειρὸς

192

emptied Himself out from His Father's bosom, Who has loved us and out of inexpressible love made us share in His Nature, is pierced by violent and bitter pains because after so much love he finds no affection in us, because after such incomparable honor bestowed upon us He finds that, so far from honoring Him, we think it no great matter to outrage Him.

And let nobody think the word too strong; it is perfectly accurate. Or is it not an outrage when, despising the Master's laws, we obey the laws of Sin; when we are deaf to His commandments but are found willing to comply with hers? What else do we do when we hate, when we envy, when we slander and indulge in abuse against one another, when not only do we fail to show compassion toward those who are in need of it, but even consider their tears a joy and a boon to ourselves? Do these things not outrage, do they not grieve, do they not hurt the Master more than the nails that pierced Him once? I think so and am convinced of it. If a lawgiver, finding that a law of his own is invalidated, considers the fact an insult to himself and a cause for grief and pain, although he did not establish that law at the cost of any toil or trouble to himself, nor of any personal suffering, but simply promulgated it from his seat of office, what are we to think of Him Who wrote the law for us at the price of such toil, such suffering? And then I do not even speak of the distance between God and men.

This is why the city of worldwide ⟨fame⟩ has been captured, this is why unfortunate Thessalonica has fallen into the cruel hands of the enemy, this is why the Martyr permitted the slaughter of the people, the outrage against the women, the deaths of the monks and priests, the profanation of the shrines, without proffering his help. This is why he tolerated all those things which to those who know how to lament pitiable events would suffice for a lifetime of lamentation.

Ἀλλὰ νήψωμεν, ἀδελφοί, διαγρηγορήσωμεν· φύγωμεν τὴν δουλείαν τῆς ἁμαρτίας, δι' ἣν πάντα τὰ κακὰ εἰς τὸν κόσμον εἰσήλασαν. Αὕτη πᾶσαν σάρκα κατέκλυσεν ὕδατι, ὅσον μόνον εἰς τὸ περιλειφθῆναι σπέρμα ζωῆς δι' ἀγαθότητα τοῦ πλάσαντος συγχωρήσασα· διὰ ταύτην πυρὸς ἐπίκλυσις τοὺς κατακριθέντας ἀνάλωσεν· αὕτη πόλεις αὐτάνδρους βυθῷ καὶ γῆς χάσματι παραδέδωκεν· αὕτη χερσὶ μ[ιαραῖς ὅπλα] κατὰ τῶν ἀσεβούντων χαρίζ[εται· αὕτη] τῆς ῥάβδου τῶν ἁμαρτωλῶν παιούσης οὐκ ἐᾷ φθέγγεσθαι τὸν κλῆρον ἡμᾶς ποιησάμενον. Ταύτην ὅλῃ δυνάμει καὶ ἀφ' ἡμῶν καὶ ἀπ' ἀλλήλων, παρακαλοῦντες, ἐκδυσωποῦντες, ἐλέγχοντες, πόρρω ποιήσωμεν, ἵνα μὴ καὶ ἡμεῖς ἐλεεινοτέρα τραγῳδία τῷ μετέπειτα βίῳ γενώμεθα καὶ τὸν δεσπότην ἐπὶ πλέον ὀργιζόμενον ἴδωμεν, ἀλλὰ τῆς φίλης αὐτῷ χρηστότητος ἀπολαύσωμεν, καὶ νῦν καὶ ἀεὶ καὶ εἰς τοὺς αἰῶνας τῶν αἰώνων, ἀμήν.

193. Letter to Andronicus Ducas

Δοὺξ ἐνδοξότατε καὶ μεγαλοπρεπέστατε, μελλοαύγουστε Ἀνδρόνικε, παρεγγυῶμαι καὶ παραινῶ σοι μὴ προέσθαι ἑαυτὸν μηδ' ὑποκαταβληθῆναι τοῖς ἀπὸ τοῦ βασιλέως μηδὲ καταπιστεῦσαι τοῖς ἐξιοῦσι πρός σε. Ψευδῆ γὰρ ἅπαντα καὶ ἕωλα τὰ δηλούμενα καὶ γραφόμενα· ὁ γὰρ Σατανώνυμος ἀκμὴν κατὰ σοῦ διαπρίεται Σαμωνᾶς. Μεῖνον τοίνυν προσκαρτερῶν καὶ ἐνδυναμούμενος καὶ κατὰ τοὔνομα καὶ τὴν πρᾶξιν ἐπιδεικνύμενος, καὶ ἡ πόλις ταχέως διὰ τῶν ἡμῶν παραινέσεων ἐπιζητήσει σε. Μὴ ἐπιλάθῃ δὲ τῆς ἡμῶν ταπεινώσεως κατευοδούμενος. Ἔρρωσο.

---

118 Ἀλλ' ἀνανήψωμεν scr. Tsaras (cf. *Letters,* Epistola 17. 119) ‖ 119 εἰσήλασαν corr. Tsaras: εἰσέλλασαν v ‖ 123–124 lac. 10 litt., ex. gr. supplevi: μιαραῖς καὶ Tsaras ‖ 124 χαριζ et lac. 7 litt., ex. gr. supplevi: χαριζομένη διὰ Tsaras ‖ 125 φθέγγεσθαι] an scr. τέγγεσθαι? ‖ 130 εὔχου καὶ τὸ γράψαντι add. scriba v

---

193: c (= *Vita Euthymii,* 69, 25–71, 1) ‖ 1 μελοαύγουστε c ‖ 6 κατὰ τοὔνομα ci. de Boor: κατ' οὔνομα c

But let us be sober, brothers, let us wake up; let us escape from the bondage of sin, because of which all evils have made their entrance into the world. It was on its account that all flesh was swept away by the flood so that only the seed of life was permitted to survive by the Creator's goodness; it was on account of sin that a deluge of fire consumed the condemned; it is sin that has made cities disappear, men and all, in the abyss and in a chasm of the earth; it is sin that arms the hands of the defiled against the impious; sin, while the rod of the iniquitous is striking us, does not allow Him Who made us His heritage to make His voice heard. Let us muster our strength to banish it from ourselves and from each other, by admonition, entreaty, reproof lest we too become an even more pitiful tragedy in the eyes of posterity and see our Master angered more and more; rather, may we enjoy the kindness so dear to Him, now and always and for ever and ever, amen.

193. Letter to Andronicus Ducas

Most glorious and illustrious Ducas, future Augustus Andronicus, I counsel and exhort you not to surrender, not to submit to the Emperor's men, nor to trust the envoys who are coming to you. All the messages and letters are false and treacherous; Satan's namesake Samonas is still raging against you. Therefore, stay where you are, holding out and gathering strength, and acting in a manner worthy of your name; then the City by our exhortations will soon ask for you. But do not forget Our Humility in the hour of achievement. Farewell.

194. First Act of Abdication

I

Ἐπειδήπερ πραγμάτων ἐναντιότητος καὶ δυσχερείας τὴν τοῦ θεοῦ καταλαβούσης ἐκκλησίαν εἰς τὸ ἀδύνατον περιέστην τοῦ οἰκονομεῖν τι περὶ τὸν φιλόχριστον βασιλέα, τὸν θρόνον παραιτοῦμαι, τὴν καθ' ἐμαυτὸν ἰδίᾳ καὶ ἀνακεχωρημένην προτιμήσας ζωὴν τῆς ἐν πράγμασιν ἀστατούσης συναναστροφῆς, μὴ τῆς θείας ἐξιστάμενος ἱερωσύνης, ἐν ᾧ ἂν τόπῳ τὴν ταπεινὴν ἡμῶν παρελκύσωμεν ζωήν.

II

Ἔγγραφος παραίτησις Νικολάου τοῦ ἁγιωτάτου πατριάρχου τοῦ Γαλακρινίτου, μεθ' ἣν ἀπεκατέστη αὖθις εἰς τὸν πατριαρχικὸν θρόνον

Νικόλαος ἀρχιεπίσκοπος Κωνσταντινουπόλεως, μόνῃ χάριτι θείᾳ τὸ μέγα τοῦτο καὶ οὐράνιον δώρημα λαβὼν καὶ παρ' ἑαυτοῦ μηδέν τι προσενεγκάμενος ἄξιον, ἐπειδὴ πραγμάτων ἐναντιότητος καὶ δυσχερείας τὴν τοῦ θεοῦ καταλαβούσης ἐκκλησίαν εἰς τὸ ἀδύνατον περιέστη τοῦ τι περὶ τὸν φιλόχριστον οἰκονομῆσαι βασιλέα, τὸν θρόνον παραιτοῦμαι, τὴν κατ' ἐμαυτὸν ἰδίαν καὶ ἀνακεχωρημένην προτιμήσας ζωὴν τῆς ἐν πράγμασιν ἀστατούσης ἀναστροφῆς, μὴ τῆς θείας ἐξιστάμενος ἀρχιερωσύνης μηδὲ τοῦ ἐπιτελεῖν ὅσα οἶδεν ἐνεργεῖν ἀρχιερωσύνη, ἐν ᾧ ἂν τόπῳ τὴν ταπεινὴν ἡμῶν παρελκύσωμεν ζωήν, εἰδότες ἀκίνδυνον οὐκ ὂν τὸ τὴν θείαν ὥσπερ ἀπαρεσκόμενον αὐτῇ

---

194 I: c (= *Vita Euthymii,* 93, 13–19) ‖ 2 καταλαβούσης infra 194 II 7: καταλαβοῦσαν c

---

194 II: p 350v z 342v k (= Papadopulos-Kerameus, *Varia graeca sacra,* 258) j 16v ‖ 1–3 Παραίτησις kj ‖ 1 γραφος p Ἡ ἔγγραφος z ‖ 2 γαλακρινίτου p: χρυσοβέργη z ‖ ἀπεκατέστη p: ἀποκατέστη z ‖ 4 Νικόλαος — 6 ἄξιον om. kj ‖ 5 ἑαυτοῦ p: ἐμαυτοῦ z ‖ 6 προσενεγκάμενος p: συνεισενεγκάμενος z ‖ 8 τοῦ — οἰκονομῆσαι] τοῦ οἰκονομεῖν τι περὶ τὸν φιλόχριστον kj ‖ τοῦ τι] τουτι p τουτὶ z ‖ 10 ἀστατούσης pz: ἀστατοῦσιν j ἀναστατοῦσιν k ‖ μὴ τῆς pz: μήτε kj ‖ 11 ὅσα οἶδεν ἐνεργεῖν pz: πάντα ὅσα ἐνεργεῖν οἶδεν kj

194. First Act of Abdication

I

Inasmuch as owing to the untoward and disturbing events that have overtaken the Church of God I have found myself unable to grant a dispensation to the Christ-loving Emperor, I resign my see, preferring a life on my own, in privacy and retirement, to the uncertainty of involvement in public affairs, without, however, renouncing the divine priesthood, in whatever place we drag out our humble life.

II

Written Abdication of the Most Holy Patriarch Nicholas of Galacrene, after which He Returned again to the Patriarchal See

I, Nicholas, Archbishop of Constantinople, who only by the Grace of God have received this great and heavenly gift and have brought to it nothing of my own to deserve it: inasmuch as the untoward and disturbing events that have overtaken the Church of God have rendered it impossible to grant a dispensation to the Christ-loving Emperor: I resign my see, preferring a life on my own, in privacy and retirement, to the uncertainty of involvement in public affairs, without, however, renouncing the divine archpriesthood or the exercise of all the functions of archpriesthood, in whatever place we drag out our humble life; for we know that it is not without peril to dismiss the divine gift as if it were not pleasing, all the

ἀποπέμπεσθαι χάριν· ἄλλως τε καὶ τοῦ ἱεροῦ κανόνος τοὺς ἐξομοσαμένους τὴν ἐν ᾗ ἐτάχθησαν ἱερὰν λειτουργίαν, κἂν φόβος ὁ ἐξ ἀνθρώπων ᾖ πρὸς τοῦτο συνωθήσας, ἀπαραιτήτως καὶ συγγνώμης ἁπάσης χωρὶς καθαιροῦντος καὶ εἰς τὴν τῶν λαϊκῶν ἀπορρίπτοντος χώραν.

195. Second Act of Abdication

Ἐπειδὴ προεπηγγειλάμην συμφωνίᾳ τῆς ἐκκλησίας περὶ τὸν φιλόχριστον οἰκονομεῖν βασιλέα χάριν τῆς συνοικούσης αὐτῷ γυναικός, ὁρῶ δὲ μακρὰν καὶ ἀκατάπαυστον διαφωνίαν πρὸς τὸ τὶ περὶ αὐτὸν οἰκονομεῖν, ἐξίσταμαι τοῦ θρόνου τῷ δυναμένῳ τὴν διαφωνίαν εἰς ὁμογνωμοσύνην ἄγειν παραχωρῶν· τὰ δὲ τῆς ἀρχιερωσύνης καὶ τῶν ταύτης ἐνεργειῶν, ἵλεω θεοῦ ὑπάρχοντος, διὰ βίου ἀναδέξομαι.

196. Third Act of Abdication

Ἐπειδὴ ἐκ διαφωνίας καὶ γνώμης πρὸς ἀλλήλους μαχομένης, ὅπερ θεοῦ ἀρχιερεῦσιν ἀνοίκειον, πρὸς συμφωνίαν καὶ φίλην ὁμογνωμοσύνην κατέστητε, διὰ τοῦτο κρίσει μιᾷ τὰ περὶ τὸν φιλόχριστον βασιλέα οἰκονομεῖτε χάριν τῆς συνοικούσης αὐτῷ γυναικός, οὐκ ἀντιφθέγγομαι ὑμῖν, ἀλλὰ στέργων τὴν οἰκονομίαν καὶ τὴν συμφωνίαν ἀποδεχόμενος ἐξίσταμαι τοῦ θρόνου, τοῦτο μὲν ὡς ἄνθρωπος ὢν καὶ ἀνθρώπινόν τι πεπονθώς, ἐφ' οἷς ἐπὶ μακρῷ χρόνῳ τὴν ψυχὴν κατετρίβην ἐπὶ ταῖς ὑμῶν ἔρισι καὶ φιλονεικίαις, τοῦτο δὲ καὶ ὅτι οὐκ οἶδα εἴ τις ἀνθρώπων ἀγαπήσας τῇ περὶ τὸν φιλόχριστον βασιλέα ἐμαυτὸν ἀγάπῃ ἀναδησάμενος ὑπὸ τῆς τῶν πραγμάτων περιηνέχθην ἀνωμαλίας, ὥστε καὶ ἡμᾶς ἐκεῖνον λυπῆσαι καὶ αὐτὸν πρὸς ἡμᾶς ἐκτραχυνθῆναι. Διὰ τοῦτο ἐξίσταμαι τοῦ θρόνου, τὴν καθ' ἑαυτὸν ἡσυχίαν προκρίνας τῆς ἀνθρωπίνης ματαιότητος καὶ τὸ τὰ οἰκεῖα καὶ καθ' ἑαυτὸν ἀσφαλίζεσθαι ἢ ἐν τοῖς ἀνθρωπίνοις στρέφεσθαι πράγμασι.

---

194 II: 14–17: *ACO*, I, 1, 7, pp. 123, 24–124, 25.

---

14 τε pz: τε δὲ kj ‖ 15 ἱερὰν λειτουργίαν] ἱερωσύνην z ‖ 16 πρὸς pz: ὁ πρὸς kj ‖ 17 ἦν δὲ οὗτος ὁ π(ατ)ριάρχης ἐπὶ τοῦ βασιλέως κῦρ λέοντος τοῦ σοφοῦ in fine add. z

195: c (= *Vita Euthymii*, 93, 22–29)

196: c (= *Vita Euthymii*, 99, 16–30) ‖ 3 διά ⟨τε⟩ coni. de Boor

more so as by the Holy Canon those who have abdicated the sacred ministry in which they were placed, even if constrained by the fear of men, are inexorably and without pardon deposed and reduced to the rank of laymen.

195. Second Act of Abdication

Inasmuch as I have undertaken, subject to the unanimous consent of the Church, to grant dispensation to the Christ-loving Emperor in the matter of the woman who shares his life, but am faced with a long and interminable discord preventing any kind of dispensation, I cede my see to one who is able to turn this discord into unanimity; however, as regards the archpriesthood and its functions, I shall, God willing, continue to exercise them as long as I live.

196. Third Act of Abdication

Since from a state of strife and contention, unworthy of archpriests of God, you have now turned to concord and friendly agreement and are therefore unanimously willing to grant dispensation to the Christ-loving Emperor in the matter of the woman who shares his life, I do not gainsay you, but acquiescing in the dispensation and commending your agreement, I resign my see; partly because, being human and having human feelings, I have suffered long mental torture by your quarrels and fights, partly also because, while attached to the Christ-loving Emperor by a love such as perhaps no other man has ever experienced, yet I was swept away by the unfortunate events to the point where I hurt him and he became embittered against me. Therefore I resign my see, choosing a state of quiet retirement in preference to the vanity of human affairs and safeguarding my own personal well-being in preference to entanglement in the troubles of man.

197

Νικολάου πατριάρχου τὰ κατ' αὐτὸν καὶ τοὺς τότε ἀρχιερεῖς διὰ τὴν τετραγαμίαν

«Υἱοὺς ἐγέννησα καὶ ὕψωσα, αὐτοὶ δέ με ἠθέτησαν,» προείρηται πάλαι περὶ ὧν προείρηκεν ὁ θεός. Νυνὶ δὲ ὡσαύτως εἴποι ἂν ἡ τοῦ θεοῦ ἐκκλησία εἰκότως περὶ τῶν ἐπὶ κακῷ τῷ οἰκείῳ γεννηθέντων αὐτῇ· κακὰ γάρ ἐπεσωρεύσατε ἑαυτοῖς, καθ' ἑτέρων ἐπισυναγαγεῖν ταῦτα σπουδάσαντες, οἱ (πῶς εἴπω οὐκ οἶδα, ἢ ποίοις κρίμασιν, ἀντὶ τέκνων ἐχθροὶ μέλλοντες ἔσεσθαι) ἐν τῇ μυστικῇ παστάδι ἀποτεχθέντες τῆς ἐκκλησίας. Ἀλλὰ γὰρ τετοκυῖα ὑμᾶς, ὡς εἴθε μὴ ὤφελε, καὶ ὑψώσασα, τῶν ὠδίνων ἔσχεν ἀμοιβὴν παρ' ὑμῶν τὴν ἀθέτησιν. Δέον γὰρ ὑπὲρ τῆς ἀκηράτου καὶ ἀχράντως τεκούσης προκινδυνεύειν ὑμᾶς καὶ πάσῃ δυνάμει τῆς δόξης καὶ τιμῆς ἀντέχεσθαι τῆς μητρός, ὑμεῖς δὲ τὴν ἐναντίαν μᾶλλον εἵλεσθε γνώμην, καὶ ἀντὶ τοῦ προκινδυνεύειν περιεστήσατε εἰς κινδύνους, καὶ τὸν ὑπὲρ αὐτῆς ὀφειλόμενον ἀγῶνα εἰς τὸν κατ' ἐκείνης μετεστρέψατε πόλεμον, καὶ ἀντὶ τοῦ τιμᾶν ὑβρίζειν ἐγνώκατε, καὶ ὕβριν ἣν μήτε ὁ προλαβὼν ἀνθρώποις ὑπέδειξε χρόνος, εἰπόντες τοῦτο δὴ τοῖς πράγμασιν, εἰ καὶ μὴ λόγοις, τὸ τοῖς πορευομένοις ὀπίσω τῶν οἰκείων θελημάτων εἰρημένον, «Τὰ χείλη ἡμῶν παρ' ἡμῶν ἐστι· τίς ἡμῶν κύριός ἐστι;» νομίσαντες πᾶσαν αἰδῶ καὶ δικαιοσύνην ἐξ ἀνθρώπων ἠφανίσθαι, μᾶλλον δέ, εἰ δεῖ τὴν πᾶσαν ὑμῶν διάνοιαν ἐξειπεῖν, μηδ' ἐν τῷ μέλλοντι δοκοῦντες πολιτεύεσθαι δικαιοσύνην αἰῶνι.

Πῶς γὰρ τοιούτων δραμάτων ἐγένεσθε ποιηταί, εἰ δίκης ἐν ὑμῖν ἀνέβαινε λογισμός, πρῶτον μὲν κατὰ τοῦ οἰκείου ἀρχιερέως καὶ διέπειν τὴν ἐκκλησίαν (εἰ καὶ ἀχρείου) λαχόντος καὶ τῆς ἰδίας κεφαλῆς ἀποστασίαν μελετήσαντες καὶ πολέμιοι ἀντὶ τέκνων γεγονότες; Ἢ οὐχὶ τοῦτο καὶ πρὶν λανθάνοντες συνεσκευάσασθε καὶ κατ' ἐκείνην δὴ τὴν ἡμέραν ὅτε ἀναίδην καὶ δημοσίᾳ ἡμῶν ἀπέστητε δήλην τὴν συσκευὴν ἐποιήσασθε; Τοῦ γὰρ βασιλέως συγκεκληκότος ἡμᾶς καὶ τοιαύτην ἀφιέντος φωνήν, «Ὅσοι τῆς μερίδος, τῆς ἡμῶν χωρίσθητε βασιλείας,» φανερῶς ἐξ ἡμῶν ἀπορραγέντες οἷόν τι πολέμιον στῖφος

197: 3: Is. 1:2. ‖ 18: cf. Sir. 18:30. ‖ 18–19: Ps. 11:5.

197: k (= Papadopulos-Kerameus, *Varia graeca sacra,* 255–59) j 16^{r-v} ‖ 6 ἐπισυναγωγῶν j ‖ 7 οἱ πῶς k: οἵπερ j ‖ 9 τῶν ἐκκλησιῶν j ‖ ὑμῶν j ‖ 11 ἀχράντου j ‖ 14 αὐτὸν j ‖ 18 τοῦ πορευομένου j ‖ 18–19 ταχίλη k ‖ 19 ἡμῶν^{2} k LXX: ἡμῖν j ‖ inter ἐστι et νομίσαντες] ὅρα ins. j ‖ 28 δὴ k: δὲ j ‖ 30 ἡμῶν k: ἐμῆς j

197

Nicholas the Patriarch on the Events Affecting Him and the Former Archpriests in the Matter of the Fourth Marriage

"I have borne and raised sons, and they have rebelled against me"—this was said long ago of those of whom God then spoke. Now, however, God's Church might well repeat it of the children born to her to their own misfortune; for you have heaped evils upon yourselves while endeavoring to bring them upon others, you that were born (I know not how, nor by what decrees of Providence, since you were to turn out enemies instead of children) in the mystical Bride chamber of the Church. Nevertheless, having borne you (as would God she had not!) and raised you, she was rewarded for her labor with rebellion; for when you should have staked your lives for the Pure One who bore you without stain, when you should with all your might have stood up for the glory and honor of your Mother, you chose the contrary course, and so far from braving dangers in her defense you imperiled her, you changed the championship due to her into warfare against her, and instead of honoring her you thought fit to insult her—an insult of which the past has not even an example to show to men; for you said by your deeds, if not in words, what was spoken by those who follow their own desires: "Our lips are our own; who is lord over us?" thinking that all decency and justice has disappeared from among men, and what is more, if I must put into words your entire thought, that neither does justice obtain in the world to come.

How, indeed, could you have written the text for such dramas as these, if the notion of a just retribution were present in your minds: conspiring, in the first place, to betray your own Archpriest, charged (in spite of his unworthiness) with the government of the Church, to betray your own Head, and becoming foes instead of sons? Or is it not true that you had for a long time been plotting this in secret and that you only brought out your plot into the open on that day when you betrayed us shamelessly and publicly? Indeed, when the Emperor had summoned us and spoke these words, "All those who are of that faction, leave our Presence," you overtly broke away from us and like a hostile force passed over

197

ἐκείνῳ προσέθεσθε· καὶ τοῦτο οὐχ ἅπαξ, ἀλλὰ καὶ πάλιν ἐν τοῖς βασιλείοις προσκεκλημένοι δὶς ἀπειργάσασθε. Καὶ ἡ ἄρνησις δὲ τῆς ὁμολογίας ὑμῶν, ἣν ἐνώπιον θεοῦ καὶ ἀγγέλων καὶ ἀνθρώπων ὡμολογήσατε, μηδὲν τῆς ἡμῶν ἔξω γνώμης πράττειν, ἀλλὰ μᾶλλον ἀκολουθήσειν ἡμῖν, εἴ τι γνοίημεν περὶ τοῦ ἐξ ἀνθρώπων ἀπελθόντος βασιλέως οἰκονομεῖν, πρὸς τί ἄλλο ἢ πρὸς τοῦτο καταστρέφει, τὸ μὴ προσεῖναι ὑμῖν ἔννοιαν δικαιωτηρίου καὶ κρίσεως; Τὸ δὲ παρὰ τῆς ἡμῶν μετριότητος, ὁπότε τὸ σχῆμα τῆς βασιλικῆς παρακελεύσεως ἅπαντας ἐξῆγε τῆς πόλεως, εἰρημένον ὑμῖν κοινῇ συνηθροισμένοις καὶ πρὸς τὴν ἔξοδον σύνταξιν ποιουμένοις, ὡς οὐδενὶ ἔξεστι χωρὶς τῆς πάντων συμφωνίας ἐπιτελεῖν τινα οἰκονομίαν, ἀλλ' εἴτε δοίη θεὸς ἐν βίῳ διαμένειν ἡμᾶς, εἴτε ἐξ ἀνθρώπων μεθίστησι, κοινῇ γνώμῃ καὶ ψήφῳ, εἴ τι γενέσθαι δεήσειε, τοῦτο ἐπιτελεῖν, καὶ ὡς εἴ τις μὴ οὕτως φρονήσειεν, ἀλλ' ἄνευ τῆς κοινῆς πάντων ἐπικρίσεως τολμήσει τι πράττειν, οὗτος ἀπαραιτήτως εἴη φέρων τὴν καταδίκην παρά τε πατρὸς καὶ υἱοῦ καὶ ἁγίου πνεύματος ἔν τε τῷ νῦν αἰῶνι καὶ ἐν τῷ μέλλοντι καὶ παρὰ τῆς ἡμῶν μετριότητος, πῶς οὐκ ἐλέγχει ὑμᾶς μηδ' ὅλως ἔννοιαν ἐσχηκότας ἢ ζωῆς μελλούσης ἢ τῆς τῶν βεβιωμένων ἐτάσεως;

Ἀλλὰ ταῦτα μὲν τοιούτους ἀποφαίνει ὑμᾶς· σκοπῶμεν δὲ καὶ τὰ ἐπὶ τούτοις προσεξειργασμένα. Ἀπηλάσατε τοῦ ποιμνίου ἡμᾶς· εἰ γὰρ καὶ βασιλεὺς τοῦτο πράττειν ἐδόκει, ἀλλ' ὑπουργὸς ἦν ἐκεῖνος τῆς ὑμῶν ἐπιτροπῆς καὶ τοῦ βουλήματος· αὐτοὶ γὰρ καὶ πρὸ ἐκείνου καὶ σὺν αὐτῷ τὴν καθ' ἡμῶν ἐπιβουλὴν ἐποιήσασθε. Δῆλον δὲ καὶ ἐκ τῶν εἰρημένων καὶ ἐκ τούτου μᾶλλον. Ἐν μεταγνώσει γὰρ τοῦ βασιλέως καταστάντος καὶ τοῦ μεγέθους τοῦ κακοῦ ταχέως αὐτὸν ἀναφρονῆσαι παρασκευάσαντος, ἐβουλεύσατο πάλιν ὅθεν κακῶς ἐξήλασεν ἐπαναγαγεῖν· καὶ γράμματι τοῦτο ἐδήλωσε καὶ ὅρκοις ἐβεβαίου τὸ δόξαν, ἀποστόλῳ χρησάμενος καὶ τοῦ γράμματος καὶ τῶν ὁρκίων διακόνῳ τῷ κατ' ἐκεῖνο καιροῦ τὸ δύνασθαι παρ' αὐτῷ λαχόντι. Καὶ ἐπεὶ κοινωνοὺς ὑμᾶς τοῦ δόξαντος προσελάβετο, μίαν ἐρρήξατε φωνὴν καὶ ἠπειλήσατε ἦ μὴν ἅπαντας ἔσεσθαι φυγάδας καὶ ἀντὶ μητροπόλεων τὰς ἐρήμους οἰκήσειν, εἰ πρὸς ὑμᾶς διαπράξει τὸν πατριάρχην ἐπανελεύσεσθαι.

---

38 παρὰ Karlin-Hayter: περὶ kj ‖ 40 συνηθροισμένον j ‖ 41 χωρὶς j: χάριν k ‖ 42 inter οἰκονομίαν et ἀλλ'] σημείωσαι, χρονικόν (leg. χρήσιμον) ἀνάξιον τοῦτο ἔργον συνοδικὸν ἦναι ins. j ‖ 42 ἐπιτελῶν j ‖ 45 τῶν κοινῶν j ‖ 48 παρὰ k: περὶ j ‖ μετριότητος k: ταπεινότητος j ‖ ἐλέγχειν j ‖ 52 τούτοις k: τούτου j ‖ προσεξειργασμένα ed. Oudot: προεξ- kj ‖ 54 ὑμῶν k: ἡμῶν j ‖ 61 αὐτοῦ j ‖ 62 ὑμᾶς j: ἡμᾶς k ‖ 64 μητροπολιτῶν j

197 to his side; and this you did not once, but a second time too, when you had again been summoned to the Palace. Further, your denial of the pledge you made before God and angels and men that you would do nothing without our approval but would follow us in whatever dispensation we should decide upon concerning the late Emperor—what else does it actually signify but that you have no consciousness of a Judgment Seat and of a Reckoning? Then there are the words of Our Mediocrity, when it was pretended that by the Emperor's order we were all to be deported from the City, words spoken to you as you were gathered together and taking leave of each other, to the effect that none must grant any dispensation without the consent of all, but whether God would permit us to live or whether He would take us away from this world, you were to take whatever measure was necessary by common and unanimous consent, and that, if anyone did not feel this way but presumed to take any step without the joint approval of us all, he would without pardon fall under the doom of the Father and the Son and the Holy Spirit, both in this world and in the world to come, as well as under the verdict of Our Mediocrity: is this not proof enough that you have no awareness whatsoever either of a life to come or of having to answer for your deeds?

That is what these events reveal about your characters; let us also review your subsequent actions. You drove us away from our flock; though it was apparently the Emperor who did this, he was no more than an executive acting upon your orders and by your will; it was you that, before him and with him, contrived the plot against us. This is proved by what I said already and even more fully by this. When the Emperor underwent a change of mind and the gravity of his misdeed made him suddenly come to his senses, he resolved to restore us to the place from which he had wrongfully expelled us; and he signified this to us in a letter and confirmed his decision by oaths, using as his messenger to convey both his letter and his oath, the man who at the time was his chief minister. Then, when he communicated his decision to you, you all spoke up with one voice and threatened that (so help you God) you would all go into exile and leave your cathedral cities to inhabit the deserts, if he should put into effect the return of your Patriarch to you.

197

Ἀλλὰ τοιούτοις καλοῖς προοιμίοις προσεθήκατε καὶ ἃ προσειρήσεται· παραίτησιν ἀπητήσατε, καὶ τοῦ θεοῦ τοὺς λογισμοὺς ὑμῶν ματαιώσαντος, οὐ παραίτησιν ἀλλ' ἀγχόνην ἐλάβετε. Ἡμῶν γὰρ εἰπόντων ὡς ἐπεὶ παρανομεῖν οὐ δεδυνήμεθα (τίς γὰρ παρανομεῖν δυνατός, εἰ μὴ ἄθεος;) καὶ τὸ τοῦ Δαυὶδ ἐγγράφως ὁμολογησάντων, εἰ καὶ λέξεσιν ἑτέραις, «Ἐμίσησα ἐκκλησίαν πονηρευομένων καὶ μετὰ ἀσεβῶν οὐ μὴ καθίσω,» αὐτοὶ ὡς ὄντως παραίτησιν περιχανόντες τοῖς γεγραμμένοις ἐπὶ μᾶλλον ἐξεβακχεύθητε πρὸς ἀπόνοιαν. Καίτοι τίς παραίτησις ὑπερορίων ὄντων, κουστωδίας στρατιωτῶν φρουρούντων, ξιφῶν μικροῦ τοῖς αὐχέσιν ἡμῶν ἐπικειμένων, ἵνα τὴν ἄλλην συνοχὴν ἐάσω καὶ βίαν, ἐρημίαν τῶν συνόντων, συμψαλλόντων, συνομιλούντων, τῶν ἄλλως ὑπηρετούντων (ἃ κἂν οἱ τῆς πίστεως ἀλλότριοι συνεχώρησαν, εἰ ταῖς χερσὶν ἐκείνων ἐγκρατεῖς ἐγεγόνειμεν), τὸν λιμόν, τὴν ὑπὸ κρυμοῦ πῆξιν; Αἰσχύνομαι λέγειν περὶ τῶν οὕτω πρὸς ἀφιλάνθρωπον γνώμην ἀποκλινάντων καὶ μόνην παραμυθίαν ἡμῖν τὴν ἐκ τῶν ἀχύρων θάλψιν παραλελοιπότων. Οὕτως συγκεκρότηται ἡμῖν ἥν φατε κατέχειν παραίτησιν· πλὴν καλὸν ἐπιμνησθῆναι ⟨τῶν⟩ ῥημάτων ἡμῶν· ἔχει γὰρ οὕτως.

Παραίτησις. «Ἐπειδὴ πραγμάτων ἐναντιότητος καὶ δυσχερείας τὴν τοῦ θεοῦ καταλαβούσης ἐκκλησίαν εἰς τὸ ἀδύνατον περιέστη τοῦ οἰκονομεῖν τι περὶ τὸν φιλόχριστον βασιλέα, τὸν θρόνον παραιτοῦμαι, τὴν κατ' ἐμαυτὸν ἰδίαν καὶ ἀνακεχωρημένην προτιμήσας ζωὴν τῆς ἐν πράγμασιν ἀστατοῦσιν ἀναστροφῆς, μήτε θείας ἐξιστάμενος ἀρχιερωσύνης μηδὲ τοῦ ἐπιτελεῖν πάντα ὅσα ἐνεργεῖν οἶδεν ἀρχιερωσύνη, ἐν ᾧ ἂν τόπῳ τὴν ταπεινὴν ἡμῶν παρελκύσωμεν ζωήν, εἰδότες ἀκίνδυνον οὐκ ὂν τὸ τὴν θείαν ὥσπερ ἀπαρεσκόμενον αὐτῇ ἀποπέμπεσθαι χάριν, ἄλλως τε δὲ καὶ τοῦ ἱεροῦ κανόνος τοὺς ἐξομοσαμένους τὴν ἐν ᾗ ἐτάχθησαν ἱερὰν λειτουργίαν, κἂν φόβος ὁ ἐξ ἀνθρώπων ᾖ ὁ πρὸς τοῦτο συνωθήσας, ἀπαραιτήτως καὶ συγγνώμης ἁπάσης χωρὶς καθαιροῦντος καὶ εἰς τὴν τῶν λαϊκῶν ἀπορρίπτοντος χώραν.»

71–72: Ps. 25:5. ‖ 84–96: supra *Op.* 194 II. ‖ 92–96: *ACO*, I, 1, 7, pp. 123, 24–124, 25.

---

69 τίς j: καὶ k ‖ 70 ὁμολογησάντων corr. Papadopulos-Kerameus: ὁμολογήσαντος kj ‖ 74–75 φρουρούσης Papadopulos-Kerameus ‖ 77 τὸν j: καὶ τὸν k ‖ 79 λέγειν k: λόγων j ‖ 80 ἡμῖν j: ἡμῶν k ‖ 82 scr. ὑμῖν ‖ τῶν add. Wk ‖ 84–96 v. Op. 194 II ‖ 88 ἀναστατοῦσιν k

197

After this commendable preamble let me tell you how you continued: you demanded an act of abdication, and God having brought your devices to naught, what you obtained was not an abdication, but a snare. For when we gave as our reason that we could not disobey the law (who indeed can do so but the godless?) and made a written declaration which, though in different terms, amounted to David's "I hate the congregation of evildoers and will not sit with the wicked," you pounced upon that statement as if it were a real abdication and were carried away to even greater frenzy. Yet what kind of abdication could this have been, when we were exiled, watched over by a posse of soldiers, with the knife, as it were, to our throat, not to mention other forms of pressure and compulsion: separation from those who kept me company, sang psalms with me, conversed with me, rendered me other services (favors which even those alien from the faith would have allowed me, had I fallen into their hands); the hunger; the numbing cold? I am ashamed to speak of those who had recourse to so inhumane a sentence and left us for our only comfort the warmth of a straw mattress. Thus you contrived the abdication which you claim to hold; however, it is good to cite our actual words, which run as follows:

Act of Abdication. "Inasmuch as the untoward and disturbing events that have overtaken the Church of God have rendered it impossible to grant a dispensation to the Christ-loving Emperor, I resign my see, preferring a life on my own, in privacy and retirement, to the uncertainty of involvement in public affairs, without, however, renouncing the divine archpriesthood or the exercise of all the functions of archpriesthood, in whatever place we drag out our humble life; for we know that it is not without peril to dismiss the divine gift as if it were not pleasing, all the more so since by the Holy Canon those who have abdicated the sacred ministry in which they were placed, even if constrained by the fear of men, are inexorably and without pardon deposed and reduced to the rank of laymen."

197

Ὁρᾷς, μᾶλλον ὁρᾶτε, οἵα ὑμῖν ἐκ τῆς παραιτήσεως ὑπάρχει ἀσφάλεια, οἷα ὑμῖν τὰ δίκαια τῆς χειροθεσίας, ἣν ὡς τῆς ἐκκλησίας προεστῶτες πεποίησθε; Ἀλλ' ὄντως τυφλὸν ἡ μανία, ἣν οὐκ οἶδα πόθεν νενοσηκότες οὐδὲ τοῦτο ἐνιδεῖν ἠδυνήθητε, ὡς τῆς δοκούσης παραιτήσεως ἡμῖν πάντα φαμένης πράττειν ὅσα θέμις πράττειν τοῖς τὸν ἀρχιερατικὸν διέπουσι θρόνον, «ἐν ᾧ ἂν τόπῳ τὴν ταπεινὴν ἡμῶν ζωὴν παρελκύσωμεν,» ὡς ἐν τῇ παραδοχῇ ταύτης, ἀνθ' ἧς ἀπελαύνειν ἐφορείας ἐγνώκειτε, πάσης ἡμῖν ἐφορείας τό γε ὑμέτερον μέρος τὴν κυριότητα ἐνεχειρίσατε, καὶ τῆς Κωνσταντινουπόλεως ὑπερορίους ποιοῦντες πάσης ἐδίδοτε πόλεως ἐπικράτειαν. Καλά γε ὑμῶν τὰ τῆς παραιτήσεως δίκαια, ἣν ὡς ἀκρόπολιν τῆς ὑμῶν τυραννίδος κατέχετε, ἐξ ἧς καὶ νομοθέται καὶ οἰκονόμοι πορνείας εἰς ὕβριν, ἵνα μὴ λέγω τοῦ ἱερατικοῦ πληρώματος, ἀλλὰ καὶ παντὸς τοῦ Χριστιανῶν γένους ἀναδειχθῆναι ἀπονενόησθε· πορνείας εἶπον, οὐ τοσοῦτον μόνον, ἀλλὰ καὶ «πλέον πορνείας,» ὡς τῷ θείῳ διδασκάλῳ καὶ τοῖς ἐκεῖνον μὴ παραλογιζομένοις δοκεῖ.

Τὰ μὲν οὖν ὑμέτερα, ἵνα μὴ ἐπὶ πλέον ὅσα κατὰ θεοῦ καὶ τῶν νόμων αὐτοῦ κατωρχήσασθε διεξερχόμενος ὁ λόγος τοῖς ἐπιεικεστέροις καὶ τὸ καθ' ὑμῶν ἀνάπτοι δίκαιον μῖσος, μὴ πλείονος ἀξιούσθω μνήμης· καίτοι γε τῶν εἰρημένων οὐκ ἐλάττω, ἀλλὰ μείζονα τὰ ὑμῖν μὲν ἐφεξῆς τετολμημένα, τῷ λόγῳ δὲ σιωπώμενα ἕνεκα τοῦ μὴ τὸ δίκαιον μῖσος παρὰ τῶν εὐσεβούντων καθ' ὑμῶν τῶν ἀρίστων ἐξαφθῆναι δραματοποιῶν. Τίς γὰρ τὴν ἄλλην πονηρίαν καὶ τὸ ψεῦδος καὶ τὴν ἀναισχυντίαν καὶ τὸν ὅλον ὑμῶν κατὰ τῆς ἐκκλησίας πολύτροπον καὶ ποικίλον τῆς κακίας ἀκούων ἀγῶνα, οὐκ εἰς ἔκπληξιν καθιστάμενος διὰ τὴν ὑπερβολὴν καὶ τὸ μηδέποτε τοιαῦτα κεκακουργῆσθαι, πόρρω τῆς ἀνθρωπίνης καὶ διανοίας καὶ πράξεως ὑπολαμβάνει τὰ γεγενημένα ὑμῖν; Ἵνα οὖν, ὅπερ ἔφην, μὴ διὰ ταῦτα τὸν δίκαιον τῶν ἀκουόντων θυμὸν ἀναφλέγῃ καθ' ὑμῶν ὁ λόγος ἐκδιηγούμενος, ἐκεῖνα παραλείψας τὴν τῶν ἱερῶν κανόνων ἀπόφασιν ἐπιφέρει καθ' ὑμῶν, καθ' ὧν καὶ τὴν τόλμαν καὶ τὸ θράσος ἀναλαβεῖν ἐνεανιεύσασθε.

Κανὼν ιη' τῶν ἐν Χαλκηδόνι, οὗ ἡ ἀρχὴ «Τὸ τῆς συνωμοσίας.»

111–112: Basil., *Ep.* 217, can. 80, PG, 32, 805B1–2. ‖ 128–129: can. Chalced. 18.

---

101 ἡμῖν Wk: ὑμῖν kj ‖ τοῖς k: τοῦ j ‖ 103–104 ἀπελαύνει j ‖ 104 ἐγνώκειτε – ἐφορείας om. j ‖ ὑμέτερον corr. Wk: ἡμέτερον kj ‖ 105 κω(νσταντίνου) j ‖ 106 καλά γε j, k mg.: ἀλλά γε k ‖ scr. ὑμῖν? ‖ 111 τοῖς k: τὴν j ‖ 114 αὐτοῦ corr. Wk: αὐτῶν kj ‖ 124 γενημένα j ‖ δίκ(αιον) j: διὰ k ‖ 125 ἀναφλέγω j

197

Do you see, or rather, do all of you see, what kind of security this act of abdication provides for you, what the rights of ordination which you have exercised as heads of the Church are worth? Truly madness blinds a man, and caught by it (I do not know through what cause) you have not even been able to discern that, since in the so-called abdication we claim the right to exercise all the functions rightfully belonging to the incumbents of the archpriestly see "in whatever place we drag out our humble life," your acceptance of this bestowed on us (in so far as it was for you to bestow), instead of the episcopal see from which you intended to expel us, sovereign power over every episcopal see: by banishing us from Constantinople you gave us authority over all cities. Precious indeed are the rights you derive from this abdication, the stronghold and base of your usurped power, from which in your frenzy you have sallied forth to be proclaimed the lawgivers and dispensators of fornication, affronting not merely the priestly order but the whole Christian community. When I said "fornication," I meant even worse: "more than fornication," as is the opinion of the Divine Doctor and of those who do not despise him.

Let this be all the comment of which your actions are deemed worthy, lest my account, by enlarging upon all your rampant outrages against God and His law, should rouse decent men to well-deserved hate against you. Yet your later misdeeds are not less, but more flagrant; they shall, however, be passed over in silence in order not to kindle the just hatred of the pious against you for your splendid performance. Who, indeed, when he hears of your further wickedness, your falsity, your insolence, and the whole versatile and subtle campaign of your malice against the Church, is not dumbfounded by such excessive and unprecedented villainy and does not refuse to believe that acts like yours could ever be either conceived or perpetrated by men? Therefore, as I said, lest by a full account I should inflame the just anger of the hearers against you because of all this, I leave it aside and bring to bear upon you the verdict of those very holy canons against which you have presumed to put in action your boldness and your effrontery.

Canon 18 of the Chalcedonian Council, beginning, "The crime of conspiracy."

197

Κανὼν ε′ τῆς οἰκουμενικῆς α′ συνόδου, οὗ ἡ ἀρχὴ «Περὶ τῶν ἀκοινωνήτων.»

Κανὼν ϑ′ τῆς ἐν Καρϑαγένῃ συνόδου, οὗ ἡ ἀρχὴ «Τοῦτο ὁρίσαι καταξιώσατε.»

Κανὼν β′ τῆς οἰκουμενικῆς β′ συνόδου, οὗ ἡ ἀρχὴ «Τοὺς ὑπὲρ διοίκησιν ἐπισκόπους.»

Ἃ δὲ περὶ πορνείας ὥρισται καὶ τῶν ἐν τῷ μύσει τούτῳ μολυνομένων, τίς τῶν πάντων ἠγνόει, καὶ μὴ ὅτι τῶν λαχόντων ἱερᾶσθαι ἢ τῶν ὁπωσοῦν εἰς ἄνδρας τελούντων, ἀλλὰ καὶ τῶν ἔτι παιδικὴν σύνεσιν ἐχόντων;

Τοίνυν διὰ ταῦτα καὶ τὰ προειρημένα τοῖς ϑείοις καὶ ἱεροῖς ἑπόμενοι κανόσιν, ἀλγοῦντες μὲν καὶ σπαρασσόμενοι τὴν ψυχήν, ὅμως δὲ κατὰ τὴν ἱερὰν ψῆφον τὴν ἀπογυμνοῦσαν ὑμᾶς τῆς ἱερατικῆς τάξεως καὶ τιμῆς, ἧς φϑάσαντες αὐτοὶ ἑαυτοὺς ἀπεγυμνώσατε, καὶ ἡ ἱερὰ αὕτη καὶ ὑπὲρ τῆς δόξης τῆς ἐκκλησίας τοὺς κινδύνους διενεγκοῦσα σύνοδος ποιεῖται τὴν ἀπόφασιν, καϑαιροῦσα καὶ ἀλλοτριοῦσα ὑμᾶς πάσης ἀρχιερατικῆς καὶ ἐνεργείας καὶ δυνάμεως.

130–131: can. Nicaen. 5. ‖ 132–133: can. Carthag. 9. ‖ 134–135: can. Constantinop. (a. 381) 2.

---

130 α′ j: om. k ‖ 132 τῆς k: τῶν j ‖ καρϑαγένει k ‖ τοῦτο k: τοῦ j

197

Canon 5 of the First Ecumenical Council, beginning, "Regarding those excommunicated."

Canon 9 of the Synod at Carthage, beginning, "May it please you to decree as follows."

Canon 2 of the Second Ecumenical Council, beginning, "Bishops outside their dioceses."

As for the decrees concerning fornication and those sullied with this stain, who ever could be ignorant of them, I do not say among ordained priests or even common adults, but among those who still have the intelligence of children?

Therefore, in view of these and the foregoing facts and in compliance with the divine and holy canons, albeit with grief and heartrending pain, yet in confirmation of the sacred decree that divests you of your priestly rank and dignity, of which you have been the first to divest yourselves, this Holy Synod, which has endured the past perils for the glory of the Church, adds its own verdict, deposing you and depriving you of all archpriestly activity and power.

198. Letter to John the Catholicus of Greater Armenia

Վսեմականի աստուածասիրի և հոգևոր Տեառն և յաւէտ սիրելի եղբօր մերում՝ Յովհաննու կաթողիկոսի Հայոց Մեծաց, ի Նիկողայոսէ ողորմութեամբն Աստուծոյ յարքեպիսկոպոսէ Կոստանդնուպոլսի և ի ծառայէ ծառայից Աստուծոյ՝ Տերամբ խնդալ։

Կարծեմ ոչ ինչ գանխուլ է՝ տէր իմ, ի քոյոյ յաստուածասիրութենէդ . յոյժ տրտմութիւն և անպակաս ցաւք սրտից մերոց յաղագս Հայոց և Վրաց և Աղուանից միահամուռ քոյդ հաւատացեալ հօտից, որ եհաս ի վերայ դառն տագնապ չարչարանաց և նեղութեանց ի Սառակինոս Իսմայելեան բռնակալացն։ Զի թէպէտև մարմնով մեկուսի եմք և աչօք ոչ տեսեալ զվտանգ հօտի ձերոյ. սակայն ի լսելն ի չարէն չարչարեալ գաշխարհդ ձեր՝ յոյժ կծծիմք անձամբք և հոգւոյ ելանեմք մեծաւ տրտմութեամբ։ Իսկ եթէ մեք հեռագոյնքս ի ձէնջ միայն ի լսելն այսպէս ընկալաք յանձինս մեր սուգ դառնութեան՝ ապա ո՞րչափ ևս առաւել դուք՝ հաղորդեալքդ ի չարչարանս ընդ հօտից ձերոց, և հալածեալքդ և գանեալքդ և հարուածեալքդ յանօրէն և ի պիղծ ապստամբացն և զինչ պարտ է և պատշաճ է լինիլ, և կամ զի՞նչ այնչափ չարութեան իմանալ մխիթարութիւն, և ո՞րպէս ուղղութիւն զհետ եկեսցէ փարատել զառաջակայն՝ որ գալոցն է գայթակղութիւն։

Արդ եթէ պատշաճ թուեսցի սրբութեանդ ձերում, պարտ է նախ զաստուածային այցելութիւնն և զօգնականութիւնն յամենայն ժամ վերակարդալ, և ձեռս ի վեր ամբառնալ և բոլորով սրտիւ ի գութ ողորմութեան կոչել զամենակալն Աստուած քոյոյդ հօտիդ Հայոց և Վրաց և Աղուանից, և խորհել զհասարակացն օգուտ. և ապա մի ևս այլ բնաւ անսալ կորստեան դոցա, և փոյթ յանձին ունել ամենայնիւ յամենայնի առհասարակ զամենեսեան խրատել յաստուածային գիտութեան, և քրիստոսաւանդ բանիւն կապել և արձակել՝ որպէս և ընկալայք պատուէր իշխանութեամբ իսկ յերկինս և յերկրի, և դադարեցուցանել գոնէ ի հակառակութենէ չարութեանդ՝ որ ընդ միմեանս. և մի՛ տար թոյլ մնալ ի վայրենի գազանութեանդ,

198: 54–58: Matth. 16:19; 18:18

198

198. Letter to John the Catholicus of Greater Armenia

To the most holy, God-loving, spiritual Father and our very dear Brother Lord John, Catholicus of Greater Armenia, from Nicholas, by the mercy of God Archbishop of Constantinople and servant of the servants of God: greetings in the name of the Lord.

I think that your God-loving Lordship is not unaware of the deep sorrow and ceaseless grief of our heart on behalf of the Armenians, the Iberians, and the Albanians, who collectively comprise your faithful flock, upon whom the Ishmaelite Saracen tyrants have inflicted severe travail and afflictions. Although we could not witness with our own eyes the visitation of danger upon your flock, as we are physically beyond range, yet, hearing of the trouble that your land is suffering at the hands of the wicked, we deplore it with deep personal grief and mourn with great sorrow. If those of us who are at a great distance from you have received these tidings through hearsay with such personal grief, then how much more severely all these must have affected you, who partook of the torments together with your flock and were persecuted as well as clubbed and beaten by the impious and wicked rebels. What could be done that might have been proper and fit? What could be said in consolation for such wickedness? How could righteousness follow this in order to dispel the scandal which is close at hand?

Now, if it seems proper to your Holiness, first of all, it is necessary to call upon the Divine Providence and succor at all times, and lifting up your arms, ask the Lord God with all your heart to have mercy on your flock, namely, the Armenians, the Iberians, and the Albanians. Think of the public welfare, and never again tolerate its abuse. Take upon yourself the task of admonishing all of them at all times in the knowledge of God, as well as that of binding and absolving them with the Christ-given authority, with which you were invested to perform matters in heaven and on earth. At least, stop the wicked hostilities that prevail among them. Do not let them remain in their wild, beastly state, whereby they fall upon one

որք բարկացեալք և դիմեալք են ի սպանումն միմեանց, և դառնալ ի մարդկային մտածութիւնս և ի քրիստոնէական հանդարտութիւնս, որով բերի իսկ ի փրկութիւն մնացելոցդ մասանց մարդկան Հայոց աշխարհիդ և Վրաց և Աղուանից։

Զայս նուաստութիւն իմ յառաջագոյն փութացաւ գրով ճեպել տալ ձեզ սուղ ինչ պատճառ յորդորման սիրոյ։ Ըստ սմին սակի առաքեցաք թուղթ և առ կուրապաղատդ և առ աւագն Ափխազաց՝ խրատելով առ ի լսել խրատուդ ձերոյ և մոռանալ զընդ միմեանս հարուածն, և նայել ի սէր ի միաբանութիւն և ի հաշտ խաղաղութիւն ընդ միմեանս և ընդ հասարակ իշխանս Հայոց և Աղուանից, և միանալ միաբան և մարտնչել ընդդէմ ամբարիշտ թշնամւոյն որդւոյն Ապուսէճայ. զի մի՛ հասարակ ձեզ կորուստ եղիցի և որ ընդ ձեօք այլ ևս մերձաւորաց ազգաց սատակումն բերցի։ Եւ արդ՝ պարտ է ձերում սրբութեանդ բերան ի բերան և թղթով և պատգամօք և եպիսկոպոսօք և քահանայիւք և սրբովք արամբք զուն գործել և ի բաց ի միջոյ բառնալ զչար հակառակութիւնս դոցա, և առանց բանի պղերգութեան հետևել յայդպիսի մատակարարութիւնն՝ և մաղթել դառնալ ի լաւագոյնսն և առ փրկական խորհուրդս և գործս։ Զի այդպէս միախոհք և միաբանք լինելով մի՛ ևս կարողասցի ինչ ի վերայ աշխարհիդ ձերոյ ապականիչ չար։ Եւ մինչ այդ այդպէս ի ձէնջ կազմիցի, ապա և ինքնակալ և աստուածապսակեալ թագաւորս մեր ի դէպ ժամանակի պիտոյից առաքեսցէ զօր բազում յօգնականութիւն ձեզ. զի և կուրապաղատդ ևս և աւագն Ափխազաց և իշխանք և մեծամեծք Հայոց միաբանեալք մերոյն զօրաց՝ մեծաւ օգնականութեամբն Աստուծոյ և ձերով մեծ քահանայագործութեամբդ պատերազմել ընդ թշնամիսն կարծեցեալ կորստեան արբանեկին սատանայի՝ վերագոյն գտցին։

Յայնժամ ապա և մեղանչականութիւն հակառակութեան, որ ընդ միմեանս եդին ապիրատութեամբ՝ և դուք և մեք առ հասարակ դոցա թողութիւն շնորհեսցուք։ Եւ զիւրաքանչիւրոցն իրաւունս յիւրաքանչիւրսն ընձեռեսցուք՝ որպէս և վայելէ իսկ ձերում սրբութեանդ. զի յառաջագոյնն իսկ ի կարգս քահանայավարութեանն իւրաքանչիւրոք տարեալ հաստատեսցի։ Յայնմհետէ խաղաղութիւնն Քրիստոսի հաստատեսցի ի ձեզ՝ և սրբափայլ աղօթք ձեր եղիցի ընդ նուաստութեանս մերում։

198 another in rage in order to kill. Let them return to human rationality and Christian serenity, wherewith salvation will be granted to the rest of the people in the lands of Armenia, Iberia, and Albania.

My Humility made haste to write to you first and give this brief friendly advice. We sent another letter like this to your Curopalate and to the Prince of Abasgia, whom we advised to listen to you, to forget their animosities, to seek friendship, unity, and peaceful coexistence with one another as well as with all the Armenian and Albanian princes, to come together unanimously and fight against the children of the ungodly enemy Aposatai so that you might not all perish and so that the kindred races that are under your sway might not be shaken. Now, your Holiness must try to extirpate the wicked animosities among the princes by talking to them face to face, or by means of letters and encyclicals, as well as with the help of bishops, priests, and holy men, and see to it that they are not negligent in this. You must encourage them to turn to better things, such as the redemptive mysteries and salutary works. For if you are thus of one accord and unified, the destructive evil will be unable to bring any kind of affliction upon your land. And while you yourself carry out these matters, our God-crowned Emperor will send large forces to your aid in accordance with the demands of the times so that your Curopalate as well as the Prince of Abasgia together with the princes and the nobility of Armenia might join our forces and, with the help of God and through your priestly intercession having fought against the enemy, the so-called accomplice of the devil, might vanquish them.

Only then, both you and we shall grant them remission for their sinful animosity, which they iniquitously allowed to prevail among themselves. And as it befits your Holiness, you may grant each one his rights so that every individual may be reinstalled in his former office. Hereafter, let there be the peace of Christ among you, and let your prayers, which shine with holiness, be with our Humility.

199. Tract on the Tetragamy

I

Ὅτι τὸ λέγειν τὸν δημιουργὸν τοῦ παντὸς περὶ τοῦ Ἀδὰμ «Ποιήσωμεν αὐτῷ βοηθὸν κατ' αὐτὸν» οὐκ ἔστι πλειόνων γάμων ἐπιτροπή, ἀλλὰ μόνου ἑνός· διὰ τοῦτο καὶ μίαν πλάττει γυναῖκα καὶ μίαν ἐξελὼν πλευρὰν τοῦ Ἀδάμ, ἣν καὶ εἰς γυναῖκα διαπλάσας νυμφαγωγεῖ αὐτῷ. Ὥστε ἡ παρὰ θεοῦ νυμφαγωγία μίαν οἶδε συνάφειαν, αἱ δὲ παρὰ ταύτην οὐκ ἤρτηνται θείου νόμου, εἰ καὶ ἀνθρωπίνως συγκεχώρηνται.

II

Ὅτι τὸ «Ποιήσωμεν αὐτῷ βοηθὸν κατ' αὐτὸν» οὐ τοσοῦτον διὰ τὴν συνάφειαν, εἰ καὶ συμβαίνει διὰ τὴν τοῦ γένους διαδοχήν, ὅσον διὰ τὴν μόνωσιν καὶ τὴν πρὸς τὸν βίον εἴρηται ἀπορίαν· ὅπερ εὖ εἰδὼς ὁ ἀπόστολος ὕστερον τῷ ἀσθενεστέρῳ μέρει καὶ ἀπορωτέρῳ τὸν δεύτερον ἐπιτρέπει γάμον, τουτέστι γυναιξί, καὶ οὐκ ἀνδράσι τοῖς μᾶλλον μὴ δεομένοις πρὸς τὸ ζῆν βοηθείας.

III

Ὅτι καὶ τὸ «Ἕνεκεν τούτου καταλείψει ἄνθρωπος τὸν πατέρα καὶ τὴν μητέρα» περὶ μονογαμίας εἴρηται. Ἢ οὐχὶ πρὸς τὴν πρώτην συνάφειαν ὁρμῶντες ἄνθρωποι καταλιμπάνουσι τοὺς οἰκείους γονέας καὶ πρὸς μίαν σάρκα συνάπτονται; Πρόδηλον οὖν ὡς ἐκείνη μόνη κυρίως ἂν εἴη γαμετή, δι' ἣν ἡ κατάλειψις τοῦ πατρὸς καὶ τῆς μητρὸς τῷ πρὸς ταύτην συναπτομένῳ διαπράττεται.

199: I 1–2: Gen. 2:18. ‖ 3–5: Gen. 2:21–22. ‖ **II** 1: Gen. 2:18. ‖ 3–5: 1 Cor. 7: 8–9. ‖ **III** 1–2: Gen. 2:24.

199: m 66^r–81^r

199. Tract on the Tetragamy

I

When the Creator of the Universe says of Adam, "Let us make a help meet for him," this is not permission for more than one marriage, but for one only; therefore He also creates one woman, having taken one of Adam's ribs, out of which He forms a woman to bring her to him as his bride. Consequently marriage as instituted by God knows one union only, and further unions do not derive from Divine Law, even though they are permitted from human considerations.

II

The words "Let us make a help meet for him" were spoken not so much in view of the union, even though this does take place for the sake of the reproduction of the kind, as in view of man's solitude and his helplessness in providing a living; later the Apostle, who understood this well, permits the second marriage to the weaker and more shiftless party, that is, to women, not to men, who are less in need of help to survive.

III

The words "Therefore shall a man leave his father and his mother" also apply to monogamy. Or is it not for their first marriage that people leave their parents and marry so as to become one flesh? It is evident, then, that only she can be the spouse properly so called for whose sake the man who becomes her husband actually leaves his father and mother.

IV

Ὅτι εἰ δέον συγχωρεῖν τέταρτον, οὐχ ἑνὶ δέον, ἀλλὰ πᾶσι· τοῦτο δέ ἐστιν ἀπάρνησις τῆς Χριστιανῶν πίστεως.

V

Ὅτι καὶ ὁ τοῦ κυρίου λόγος, εἰπόντος «Ὃ ὁ θεὸς συνέζευξεν, ἄνθρωπος μὴ χωριζέτω,» ἐπ᾽ ἐκείνην τὴν πρώτην ἀνάγει μνηστείαν ἣν ὁ πλάστης καὶ νυμφαγωγὸς τῷ Ἀδὰμ ἐμνηστεύσατο, ἀλλ᾽ οὐ περὶ δευτέρου ἢ τρίτου ὁ λόγος αὐτῷ.

VI

Ὅτι καὶ ἐκ τῆς τοῦ κυρίου σαρκώσεως ἡ μονογαμία νενομοθετημένη παρὰ θεοῦ μόνη γινώσκεται. Μιᾶς γὰρ ἐκ τοῦ ἀνδρὸς πλευρᾶς εἰς διάπλασιν ληφθείσης τῆς γυναικὸς καὶ ὀφλήματος ἑνὸς ὄντος τῇ Εὔᾳ πρὸς τὸν Ἀδάμ, μία παρθένος ἐκ τῶν αὐτῆς ἀχράντων αἱμάτων ἑνὶ ὑπὲρ τοῦ Ἀδὰμ σαρκωθέντι υἱῷ ἀντιδοῦσα τὴν ὕλην εἰς διάπλασιν τῆς ἁγίας σαρκὸς ἀνεπλήρωσε τὴν ὀφειλὴν τῆς προμήτορος. Ὥστε εἰ ἓν ὄφλημα τὸ τῆς γυναικὸς πρὸς τὸν ἄνδρα καὶ μία ἀνταπόδοσις τοῦ ὀφλήματος, οὐ δύο γυναῖκες ἁρμόσουσι τῷ ἀνδρί, ἀλλὰ μία.

VII

Ὅτι ⟨εἰ⟩ ἡ τοῦ κυρίου παρουσία βελτίωσις γέγονε καὶ τελείωσις τῷ ἀνθρωπείῳ βίῳ, πῶς ἔχει λόγον τὸν ἐκ τῆς ἀτελοῦς πολιτείας ἀνάγοντα μὴ κωλύειν ἐπὶ πλείονας προέρχεσθαι γάμους; ὁπότε μηδὲ ὁ νόμος τοιοῦτον ἐπιτρέπει, πλὴν ὅσον ἐπ᾽ ἀδελφοῦ ὁμοιότητος ἔγερσιν, κἂν τινες ἐν νόμῳ τελοῦντες διαφόροις ὡμίλησαν γάμοις.

V 1–2: Matth. 19:6; Marc. 10:9. ‖ **VII** 3–5: Deut. 25:5–6 (Matth. 22:24; Marc. 12:19; Luc. 20:22).

VII 1 εἰ add. Wk ‖ 2 βίῳ Wk: λόγῳ m

IV

If we are to permit a fourth marriage, we must do so not for one, but for all; this, however, is a denial of the Christian faith.

V

The saying of the Lord, "What God has joined together, let not man put asunder," also brings us back to that first betrothal arranged for Adam by the Creator and Giver of his bride; He does not speak of a second or third.

VI

From the Lord's incarnation, too, we learn that only a single marriage is the law laid down by God. For since it was only one man's rib that was taken to shape woman and thus there was only one debt that Eve owed to Adam, it was one Virgin who in return gave to one Son, incarnated on behalf of Adam, the matter for the formation of His Holy Flesh from her immaculate blood, and thereby repaid the debt owed by the first mother. Consequently, if the debt of woman to man is one and the repayment of the debt is one, not two women shall be joined to a man, but one only.

VII

If the Lord's coming meant an improvement and a perfection for human society, how is it conceivable that He Who lifted man up from an imperfect way of life should not prevent him from entering into a succession of marriages? Even the Law does not permit such a thing, except to preserve a brother's image in a child, although some who lived under the Law did contract several marriages.

VIII

Ὅτι ὁ κύριος τῆς ἐξ ἀρχῆς παρ' αὐτοῦ δεδομένης τῷ πλάσματι διατάξεως ἐλθὼν πρὸς ἡμᾶς ὑψηλοτέραν, ἀλλ' οὐκ ἐλάττονα τὴν διάταξιν δίδωσι. Τότε γὰρ τὴν γυναῖκα τῷ ἀνδρὶ συνάψας νῦν φησιν ἥκειν (ἤγουν «ἐλθεῖν») διαχωρίσαι ἄνδρα τῆς γυναικὸς καὶ υἱὸν καὶ θυγατέρα ἀπὸ πατρὸς καὶ μητρός. Τίνα οὖν ἔχει λόγον τὸ νομίζειν μὴ παρὰ τοῦ κυρίου κεκωλῦσθαι πολυγαμίαν;

IX

Ὅτι ὁ θεὸς τὰ δημιουργήματα ὑποστήσας ἅπαξ ἔδωκεν αὐτοῖς τάξιν καθ' ἣν δεῖ ῥυθμίζεσθαι καὶ διατελεῖν, οἷον σπόρῳ θέρει, ἔαρι χειμῶνι, νυκτὶ ἡμέρᾳ, ὡσαύτως καὶ τῇ γενέσει τῶν ζῴων. Παρεσχέθη οὖν καὶ τῷ ἀνθρώπῳ γυνὴ μία, μεθ' ἧς δεῖ αὐτὸν μέχρις ἂν τὸ βούλημα τοῦ παρασχόντος ἐπιτρέπει συζῆν· οἱ δὲ παρὰ τοῦτον γάμοι ἀνθρωπίνης συγκαταβάσεως, ἀλλ' οὐ θεϊκῆς διατάξεως.

X

Ὅτι καὶ ἡ τοῦ θείου ἀποστόλου περὶ χειροτονίας νομοθεσία, δι' ὧν ὁρίζει τοὺς μιᾶς γυναικὸς ἄνδρας πρὸς θείαν λειτουργίαν ἀναλαμβάνεσθαι, τί ἄλλο ἢ τοῦτο ἡμᾶς διδάσκει, ὅτι εἷς γάμος ὁ παρὰ θεοῦ ὁρισθεὶς τῇ φύσει; Καὶ διὰ τοῦτο ὡς ἀμέμπτου ὄντος οὐκ ἀνάξιοι πρὸς χειροτονίαν οἱ νομίμως αὐτῷ ὑπουργήσαντες, οἱ δὲ παρὰ τοῦτο ὑπὸ μέμψιν· καὶ διὰ τοῦτο οὐδεὶς τῶν ἐκ δευτέρου γάμου τῇ ἱερᾷ προσάγεται ὑπηρεσίᾳ. Εἰ δὲ μὴ ὁ δεύτερος ἄμεμπτος ὡς μὴ θεόθεν διδόμενος (ἐποίησε γὰρ ὁ θεὸς πάντα «καλὰ λίαν»), πῶς ἄν τις εἴποι γ' ἢ τέταρτον μὴ παρὰ θεοῦ κωλύεσθαι;

VIII 3–5: Matth. 10:35. ‖ **IX** 1–3: Gen. 8:22. ‖ **X** 1–3: 1 Tim. 3:2. ‖ 8: Gen. 1:31.

VIII

When the Lord came to us, he established a higher, not a lower, standard than the one He had set for His creature originally. Whereas He then joined woman to man, He now says that He has arrived (or "come") to sever the man from his wife and the son and the daughter from their father and mother. What sense does it make, then, to hold that polygamy was not forbidden by the Lord?

IX

When God had wrought His creatures, He gave them once and for all an order to which they must conform and by which they must abide, such as seedtime and harvest, spring and winter, night and day, and so too for the generation of animals. As for man, he was given one wife, with whom he must live as long as the Giver's will allows him; marriages in excess of this are a matter of human indulgence, not of Divine Ordinance.

X

Further, the Divine Apostle's decree on ordination, where he prescribes that only husbands of one wife are acceptable for the divine service, teaches us precisely this: that marriage as ordained by God is by its nature only one. For this reason, because such a marriage is irreproachable, those who have lawfully fulfilled their duty in it are not unworthy of ordination, while marriages beyond this are subject to censure; therefore no one who has remarried is admitted to the holy ministry. But if even the second marriage is not blameless inasmuch as it is not instituted by God (since all that God made is "very good"), how can anybody say that a third or fourth marriage is not forbidden by God?

XI

Ὅτι τὸ τοῦ ἀποστόλου «Καλὸν ἀνθρώπῳ γυναικὸς μὴ ἅπτεσθαι» τὴν ἀγαμίαν προτιμῶντος εἴρηται· ὁ δὲ τῆς νομίμου συζεύξεως τὴν ἀγαμίαν προκρίνων πῶς ἐπιτρέψει παρανόμως συνάπτεσθαι; Σφάλλονται οὖν οἱ λέγοντες τὸν ἀπόστολον διὰ τοῦ λέγειν «Κρεῖσσον γαμῆσαι ἢ πυροῦσθαι» πλείοσιν ἐπιτρέπειν ὁμιλεῖν γάμοις, ἀλλ' ἡ παραίνεσις τὸν ἕνα μόνον διδάσκει.

XII

Ὅτι ὁ μέγας ἀπόστολος Παῦλος παραινῶν δεῖν τοὺς ἄνδρας ἀγαπᾶν τὰς γυναῖκας ὡς τὰ ἑαυτῶν σώματα, καθὼς καὶ ὁ Χριστὸς τὴν ἐκκλησίαν, δείκνυσι τηλαυγῶς τοῖς μὴ παντελῶς ἀποτετυφλωμένοις μίαν καὶ μόνην ἀνδρὶ συνάπτεσθαι ὀφείλειν γυναῖκα· οὐδὲ γὰρ δύο τοῦ Χριστοῦ ἐκκλησίαι, ἀλλὰ μία παραδέδοται καθολικὴ καὶ ἀποστολικὴ ἐκκλησία. Φησὶ δὲ οὕτως· «Ὀφείλουσιν οἱ ἄνδρες ἀγαπᾶν τὰς ἑαυτῶν γυναῖκας ὡς τὰ ἑαυτῶν σώματα· οὐδεὶς γάρ ποτε τὴν ἑαυτοῦ σάρκα ἐμίσησεν, ἀλλ' ἐκτρέφει τε καὶ θάλπει αὐτήν, καθὼς καὶ ὁ κύριος τὴν ἐκκλησίαν.» Καὶ τὸ ἑξῆς δέ, «Τὸ μυστήριον τοῦτο μέγα ἐστίν, ἐγὼ δὲ λέγω εἰς Χριστὸν καὶ τὴν ἐκκλησίαν,» φανερῶς ἀποτρέπει τὴν ἐπὶ δευτερογαμίαν πρόοδον. Εἰ δὲ μὴ χώρα τῷ δευτέρῳ γάμῳ, τίς ἂν ὑπολείποιτο τοῖς πλείοσιν;

XIII

Ὅτι διὰ τοῦ εἰπεῖν τὸν θεῖον Βασίλειον «πορνείαν κεκολασμένην» τὴν τριγαμίαν κεκώλυται ἡ τετάρτη συνάφεια, καὶ μόνως ὀνομαζομένη «πολυγαμία,» κἂν μηδὲν ἕτερον περὶ ταύτης εἴρητο. Ἔφη γὰρ «κεκολασμένην πορνείαν» τὴν τριγαμίαν, ἵνα σαφῶς εἰδεῖεν οἱ πλέον ἐπεκτεινόμενοι ὡς πρὸς φανερὰν ἐξελαύνουσι πορνείαν, εἰ καὶ ταύτης φησὶ «πλέον» ἔχειν τὴν πολυγαμίαν ὁ μετὰ ταῦτα ἐντεταγμένος κανών.

XI 1: 1 Cor. 7:1. ‖ 4–5: 1 Cor. 7:9. ‖ **XII** 1–9: Ephes. 5:28–29. ‖ 9–10: Ephes. 5:32. ‖ **XIII** 1–3: Basil., *Ep.* 188, can. 4, PG, 32, 673A6–7. ‖ 5–6: Basil., *Ep.* 217, can. 80, PG, 32, 805B1–2.

XI

The Apostle's word, "It is good for a man not to touch a woman," expresses his preference for the single state; now how can he who prefers this state to lawful wedlock permit illegal marriages? Accordingly those who maintain that the Apostle, by saying "It is better to marry than to burn," encourages a plurality of marriages are wrong; the advice pertains to the one marriage only.

XII

The great Apostle Paul, admonishing men to love their wives as their own bodies as Christ loves the Church, makes it manifest to those who are not totally blinded that a man should wed one wife only: there are not two Churches of Christ either, since tradition acknowledges one Catholic and Apostolic Church. He expresses himself thus: "Men ought to love their wives as their own bodies; for no man ever yet hated his own flesh, but he nourishes and cherishes it, even as the Lord the Church." And the sequel, too, "This is a great mystery, but I speak concerning Christ and the Church," obviously dissuades the step of a second marriage. But if there is no place for the second marriage, what can there be for more?

XIII

By the fact that the Divine Basil calls the third marriage "restricted fornication" the fourth union is forbidden; also by the mere fact that it is called "polygamy," even if nothing else were said about it. He calls the third marriage "restricted fornication" to make those inclined to exceed even this realize clearly that they are passing the limit of open fornication, since the canon placed after this one states that polygamy is something "more" even than fornication.

XIV

Ὅτι «πλέον πορνείας» ἡ πολυγαμία, διότι ὁ πόρνος, εἰ καὶ πράττει τὸ παράνομον, μεταδιώκει τὸ κρύφιον· ἡ δὲ πολυγαμία δημοσιευομένην εἰσάγει καὶ παρρησίᾳ πολιτευομένην τὴν παρανομίαν.

XV

Ὅτι μὴ διότι τινὲς πολλάκις τῶν κατεχόντων τοὺς νόμους παρορῶσι τὴν παράβασιν αὐτῶν, διὰ τοῦτο δεῖ καὶ ἄλλους ἀτιμάζειν τὸν νόμον καὶ ποιεῖσθαι τύπον τὰ παραβαθέντα καὶ παράδειγμα.

XVI

Ὅτι ἡ οἰκονομία οὐκ ἐπὶ βεβαιώσει τῶν ἁμαρτανομένων γίνεται, ἀλλ' ἐπὶ ἀπαλλαγῇ τῆς ἁμαρτίας καὶ σωτηρίᾳ τοῦ ἁμαρτάνοντος· ὅτι ἡ οἰκονομία ἐπὶ καταγνώσει τοῦ σφάλματος γίνεται ἐφ' ᾧ ἀξιοῦνται τῆς οἰκονομίας διὰ φιλανθρωπίαν οἱ ἐχόμενοι τῷ ἁμαρτήματι· ὅτι ἡ οἰκονομία κοινή τίς ἐστι καὶ διάδοσις ἐπὶ πάντας τοὺς ἐφ' ὧν ἐπὶ εὐεργεσίᾳ καὶ σωτηρίᾳ τελεῖται, ἀλλ' οὐκ ἰδία τις καὶ ἀποτεταγμένη τοῖς λαμβάνουσι χάρις.

XVII

Ὅτι τὴν διάζευξιν εἰ καὶ μὴ λόγῳ, ἀλλὰ πράγματι, ὅπερ ἐστὶ τρανότερον τῆς ἐκ λόγων παρακελεύσεως, παρακελεύεται ὁ κανών. Τί γὰρ ἕτερόν ἐστιν ἐκ τῶν ἱερῶν περιβόλων ἀφορισμός, τουτέστιν ἡ τοῦ σώματος τῆς ἐκκλησίας ἐκτομή, ἢ πρόσταξις διαζεύξεως; Ἐπεὶ γὰρ ἡ ἁμαρτία ἐπισπασαμένη ἥνωσεν ἑαυτῇ, ἀνάγκη τῆς ἐκκλησίας, τουτέστι τοῦ σώματος τῶν πιστῶν ἐκτέμνεσθαι τὸν ἡνωμένον τῇ ἁμαρτίᾳ, καὶ οὐκ ἄν ποτε συναφθείη τῷ ἐξ οὗ διετμήθη σώματι μὴ τῆς πρὸς τὴν ἁμαρτίαν ἑνώσεως διαστάς. Ὥσπερ γὰρ ὁ ταύτῃ ἑνωθεὶς τὴν ἀρχὴν ἀπέστη τῆς ἐκκλησίας, οὕτω πάλιν ὁ μέλλων συναφθῆναι τῷ πληρώματι τῆς ἐκκλησίας, ἀνάγκη τῆς ἁμαρτίας τοῦτον διΐστασθαι· ἀμήχανον δὲ ἀμφότερα συνδραμεῖν, τό τε τῇ ἁμαρτίᾳ ἡνῶσθαι καὶ τὸ μὴ τοῦ σώματος τῶν πιστῶν κεχωρισμένον γνωρίζεσθαι.

XIV 1: ibid.

XVI 3 ᾧ Karlin-Hayter: ὃ m ‖ **XVII** 5 ἑαυτῇ Karlin-Hayter: -ὴν m ‖ 12 τὸ Karlin-Hayter: τοῦ m

XIV

Polygamy is "more than fornication," because the fornicator, in spite of his lawless behavior, still seeks secrecy, whereas polygamy introduces sin practiced openly as an acknowledged social institution.

XV

The face that some of those charged with enforcing the laws often connive at their being transgressed, is no reason for others to despise the law and make the transgression a pattern and an example.

XVI

Dispensation is not granted to support sin, but to free from sin and save the sinner; dispensation aims at the condemnation of the error for which it is extended, out of clemency, to those in the grip of that sin; dispensation is universal and distributed to all those for whose benefit and salvation it is given; it is not a personal favor restricted to the receivers.

XVII

Though the canon does not prescribe separation in so many words, it does so in fact and in a way clearer than a mere verbal command. What else, indeed, is exclusion from the sacred precincts, in other words, excision from the body of the Church, but an order of separation? For since sin has seduced the man and united him to herself, the one so united with sin must be severed from the Church, that is, from the body of the faithful, and he can never be united again with the body from which he was cut off, unless he detaches himself from the union with sin. In the same way as at the beginning the man who united himself with sin removed himself from the Church, so the one who is to rejoin the community of the Church must separate himself from sin; it is impossible for the two to go together, being united with sin, and not being found severed from the body of the faithful.

XVIII

Ὅτι οἱ ληροῦντες ὡς τὸ «πλέον πορνείας» εἶναι τὸ ἁμάρτημα οὐκ ἔστι πλέον τῆς ἀνειμένης, ἀλλὰ τῆς κεκολασμένης, τουτέστι τῆς τριγαμίας, εἰπάτωσαν τί τὸ πλέον λογίζονται πρὸς τὴν ἀνειμένην. Εἰ γὰρ μὴ πλέον ἐκείνης, πάντως ἕξει τὸ ἴσον πρὸς αὐτὴν ἢ τὸ ἔλαττον. Τί δή ποτ᾽ οὖν ἡ μείζων, τουτέστιν ἡ ἀνειμένη, ἀνθρώπινον λογίζεται ἁμάρτημα καὶ μνήμης τυγχάνει παρὰ τῶν πνευματικῶν ἰατρῶν καὶ θεραπείας ἀξιοῦται (τέθεινται γὰρ περὶ ταύτης κανόνες καὶ μέθοδοι σωτηρίας καὶ οὐδεὶς αὐτὴν εἴρηκεν οὔτε «ἀλλότριον φύσεως ἀνθρωπίνης» οὔτε «κτηνῶδες», ἀλλ᾽ οὐδὲ «βίον χοιρώδη», ἀνθρώπινον δὲ τὸ παράπτωμα ἴσασι καὶ τῆς ὀφειλομένης ἀξιοῦσι μεθοδείας), ταύτην δὲ τὴν νομιζομένην ἐλάττω παρὰ τοῖς σοφοῖς τούτοις, μᾶλλον δὲ ἀνοήτοις, οὔτε τις τῶν θείων πατέρων μνήμης ἠξίωσεν οὔτε τρόπος θεραπείας περὶ αὐτῆς ἐγνώρισται, ἀλλ᾽ οἷα ἀλλότριον τοῦ ἀνθρωπίνου γένους καὶ πρὸς τὸν βίον τῶν κτηνῶν ἀπερριμμένον παντελῶς ὀπίσω μνήμης καὶ συνόδοις ἁπάσαις καὶ ἰδίᾳ τοῖς πατράσι μέχρι τοῦ θείου καταλέλειπται Βασιλείου; Ἀλλ᾽ εἰ μὲν ἔλαττον, τί δή ποτε τούτων οὐ τυγχάνει ὧν τὰ μείζω; Εἰ δὲ ἴσα, πάλιν ἁρμόσει ταῦτα δὴ τὰ εἰρημένα καὶ ἐπὶ τούτοις ἔλεγχος ἕτερος.

XIX

Ὅτι πρὸς τὴν ἀπόνοιαν τῶν λεγόντων δεδυνῆσθαι οἰκονομεῖν, ὃ ἀδύνατον ἡμῖν εἴρηται, ῥητέον· Πόθεν αὐτοῖς ἐπῆλθε τῆς οἰκονομίας ἡ δύναμις; Τῷ γὰρ εἰπόντι μὴ δύνασθαι οἰκονομεῖν τοῦτο εἴρηται διὰ τὸ μὴ εἶναι τῆς ἐκκλησιαστικῆς θεσμοθεσίας τοιαύτην λαμβάνειν ἐπιτροπήν. Πόθεν οὖν ἐκείνοις τῆς οἰκονομίας ἡ παρουσία; Εἰ μὲν ἀπὸ τῆς ἐκκλησίας, δῆλον ἀπὸ τῶν θεσμῶν τοῦ πνεύματος ὃ ἐν τῇ ἐκκλησίᾳ θεσπίζει· καὶ δεικνύτωσαν ποῦ τοῦτο τεθεσπισμένον εὑρήκασιν. Εἰ δὲ ἡ δεῖξις ἀμήχανος (πῶς γὰρ δείξουσι τὸ μὴ ὄν;), πρόδηλον ὡς ἐκ τοῦ ἐναντίου πνεύματος καὶ ἡ δύναμις αὐτοῖς καὶ τὸ οἰκονόμημα. Ἐφ᾽ ᾧ δέον αὐτοὺς οἰμώζειν ὡς κατακρίτους, ἀλλ᾽ οὐχ ὡς ἀθῴους θρασύνεσθαι.

XVIII 1: ibid. ‖ 2: cf. Basil., *Ep.* 188, can. 4, PG, 32, 673A6–7. ‖ 8–9: Basil., *Ep.* 217, can. 80, PG, 32, 805A15–B1. ‖ 9: Greg. Naz., *Or.* 37.8, PG, 36, 292B9–10. ‖ **XIX** 1–2: cf. supra *Op.* 194 I, 2–3; II, 7–9.

XVIII 13 οἷα e corr. (dub.) m ‖ 15 ἁπάσαις Karlin-Hayter: –σας m ‖ **XIX** 5 παρουσία] fort. ἐξουσία ‖ 6 ὃ Karlin-Hayter: ὁ m

XVIII

Let those who hold the ridiculous view that, when the sin is described as "more than fornication," this does not mean more than unrestrained, but more than restricted fornication, i.e., a third marriage, explain what they consider as "more" in respect of unrestrained fornication. If a fourth marriage is not "more" than this, it will necessarily be either equal or less. Why then is the greater sin, i.e., unrestrained fornication, regarded as a human failing and is it found worthy of mention and of treatment by the spiritual physicians (there are canons for it and ways of salvation, and nobody has called it "alien from human nature" or "beastly," or again "a swinish way of life," but they recognize the error as human and allow it the necessary treatment), and why, on the other hand, is this sin, which is looked upon as less serious by these wise men—or rather, by these fools—not deemed worthy of mention by any of the holy Fathers, nor has any cure for it been indicated? Why is it considered "alien from mankind" and rejected as bestial and therefore passed over in complete silence by all the councils as well as by the individual Fathers up to St. Basil? If it is less grave, why ever is it not granted the same treatment that graver sins are? If, however, it is equal, these same points will apply, and another argument may be added.

XIX

In response to the mad conceit of those who say that they were able to grant a dispensation, which we declared to be impossible, one should ask: Whence have they obtained this power of dispensation? He who declared himself unable to give despensation said so on the ground that it is not for ecclesiastical legislation to assume such competence. Where, then, did they acquire the authority for dispensation? If from the Church, it must be from the commandments of the Spirit Which dictates the laws of the Church; in which case let them show where they have found such a commandment. If, on the contrary, this is impossible to show (how can they show what is not there?), then obviously both their power and their dispensation come from the contrary spirit. This should make them wail for their damnation, not pride themselves on their blameless conduct.

XX

Ὅτι πρὸς τὴν ἀπονενοημένην αὐτῶν προβολὴν τῆς συμφωνίας (φασὶ γὰρ ὅτι συμφώνῳ ψήφῳ αὐτῶν τε καὶ ἄλλων δή τινων, οἷς τὸ κράτος τῆς συμφωνίας αὐτῶν ἐγχειρίζουσι, τὴν παραδοχὴν πεποιῆσθαι τοῦ ἀλλοτρίου γάμου τοῦ τῶν ἀνθρώπων γένους) ἀποκριτέον ὡς οὐ δεῖ συμφωνίᾳ πείθεσθαι πονηρᾷ, ἀλλὰ μᾶλλον ἀκολουθεῖν διαφωνίᾳ τῆς πονηρίας ἀμετόχῳ. Ἐξ ἀρχῆς γὰρ καὶ μέχρι τοῦ νῦν οἱ συμφωνήσαντες ἐπὶ κακῷ οὐδεμίαν εὑρήσουσιν ἐκ τῆς συμφωνίας παραίτησιν τῆς κατακρίσεως. Συνεφώνησε γὰρ πρῶτος ὁ ὄφις καὶ ἡ Εὔα, καὶ διὰ βίου πᾶσι ζωῆς δέδοται ἡ κληρονομία. Συνεφώνησαν ἐπὶ τῇ τοῦ πύργου οἰκοδομῇ, ἀλλὰ θεομαχία ἦν ἡ συμφωνία. Συνεφώνησαν ἐπὶ τῇ τοῦ Ἰωσὴφ ἐπιβουλῇ οἱ ἀδελφοί, ἀλλ' ἀδελφοκτόνος ἡ συμφωνία. Τί λέγω ταῦτα; συνεφωνήθη πάσῃ σαρκὶ τὸ ἀσεβεῖν, διεφώνει δὲ μόνος Ἀβραὰμ τῇ θεομάχῳ συμφωνίᾳ, ἀλλ' ὅμως εἷς ὢν διὰ τὴν εὐσεβῆ διαφωνίαν θεοῦ φίλος ἐκλήθη καὶ ἔστιν, οἱ δὲ ἀλλότριοι καὶ τοῦ θεοῦ καὶ τῆς αὐτῶν σωτηρίας. Οὐ τοίνυν πρὸς τὴν συμφωνίαν ἁπλῶς δεῖ ὁρᾶν, ἀλλὰ πρὸς τὸ ἔργον δι' ὃ ἡ συμφωνία. Συνεφώνησε πᾶς ὁ λαός, ναὶ δὴ καὶ Ἀαρὼν ὁ τοῦ θεοῦ ἱερεὺς ἐπὶ τῷ μόσχῳ, ἀλλ' οὔτ' Ἀαρὼν διὰ τοῦτο ἀνέγκλητος καὶ ὁ λαὸς ἀπώλετο πεσόντων ἐν μιᾷ ἡμέρᾳ χιλιάδων εἴκοσι καὶ τριῶν. Συνεφωνήθη προσκυνῆσαι τῇ εἰκόνι πᾶσιν οἷς ἐθέσπιζε Ναβουχοδονόσορ, μόνοι δὲ οἱ τρεῖς διεφώνησαν παῖδες· ἀλλ' οἱ μὲν ὑπὸ θεῷ μάρτυρι διὰ τῆς παραδόξου σωτηρίας ἔτυχον θείας ἀποδοχῆς, τῶν δὲ ἀσεβῶν ἡ ὁμοφωνία στηλὶς ἀκατάλυτος καὶ σωρὸς καταγνώσεως.

XXI

Ὅτι τοὺς λέγοντας συμπαθῶς διατεθῆναι καὶ διὰ τοῦτο συνελθεῖν τῷ βουλήματι τῶν γεγαμηκότων ἐρωτητέον τίνος ἕνεκεν συνεπάθησαν. Εἰ μὲν διὰ θεόν, δέον καὶ τοῖς λοιποῖς συγχωρεῖν πρὸς τοιοῦτον γάμον βουλομένοις μεθίστασθαι, καὶ μᾶλλον τὸ συμπαθὲς ἐπιδείκνυσθαι πρὸς τοὺς ἀσθενεστέρους καὶ ὧν ἴσως ἡ ἀπορία τοῦ βίου ἔχει τινὰ πρὸς τὴν συμπάθειαν προσιόντα λόγον. Εἰ δὲ οὔ (καὶ γὰρ οὐκ ἂν τοῦτο φαῖεν), πῶς οὐ κατάκριτος καὶ ἡ συμπάθεια καὶ οἱ συμπαθοῦντες;

XX 4: cf. Basil., *Ep.* 217, can. 80, PG, 32, 805A15–B1. ‖ 8–9: Gen. 3:1–6. ‖ 9–10: Gen. 11:1–11. ‖ 10–11: Gen. 37:18–20. ‖ 14: Iac. 2:23. ‖ 17: Exod. 32:1–6. ‖ 18: Exod. 32:21. ‖ 18–19: Exod. 32:28. ‖ 20–22: Dan. 3. ‖ 22–23: cf. Ios. 7:26.

XX 2 ὅτι del.? ‖ 10 θεομαχία ἦν Karlin-Hayter: θεομαχίᾳ, ἣν m

XX

As for their absurd plea of unanimity (they claim that it was by a unanimous vote of themselves and of certain others, to whom they assign the decisive voice in their unanimous decision, that this marriage alien from mankind was declared acceptable), the answer should be that one must not obey a unanimous evil decision, but rather take a course of dissent that is free from evil. Indeed, from the beginning of things and down to this day, those who are unanimous in an evil purpose will find no excuse in this unanimity to escape condemnation. The first to be unanimous were the snake and Eve, and we all inherit the consequences as long as we live. There was unanimity in the building of the Tower, but that unanimity was war against God. Joseph's brothers were unanimous in their plot against him, but their unanimity was fratricidal. Why should I mention these cases? All mankind was unanimous in the matter of idolatry, and the only one to dissent from this unanimous alliance against God was Abraham; yet he alone because of his pious dissent received the name and rank of God's friend, whereas the others were alienated from God and from their own salvation. One should therefore not consider unanimity by itself, but in reference to the action for which unanimity exists. The whole people, and even Aaron, the priest of God, were unanimous with regard to the Calf, but in spite of this Aaron was called to account and the people perished, twenty-three thousand of them falling on one day. There was unanimous willingness to worship the image among all to whom Nebuchadnezzar issued his command, only the three young men dissented; but they, with God testifying for them, found divine approval in their miraculous rescue, while the consent of the impious became an everlasting pillory and a mound of condemnation.

XXI

Those who say that they were moved by compassion and therefore acceded to the wish of the married couple, should be asked what was the reason for their compassion. If it was for God's sake, permission must be given also to all others who wish to enter into such a marriage, and compassion should be shown in the first place to the weaker, whose needy condition perhaps provides some ground for acting in a spirit of compassion. If it was not for God's sake (and they cannot possibly say it was), it is clear that the sympathy and the sympathizers are jointly condemned.

XXII

Ὅτι ὁ περὶ τῆς ἀνθρωπίνης ζωῆς ὅρος οὐκ εἰς ἀνάγκην περιγράφεται, ὡς ἡ τῶν Ἑλλήνων εἱμαρμένη, ἀλλ' εἴς τε τὸν πλάστην ὁρᾷ καὶ τὴν ἑκάστου ἡμῶν προαίρεσιν, ὡς ἐξ ἀρχῆς ἐπὶ τῶν πρωτοπλάστων γέγονε. Καὶ γὰρ ἐπὶ ἐκείνων ὅρος ἐτέθη ἀθανασίας καὶ θνητότητος οὐκ ἐκ μόνου τοῦ θείου κελεύσματος, ἀλλ' ἐξ ἀμφοτέρων, τῆς θείας ἐντολῆς καὶ τῆς αὐτῶν προαιρέσεως. Ὅπη οὖν ὑπῆρξε τότε, καὶ νῦν τοῦτο ἐπὶ τῇ ἑκάστου γενέσει, κἂν μὴ τοῦ προστάγματος ἡ φανέρωσις γίνηται· ὁρίζεται μὲν τὰ τῆς ζωῆς ἡμῶν παρὰ τῷ θεῷ καθὼς πρὸς τὸ συμφέρον ἐστίν, ἡμῶν δὲ τῇ αὐτεξουσίῳ ῥοπῇ πρὸς τοῦτο ἢ πρὸς τὸ χεῖρον φερομένων κατὰ τὴν ἑκάστου προαίρεσιν καὶ ἡ θεϊκὴ συνένδοσις οὐχ ἁπλῶς ἀλλὰ δικαίως συνεπιρρέπει.

XXIII

Ὅτι τοῖς λέγουσι τὸ «πλέον τῆς πορνείας» πρὸς τὴν τριγαμίαν εἰρῆσθαι τῷ κανόνι οὐ μόνον συμβαίνει τὸ λῆρον, ἀλλὰ καὶ κατηγορεῖν τοῦ τὸν κανόνα ἐκτεθεικότος πατρός. Εἰ γὰρ καί, ὡς αὐτοί φασι, τὸν ἐπέκεινα τοῦ γ' γάμου πλέον ἔχειν εἰς πορνείαν φησὶν ὁ κανών, πῶς οὐχὶ ἑκόντες καὶ ἄκοντες τὴν κατηγορίαν ταύτην κατὰ τοῦ θείου παρέξονται Βασιλείου; Τίς γὰρ τῶν πάντων ἀνθρώπων ἠγνόηκεν ὡς τὰ τέσσαρα τοῦ τρίτου πλέον καὶ ὅτι ὁ τετράκις ἁμαρτήσας τοῦ τρίτον ἁμαρτάνοντος ἐπὶ τὸ πλέον ἐξήμαρτε, καὶ τότε τοῦ αὐτοῦ ἁμαρτήματος τὴν πρᾶξιν ἔχοντος; Οὐ τοίνυν ἔχει λόγον πρὸς τὴν τριγαμίαν ὁρῶντα τὸ «πλέον τῆς πορνείας» εἰπεῖν τὸν μέγαν ἀρχιερέα· τοῦτο γὰρ παντὶ γνώριμον καὶ οὐδεὶς οὐδὲ τῶν μεμηνότων εἰς χρείαν τοιαύτην καθέστηκε διδασκαλίας· ἀλλ' εἰς τὴν ἀπόλυτον καὶ ἀνειμένην πορνείαν ἔχει τὴν ἀναφορὰν ἡ τοῦ κανόνος ἐξήγησις, εἰ καὶ μὴ οὕτως δοκεῖ, οὐχ ὡς ἀγνοοῦσιν, ἀλλ' ὡς κακούργοις τοῖς πλέον εἰς ἀναισθησίαν τῶν μεμηνότων ἀποφερομένοις δι' ὧν ποιοῦνται τὴν περὶ τοῦ κανόνος ἐξήγησιν.

XXII 4–6: Gen. 2:16–17. ‖ **XXIII** 1: Basil., *Ep.* 217, can. 80, PG, 32, 805B1–2.

XXII 3 καὶ Wk: ἢ m ‖ **XXIII** 12 fort. τοιαύτης

XXII

The limit of human life is not determined by necessity, as the Greek doctrine of fate declares, but it depends, on the one hand, on the Creator, and on the other hand, on the freewill of each of us, just as it was originally, in the case of the first-created. For them, too, a limit was set for immortality and mortality, resting not only on the Divine Ordinance but on both, God's commandment and their own freewill. As it was then, so it is now at the moment of each man's birth, though the decree is not revealed: the course of our lives is determined by God for our good, and according as by voluntary inclination we tend either toward the good or toward the worse, Divine permission follows our trend, not arbitrarily, but justly.

XXIII

Those who maintain that in the canon "more than fornication" is said in reference to the third marriage, besides talking nonsense themselves, also accuse the Father who formulated the canon of doing so. If, indeed, according to them the canon says that the marriage after the third adds to the sin of fornication, are they not evidently exposing St. Basil to this charge, whether they intend to or not? Who on earth does not know that four is more than three, and that a man who sins four times has sinned more than the one who does so for the third time, provided the sin is the same? Consequently, it makes no sense to say that the great archpriest used the phrase "more than fornication" in view of the third marriage, since this is obvious to anyone and not even a madman needs that kind of instruction; rather, the canon should be interpreted with reference to unbounded and unrestrained fornication, though they refuse to recognize this, not because they do not know, but because they are quibblers who let themselves go beyond the obtuseness of madmen in their interpretation of the canon.

XXIV

Ὅτι πρὸς ὅ φασιν οὗτοι, ἀλλ' οὐχ ὁ ἀπόστολος, «Κρεῖσσον γαμῆσαι ἢ πυροῦσθαι» (εἰ γὰρ καὶ τὰ αὐτὰ φθέγγονται, ἀλλ' ἑτέρα μὲν ἡ τοῦ ἀποστόλου τῆς ἀληθείας φθογγή, ἑτέρα δὲ ἡ τῶν ἀπὸ τοῦ ψεύδους), φατέον ὡς «Εἰ παραμύθιον τοῦ πυροῦσθαι διδόατε τὴν πρὸς τετάρτην γυναῖκα συνάφειαν, δώσετε πάντως καὶ ἐπὶ πέμπτην καὶ ἕκτην καὶ ἐφεξῆς, μέχρις ἂν ἡ πύρωσις ἡ παρενοχλοῦσα στήσεται.» Οἱ δὲ οὐ μέχρι *** πάντως, μιᾷ κατὰ διαφόρους γάμους συνάπτεσθαι γυναικί, ἀλλὰ τὴν παραμυθίαν ταύτην πάντως καὶ γυναικὸς προσούσης διὰ τὴν πύρωσιν συγχωρήσουσιν, ὑπομένοντες οὐ μιᾷ γυναικί, ἀλλὰ κατὰ τὸ αὐτὸ δυσὶ καὶ τρισὶ καὶ πλείοσιν, ἂν οὕτω τύχοι. Πολλοὶ γὰρ γαμεταῖς συνοικοῦντες πρὸς μὲν τὰς ἰδίας ἔχουσιν ἀηδῶς, πρὸς δὲ τὰς ἀλλοτρίας πυροῦνται σφοδρῶς. Τί οὖν κωλύει τοὺς φιλανθρώπους τούτους νομοθέτας πλείοσι γυναιξὶ κατὰ τὸ αὐτὸ συναρμόζειν τοὺς πυρουμένους, καὶ ἀποπηδᾶν, ἂν οὕτως ἡ πύρωσις βιάζηται, τοῦ ἰδίου γαμετοῦ τὴν γυναῖκα, συνοικίζειν δὲ τῷ πυρουμένῳ;

XXV

Ὅτι πρὸς τοὺς λέγοντας «Ἐπὶ μόνου τοῦ βασιλέως συγκεχώρηται ἡ τετάρτη γαμετή, ἐπὶ δὲ τῶν λοιπῶν ἀπείρηται προσώπων καὶ νόμος φοβερὰν τὴν ἀπειλὴν ἔχων ἐκτέθειται» ἁρμόσει τὸ τοῦ ἀποστόλου «Λογίζῃ τοῦτο, ὦ ἄνθρωπε κενέ, ὁ κρίνων τοὺς τὰ τοιαῦτα πράσσοντας καὶ ποιῶν αὐτά, ὅτι σὺ ἐκφεύξῃ τὸ κρίμα τοῦ θεοῦ;» ἔτι δὲ καὶ τὸ τοῦ κυρίου «Ἰατρέ, θεράπευσον ἑαυτόν,» καὶ «Ἔξελε τὴν δοκὸν ἐκ τοῦ ὀφθαλμοῦ σου καὶ τότε βλέψεις τὸ κάρφος τὸ ἐν τῷ ὀφθαλμῷ τοῦ ἀδελφοῦ σου.» Εἰ δὲ «ὅσα ὁ νόμος λέγει, τοῖς ἐν τῷ νόμῳ λαλεῖ,» εἰ μὲν ὁ τὸν νόμον τιθεὶς τῆς τοῦ νόμου πεφρόντικε φυλακῆς, ἔσται καὶ αὐτὸς ὑπὸ τὸν νόμον καὶ ἀνάγκη ἀκούειν αὐτοῦ· εἰ δὲ πρῶτος αὐτὸς λῆρον τὸ τοῦ οἰκείου νόμου ἐπίταγμα ποιεῖται δι' ὧν παρὰ φαῦλον ἔρριψε τὴν παραγγελίαν, πῶς οὐχὶ μᾶλλον πρὸς παράβασιν ἢ πρὸς συντήρησιν τοῦ νόμου προτρέπεται τοὺς ἀκροατάς;

XXIV 1–2: 1 Cor. 7:9. ‖ **XXV** 3–5: Rom. 2:3. ‖ 6: Luc. 4:23. ‖ 6–8: Matth. 7:5. ‖ 8–9: Rom. 3:19.

XXIV 7 lac. indic. wk, supple ex. gr. τούτου στήσονται

XXIV

The answer to *their* contention, *not* to the Apostle's words "It is better to marry than to burn" (for though the sounds are the same, the utterance of the apostle of truth is one thing, and that of the disciples of falsehood another), must be as follows: "If you allow the union with a fourth wife to relieve burning passion, you will necessarily also allow it for a fifth, a sixth, and so on, until the burning that troubles a man comes to an end." But surely they will not ⟨stop at allowing him⟩ to marry one wife in successive marriages; of course, they will grant such relief for his burning passion also when there is a wife available, permitting him to have, instead of one wife, two and three and more simultaneously, if things happen to be that way. Many married men, indeed, dislike their own wives, while burning with passion for those of others. So what prevents these humane lawgivers from marrying such cases of "burning" to several wives at a time, and from allowing the wife, if the burning passion demands this, to run away from her own husband and to live with her burning lover?

XXV

To those who declare, "The fourth wife is permitted only in the emperor's case, but forbidden to all other persons, and a law is in force which contains a fearful sanction," the Apostle's word is applicable: "Thinkest thou this, vain man, that judgest them which do such things, and doest the same, that thou shalt escape the judgment of God?" and also the Lord's "Physician, heal thyself" and "Cast out the beam out of thine own eye and then shalt thou see clearly to cast out the mote out of thy brother's eye." Now if "whatever the law says, it speaks to those who are under the law," the lawgiver, assuming that he cares for the observance of his law, will submit to the law himself and thus compel obedience; but if he is the first himself to make nonsense of what his own law prescribes by scorning its command, is it not evident that he encourages the public to transgress the law rather than to observe it?

XXVI

Ἔτι δὲ εἰ συγχωρεῖται τῷ βασιλεῖ ὁ γάμος, πάντως ἔσται καὶ τοῖς λοιποῖς βασιλεῦσι συγκεχωρημένος. Οὐ γὰρ δὴ τῷ μὲν διὰ τὴν βασιλείαν συγχωρηθήσεται, τοῖς δὲ οὐχί, ἀλλ' ὥσπερ ἔχουσι τὸ ἴσον τοῦ ἀξιώματος, οὕτω κληρονομήσουσι καὶ τῆς ἴσης ἐξουσίας περιστάσεως ὁμοίας συμπιπτούσης· τοῦτο δὲ πῶς ἂν ᾖ περιγραφόμενον ἐφ' ἑνὶ προσώπῳ καὶ οὐκ εἰς πλείονας διαβαῖνον; Ἀφ' ὧν ἀνάγκη ὥσπερ ἀπό τινων μετεώρων καὶ ὑψηλῶν χωρίων ῥεῦσαι ῥᾳδίως τὸ κακὸν ἐπὶ τοὺς ταπεινοτέρους. Καὶ ἄλλως δὲ τίς οὗτος ἕτοιμος πείθεσθαι νομοθεσίᾳ ἣν ὁρᾷ ὑπὸ τοῦ νομοθετοῦντος ὑβριζομένην, ὅπου γε μᾶλλον πέφυκε τὸ τῶν ἀνθρώπων ἀνάγωγον μηδὲ λίαν τιμωμένης ἐντολῆς ὑπὸ τοῦ ταύτην ἐντειλαμένου ἀσφαλῶς πρὸς αὐτὴν διατίθεσθαι; Καὶ ὅρα μοι τὰ θεῖα νομοθετήματα, τὰ τῶν θείων ἀποστόλων, τὰ τῶν πατέρων, ἃ πράξεσιν αὐτῶν μᾶλλον ἢ λόγοις νενομοθετημένα παραμελεῖται ὑπὸ τῆς ἐπὶ τὰ χείρω τῶν ἀνθρώπων ῥοπῆς.

XXVII

Ὅτι πρὸς τοὺς λέγοντας μὴ χρῆναι δι' ἕνα σφαλλόμενον ἀκριβολογεῖσθαι ῥητέον· δι' ἑνὸς ἀνθρώπου ἁμαρτίαν θάνατος εἰς τὸν κόσμον εἰσῆλθεν καὶ οὐκ ἐφείσατο δὲ διὰ πταῖσμα ἑνὸς ὁ πλάστης καίτοι πταίσαντος ἅπαξ, ἀλλ' εἰς θάνατον παραδέδωκε.

XXVIII

Ἔτι δέ, τὸ τοῦ ἀποστόλου, «μικρὰ ζύμη ὅλον τὸ φύραμα ζυμοῖ»· ἐνταῦθα δὲ οὐ μικρὰ ζύμη, ἀλλ' ἡλίκον τὸ μέγεθος. Καὶ εἰ μικρὰ ζύμη ὅλον τὸ φύραμα ζυμοῖ, τί ποιήσει τῆς τοιαύτης ζύμης ὁ ὄγκος;

XXIX

Ὅτι τὸ «Διαμαρτύρομαι ἐνώπιον τοῦ θεοῦ καὶ τῶν ἐκλεκτῶν αὐτοῦ ἀγγέλων, ἵνα ταῦτα φυλάξῃς χωρὶς προκρίματος,» πῶς οὐκ ἔστι φρικτὸν ἀκοῦσαι, μὴ ὅτι γε πρᾶξαι τὴν λεγομένην τοῖς ἀθλίοις νυμφοστόλοις οἰκονομίαν;

XXVII 2–3: Rom. 5:12. ‖ **XXVIII** 1–2: 1 Cor. 5:6. ‖ **XXIX** 1–2: 1 Tim. 5:21.

XXVI 4–5 περιστάσεως corr. Karlin-Hayter: περὶ στάσεως m ‖ 8 fort. οὗτως

XXVI

Further, if the marriage is permitted to the emperor, it will inevitably be permitted also to other emperors. Surely it cannot be permitted to the one on the ground of his imperial dignity and refused to the others: as they hold equal rank, so they will also inherit equal freedom of action when a similar situation presents itself; and why should such a case be limited to one person and not extend to several? Then, necessarily, just as water flows down from elevated points high up in the mountains, the evil will spread unchecked to the lower classes. Besides, what man is willing to obey a legislation which he sees is despised by the lawgiver? On the contrary, man's unruly nature cannot be trusted to conform even to a command that is held in the highest honor by the one who gave it. Look at the Divine Commandments, those of the Holy Apostles, of the Fathers, which, though promulgated by their deeds rather than by their words, are slighted owing to man's bent toward the inferior.

XXVII

Against those who argue that we should not draw up strict rules on account of one man's error, we must say: By the sin of one man death has entered into the world, and for the sake of one man's fault the Creator did not spare it, though he sinned only once, but abandoned it to death.

XXVIII

Further, as the Apostle has it, "A little leaven leaveneth the whole lump"; but this is not a case of a little leaven, there is only too much of it! And if a little leaven leaveneth the whole lump, what will a mass like this do?

XXIX

Are not the words, "I charge thee before God and His elect angels that thou observe these things without preferring one before another," frightful even to hear? How much more frightful, then, to put into actual practice what these wretched matchmakers call dispensation!

200. The Tome of Union

A. Argument

Εἴδησις πῶς ἡ τετραγαμία τῷ βασιλεῖ κυρῷ Λέοντι τετόλμηται καὶ ὅπως κατήργηται διὰ τοῦ τόμου τῆς ἑνώσεως

Λέων ὁ σοφώτατος εἶχε μὲν πρώτην γαμετὴν τὴν ἁγίαν Θεοφανώ, μεθ' ἧς καὶ θυγατέρα ἔτεκεν· ἀλλὰ τάχιον ἐτεθνήκει. Καὶ αὐτῆς δὲ πρὸς κύριον ἀπελθούσης τῆς ἁγίας ζεύγνυται Ζωῇ τῇ θυγατρὶ τοῦ Τζαουτζᾶ Στυλιανοῦ, ἑνὸς τῶν ἀρχόντων καὶ φίλων τοῦ βασιλέως. Κἀκείνης συντόμως ἄπαιδος τελευτησάσης καὶ τρίτην ἠγάγετο γυναῖκα, Εὐδοκίαν, τὴν ἀπὸ τοῦ θέματος Ὀψικίου ἐπιλεγεῖσαν διὰ τὸ κάλλος, ἥτις ἐν αὐταῖς ταῖς ὠδῖσι θνήσκει σὺν τῷ βρέφει. Ὁ δὲ βασιλεὺς ἀφάτῳ συσχεθεὶς λύπῃ ἐπὶ τῷ καταλειφθῆναι ἄπαις, ἐφέσει τεκνογονίας καὶ τετάρτην λαμβάνει γυναῖκα, τὴν τῆς Καρβωνοψίνης Ζωήν, καὶ τίκτει μετ' αὐτῆς τὸν Κωνσταντῖνον.

Ὁ πατριάρχης δὲ Νικόλαος καὶ οἱ μητροπολῖται ἀφορίζουσι τὸν βασιλέα τῆς ἐκκλησίας. Καὶ τὸν ἀφορισμὸν οἱ μέν τινες τῶν ἀρχιερέων συντεμεῖν ἔλεγον δεῖν καὶ μὴ ἐπὶ πλείονα παρατείνειν καιρόν, οἱ δὲ οὐκ ἐπείθοντο· καὶ σχίσματα ἦν ἐν αὐτοῖς καὶ στάσις πολλή. Καὶ πολλὰ δεόμενον τὸν βασιλέα καὶ παρακαλοῦντα οἱ μὲν προσεδέχοντο, οἱ δὲ ἀπειθεῖς ἦσαν καὶ ἄτεγκτοι. Ὁ δὲ βασιλεύς, συνετὸς ὢν καὶ ὅθεν ἀνεφύη τὸ ἀσύμφωνον τῶν ἀρχιερέων οὐκ ἀγνοῶν, μεθίστησι τὸν πατριάρχην Νικόλαον καὶ ἐξορίζει τῆς ἐκκλησίας, ὡς ψεύστην καὶ πολλάκις μὲν ὅρκοις διαβεβαιοῦντα καὶ ὑποσχόμενον δοῦναι τῷ βασιλεῖ τὴν τοῦ ἐπιτιμίου συμπάθειαν, τοσαυτάκις δὲ μεταμελόμενον καὶ ἀναβαλλόμενον ἐπίτηδες· προβάλλεται δὲ πατριάρχην τὸν ἑαυτοῦ πνευματικὸν πατέρα Εὐθύμιον, ἄνδρα πολλοῖς ἔτεσι τῇ μοναχικῇ διαπρέψαντα ἀσκήσει καὶ προφητικοῦ χαρίσματος ἠξιωμένον. Οὗτος ἐλεύθερον τοῦ ἐπιτιμίου δείκνυσι τὸν βασιλέα καὶ τοῦ χρονίου δεσμοῦ ἀπολύει καὶ εἰς κοινωνίαν δέχεται.

Ἀλλ' ἦσαν ἔτι πολλοὶ τῶν ἀρχιερέων οἱ μὴ συνελθόντες τῇ τοῦ πατριάρχου οἰκονομίᾳ, καὶ μᾶλλον οἱ τοῦ μέρους τοῦ ἐκβληθέντος Νικολάου. Ἐπεὶ δὲ ὁ μὲν βασιλεὺς Λέων μετέστη πρὸς κύριον καὶ ὁ ἀδελφὸς ἐκείνου Ἀλέξανδρος τῆς βασιλείας ἐγκρατὴς ἦν, τὸν μὲν πατριάρχην Εὐθύμιον

---

200 A: L 328^{v}–329^{r} H 374^{r-v} Z 27^{r-v} ‖ 1–2 περὶ συνόδου γεγονυίας ἐν κωνσταντινουπ(ό)λ(ει) εἰς τὴν μεγ(ά)λ(ην) ἐκκλησίαν· ἐπὶ κωνσταντίνου τοῦ πορφυρογεννήτου καὶ ῥωμανοῦ, τοῦ μὲν βασιλεύοντος· τοῦ δὲ τοτηνικαῦτα ὄντος βασιλεωπάτ(ο)ρος· περὶ τῆς ἑνώσεως τῆς ἐκκλησίας H Σύνοδος ἑτέρα ἐπὶ κω(νσταντίνου) βασιλέως τοῦ α′ πορφυρογεννήτου ἐπικληθ(έν)τος· υἱοῦ λέοντος βασιλέως τοῦ σοφοῦ· καὶ νικολ(άου) π(ατ)ριάρχ(ου) κω(νσταντινου)πόλ(εως)· ἀθροισθεῖσα ἐν ταύτη τῇ μεγ(ά)λ(η) ἐκκλησ(ία) τῆς ἁγίας σοφίας· ἐπὶ τῇ ἑνώσει τῶν ἀποσχισθ(έν)των ἐπισκόπων· διὰ τὴν τετραγαμίαν τοῦ βασιλέως λέοντος· ἐν ἔτει τῷ ‚ϛυκη′ μήπω βασιλεύσαντος ῥωμανοῦ τοῦ λακαπη(νοῦ)· ἀλλ' ἔτι τῷ βασιλεωπάτ(ο)ρ(ος) ἀξιώματι διαπρέποντος Z ‖ 3 σοφώτατος] βασιλεὺς add. HZ ‖ 5 τῆς ἁγίας om. H ‖ τζαουτζᾶ L: ζαούτζ( ) H -η Z ‖ 10 ἐν ἐφέσει H ‖ 17–18 τὸ ἀσύμφωνον ἀνεφύη colloc. HZ ‖ 20 ὑπισχνούμενον H

200. The Tome of Union

A. Argument

An account as to how the Emperor, Lord Leo, ventured upon the fourth marriage and how it was abolished by the Tome of Union

Leo the Most Wise had for his first consort Saint Theophano, who bore him a daughter; the child, however, died soon. When the Saint herself, too, had departed to the Lord, he wedded Zoe the daughter of Stylianus Tzaoutzas, one of the Emperor's magistrates and friends. When she also died childless after a short time, he married a third wife, Eudocia, from the theme of Opsikion, chosen because of her beauty; she died in childbirth with the baby. The Emperor, afflicted by inexpressible sorrow at being left without a son, was driven by his desire for a child to take a fourth wife, Zoe Carbonopsina, who bore him Constantine.

The Patriarch Nicholas, however, and the metropolitans excommunicated the Emperor. The excommunication, in the opinion of some of the archpriests, was to be brief and not to be extended over a longer period of time, while others did not share this view; and there were schisms between them and great discord. So when the Emperor begged and entreated them urgently, the one group was willing to admit him, the others refused and were adamant. Then the Emperor, intelligent enough to be aware of the origin of the dissension between the archpriests, removed the Patriarch Nicholas and banished him from the Church as a liar, who again and again assured and promised under oath to grant the Emperor indulgence of his penance, but as many times changed his mind and delayed intentionally; as patriarch he appointed his own spiritual father Euthymius, a man who had distinguished himself for many years as a monk and ascetic and had been deemed worthy of the gift of prophecy. He declared the Emperor free from the penance, released him from the long interdict, and admitted him to Communion.

However, there were still many of the archpriests who had not acceded to the Patriarch's dispensation, especially the party of the ex-Patriarch Nicholas. When the Emperor Leo had departed to the Lord and his brother Alexander held the imperial power, the latter expelled the Patriarch Euthymius ignominiously

ἐξωθεῖ τῆς ἐκκλησίας μεθ' ὕβρεων, ἀντεισάγει δὲ πάλιν τὸν προεκβεβλημένον Νικόλαον. Καὶ ἔτι μᾶλλον τὰ τῆς ἐκκλησίας ἐστασίαζε πράγματα, διαιρεθέντων τῶν μητροπολιτῶν, καὶ τῶν μὲν τῷ ἐκβληθέντι πατριάρχῃ, τῶν δὲ τῷ ἀντεισαχθέντι προσκειμένων.

Οὐ πολὺ τὸ ἐν μέσῳ, καὶ ὁ μὲν Ἀλέξανδρος ἐτεθνήκει, ὁ δὲ Κωνσταντῖνος τῆς βασιλείας κληρονόμος ἐγεγόνει. Ὃς συγκαλέσας τόν τε πατριάρχην Νικόλαον καὶ σύμπαντας τοὺς ἀρχιερεῖς (ὁ γὰρ Εὐθύμιος ἤδη πρὸς κύριον ἐξεδήμησε) πείθει τούτους πρὸς μίαν γνώμην συνελθεῖν καὶ ὁμόνοιαν, καὶ δοῦναι τῷ πατρὶ αὐτοῦ καὶ μετὰ θάνατον κοινῇ ψήφῳ τὴν ἄφεσιν, κανονικὴν δὲ ψῆφον ἐκθεῖναι τοῦ μηκέτι τολμᾶν τοιοῦτον ἢ πραχθῆναι ἁμάρτημα· ἐφ' οἷς ὁ λεγόμενος οὑτοσὶ τῆς ἑνώσεως τόμος προέβη.

B. Text

Ἔκθεσις ἤτοι ἀνάμνησις τῆς γενομένης τῆς ἐκκλησίας ἑνώσεως ἐπὶ Κωνσταντίνου καὶ Ῥωμανοῦ, τοῦ μὲν βασιλεύοντος, τοῦ δὲ τὸ τηνικαῦτα τῷ τοῦ βασιλεοπάτορος ἀξιώματι διαπρέποντος

Ὁ κύριος ἡμῶν Ἰησοῦς Χριστὸς καὶ θεὸς τοῖς ἑαυτοῦ μαθηταῖς καὶ ἀποστόλοις καὶ τοῖς ὅσοι μετ' ἐκείνους ἄξιοι γεγόνασι τῆς κληρονομίας αὐτοῦ, ἐξαίρετόν τινα κλῆρον τὴν εἰρήνην κατέλιπε, τοῦτο γνώρισμα παρασχόμενος τοῖς οἰκείοις τῆς πρὸς αὐτὸν οἰκειότητος, εἰ τῷ συνδέσμῳ τῆς εἰρήνης σφιγγόμενοι μὴ τὴν τοῦ πνεύματος διασπῶσιν ἑνότητα· πρότερον αὐτὸς οἰκείῳ ὑποδείγματι δείξας

---

200 B: 7: Ioann. 14:27. ‖ 8–9: cf. Ioann. 13:35. ‖ 9–10: Ephes. 4:3.

---

30 μεθ' ὕβρεων ἐξωθεῖ τῆς ἐκκλησίας colloc. HZ ‖ 30–31 προεκβεβλημένον om. H ‖ 31 καὶ om. Z διὸ καὶ H ‖ 35 τῆς — ἐγεγόνει LZ: βασιλεύει H ‖ τε om. H ‖ 39 ψῆφον L: νομοθεσίαν HZ ‖ ἐκθεῖναι L: ἐκτιθέασι HZ ‖ τολμᾶν L: τολμηθῆναι HZ ‖ 39–40 ἢ πραχθῆναι om. H: ἢ om. Z ‖ 40 ἐφ' — προέβη L: ἢ καὶ ἔχει οὕτως H om. Z

200 B: J 265^{v}–267^{r} W 68^{r}–70^{r} G 230^{r}–232^{v} U 1^{r}–16^{v} N 201^{r}–203^{v} O 125–127 M 114^{r}–116^{v} P 39^{r}–40^{v} V 114–120 F 315^{v}–317^{v} S 186^{v}–188^{r} T 397^{v}–399^{r} L 329^{r}–330^{r} H 374^{v}–376^{v} Z 27^{v} ‖ ante 1 ἀναγινώσκετ(αι) ἡ σύνοδ(ος) αὕτη κυ(ριακῇ) τῆς ἑνώσεως G ἀναγινώσκ(ε)τ(αι) καὶ ἡ κειμ(έ)νη ἑξῆς ἕνωσις αὕτη κατὰ μῆ(να) ἰούλ(ιον) ἀπὸ τ(οῦ) ἁγ(ίου) προκ(ο)π(ίου) mg. N Ἡ σύνοδ(ος) τῆς ἑνώσεως· ἥτις ἀναγινώσκεται τῇ κυριακῇ τῶν προαλλάκτων O ‖ 1–4 om. HZ ‖ 1 ἤτοι ἀνάμνησις om. S ‖ τῆς^{2} — 2 ἑνώσεως] ἑνώσεως τῆς ἁγίας ἐκκλησίας S ‖ 3 τὸ τηνικαῦτα om. OT ‖ τῷ — 4 διαπρέποντος] τὸ τοῦ βασιλεοπάτορος ἀξίωμα ἔχοντος T ‖ τῷ] ante ἀξιώματι pon. S ‖ 4 βασιλεοπάτορος WGOMPST: βασιλεωπάτορος UL (cf. HZ ad Op. 200 A lin. 1–2) βασιλειοπάτορος J βασιλοπάτορος N ‖ 5 καὶ θεὸς] post κύριος pon. T om. S ‖ 6 ἐκείνους NOH^{pc}FST: ἐκεῖνον JGUVL ἐκείνων MPZ ‖ 7 αὐτῶν H ‖ κατέλιπε] hinc usque ad 53 συνα- deest U ‖ 8 τῆς οἰκείας S ‖ 9 δεσμῷ F ‖ σφιγγόμενοι] σφραγιζόμενοι FS ‖ 10 διασπῶσιν – 11 προαίρεσιν om. H ‖ 10 αὐτοῖς J

from the Church and reinstated Nicholas who had been removed from his office. Then the situation in the Church was even more turbulent, for the metropolitans were divided, some siding with the deposed Patriarch, some with the one that had replaced him.

Shortly after, Alexander died, and Constantine succeeded to the throne. Having convoked the Patriarch Nicholas and all the archpriests (Euthymius had meanwhile departed to the Lord), he persuaded them to join in one unanimous resolution, granting by common consent absolution to his Father even after death, but also passing a canonical decree to the effect that no one should dare to commit this sin again. On this understanding the present "Tome of Union" was issued.

B. Text

Decree or Record of the Union of the Church under Constantine and Romanus, the Former Being Emperor, the Latter at the Time Distinguished by the Rank of Basileopator

Our Lord and God Jesus Christ left to His disciples and apostles and to all those who after them were found worthy of guarding His inheritance, the gift of peace as a unique heritage, making this the mark whereby His own people should be recognized as belonging to Him, if they were tightly joined together by the bond of peace and never disrupted the unity of the Spirit. First, He showed us by His own example what value He sets upon

ἡμῖν ἣν ἔχει περὶ τῆς εἰρήνης προαίρεσιν, δι' ὧν ὑπεράνω παντὸς ὕψους τελῶν ἐπὶ τὴν ἐσχατιὰν κατῆλθε τὴν ἡμετέραν καὶ παραπλησίως ἡμῖν σαρκὸς καὶ αἵματος ἐκοινώνησεν, ἵνα τοὺς ἐξ ἀλλήλων διηρημένους εἰς ἑνότητα καταστήσῃ· ἔπειτα καὶ τοῖς τὰ ἐκείνου μαθήματα πεπαιδευμένοις ταύτην κατέλιπε τὴν κληρονομίαν, τὸ εἰρηνεύειν ἐν ἀλλήλοις, καὶ οὐ τοσοῦτον μόνον, ἀλλὰ καὶ τὸ πρὸς εἰρήνην ἄγειν ἑτέρους πρὸς ἑαυτοὺς στασιάζοντας.

Ἀλλὰ γὰρ τοιούτου ὄντος τοῦ πράγματος, ἐξ ἀρχῆς καὶ μέχρι τοῦ νῦν οὐ διέλιπεν ἡ τοῦ πονηροῦ στασιώδης κακία τὸ ἱερὸν τῆς ἐκκλησίας διαταράττουσα πλήρωμα, νῦν μὲν ταύτην, νῦν δὲ ἐκείνην ἀνακινοῦσα τὴν πρόφασιν· ἀλλ' ὁ μὲν τοιοῦτος, ὁ δὲ τῆς εἰρήνης αἴτιος καὶ διδάσκαλος Χριστὸς ὁ θεὸς ἡμῶν, ὁ πύλας εἰπὼν ᾅδου μὴ κατισχύσειν τῆς ἐκκλησίας αὐτοῦ, ἀεὶ τὰ σκάνδαλα εἰς τὴν τοῦ πονηροῦ κεφαλὴν περιτρέπων τὴν εἰρήνην τῇ ἐκκλησίᾳ διαφυλάττει ἀλύμαντον. Οὗτος ἐκεῖνος, ἡ εἰρήνη ἡμῶν, Χριστὸς ὁ θεός, ὁ πατήρ, ὁ ἀρχιερεύς, ὁ ποιμὴν ὁ ἀληθινός, τῶν ἱερῶν τέκνων τῆς πανάγνου νύμφης αὐτοῦ τῆς ἐκκλησίας ἐξ ἀλλήλων διασπασθέντων, τῇ αὐτοῦ προνοίᾳ καὶ χάριτι τὴν ἕνωσιν αὐτοῖς κατεπράξατο καὶ τοῖς ἀχράντοις κόλποις πάλιν συνήγαγε τῆς μητρός, διδοὺς ἐκείνῃ μὲν χαίρειν ἐπὶ τῇ συναγωγῇ τῶν τέκνων, ἑαυτῷ δὲ τὴν ἐξ ἑνὸς στόματος καὶ μιᾶς καρδίας προσάγεσθαι τῆς δόξης ἀναφοράν, πᾶσι δὲ τοῖς ὅσοι μὴ πρὸς τὴν ταραχώδη τοῦ δαίμονος προαίρεσιν ἀποκλίνουσιν, ἀλλὰ τοῦ τῆς εἰρήνης αἰτίου τὸ παράγγελμα τιμῶσι, τὴν εὐχαριστίαν προσάγειν.

Ἀλλ' ἐπὶ μὲν τῶν ἄνω χρόνων ἐγένοντο σκανδάλων ἀφορμαί, ὁποῖαι δὴ καὶ γεγόνασι, καὶ πρὸς τὴν ἑκάστοτε κίνησιν τοῦ κακοῦ τοῖς σοφοῖς τῶν ἐκκλησιῶν οἰκονόμοις ἡ πρόσφορος ἐξεύρηται θεραπεία. Νῦν δέ, ὅτι συμβέβηκε τεταράχθαι τὴν ἐκκλησίαν ἐξ ἀφορμῆς γαμικῆς, ἐν τῷ μὴ τυγχάνειν τὸν γάμον ἐλεύθερον μέμψεως, πρὸς

22–23: Matth. 16:18. ‖ 25: Ephes. 2:14.

---

13 κεκοινώνηκεν S ‖ ἐξ] ἀπ' FS ‖ 15 παθήματα HZFS ‖ παιδευομένοις VT ‖ τὸ] τοῦ V ‖ 16 ἐν om. T ‖ τοσοῦτον WGNMPVS: τοῦτο JOFTLHZ ‖ 17 ἄγειν om. VT ‖ 18 γὰρ om. F ‖ τοῦ om. S ‖ 23 κατισχύειν OSL ‖ τὴν ἐκκλησίαν T ‖ 25 ἡμῶν] post θεός pon. FS om. VT ‖ 26 ὁ ἀληθινὸς ποιμὴν HZ ‖ 28 αὐτῆς WOM[pc] ‖ 29 πάλιν om. FS ‖ 30 δὲ] δὲ καὶ FS ‖ στόματος NOFSTLH: om. JWGMPVZ ‖ 32 προαίρεσιν τοῦ δαίμονος colloc. T ‖ 33 τιμῶσι] τολμῶσι HZ[ac] τιμῶσιν, ἀπὸ ψυχῆς S ‖ 35 ἄνω] ἄλλων F ‖ 37 τῆς ἐκκλησίας HZ ‖ 38 ὅτε H ‖ 39 γάμον] ἐκεῖνον add. S

200 B

peace by the fact that, though being above all that is high, He came down to our lowest depth and shared our flesh and blood so that He might establish unity among those who were divided from each other; then, to those instructed in His teachings, he left this as their inheritance, to live in peace with one another and, what is more, also to bring peace to others who are at strife.

However, this being so, the rebellious malice of the Evil One has never ceased, since the beginning and until this day, from disturbing the holy complement of the Church by stirring up now one occasion, then another. Such is his nature; but Christ our God, the Cause and Teacher of peace, Who has said that the gates of hell shall not prevail against His Church, always turns the machinations of the Evil One upon his own head and preserves the peace of the Church unscathed. It is He, our Peace, Christ our God, the Father, the High Priest, the True Shepherd, Who when the holy children of His most pure Bride the Church had been torn from each other, brought about their union by His Providence and Grace and gathered them together again in the immaculate bosom of their Mother, thereby granting that she might rejoice in the gathering of her children, that He Himself might receive the offering of praise from one mouth and one heart, and that all those who do not swerve toward the subversive purpose of the devil but honor the commandment of Him Who is the Cause of peace, might offer up thanksgiving to Him.

In the olden times there were various causes for scandals, whatever they may have been, and on each occasion when evil reared its head, the wise stewards of the Church found the appropriate cure. In the present case, since the disturbance in the Church is occasioned by a marriage, inasmuch as the marriage is not exempt from blame, the holy decree of the

τὴν ἐκείνου κώλυσιν ἡ τῆς ἐκκλησίας ἱερὰ κρίσις φέρει τὴν γνώμην καὶ τοῦ μὴ προέρχεσθαι τοῦτον ἔτι χώραν εὑρίσκειν. Οὕτω γὰρ καὶ νῦν καὶ μετέπειτα τῶν κατεχόντων σκανδάλων ἀπηλλάχθαι περιγενήσεται τοῖς ὅσοι μὴ τὸ φιλόνεικον καὶ τὴν ἔριν ἀντὶ τῆς εἰρήνης ἠγάπησαν τοῦ Χριστοῦ· τῆς γὰρ προφάσεως ἐκποδὼν γεγενημένης ἀφ' ἧς ἐξέφυ τὰ σκάνδαλα, τοῦ εἰρηνεύειν τοῖς ἀγαπῶσιν εἰρήνην οὐδεμία ἐστὶν ἡ κωλύουσα πρόφασις. Καὶ γὰρ ἐν παντὶ πράγματι οὕτως ἔχει· τῆς σφαλερᾶς αἰτίας τῆς τῶν ἀτόπων γενέσεως ἐκποδὼν καθισταμένης πρὸς τὴν ἐξ ἀρχῆς εὐταξίαν ἀποκαθίσταται τὰ τέως ἐκεῖθεν λαβόντα τὸ πονηρῶς διακεῖσθαι. Οὕτω καὶ σώματι νόσου προσγινομένης, τοῦ αἰτίου ταύτης ἀναχωρήσαντος τὸ ὑγιαίνειν ἐπανέρχεται, καὶ θαλάσσῃ ἐξ ἀνέμων βιαιότητος ταραττομένῃ, τῆς καταιγίδος πεπαυμένης ἡ γαληνιῶσα κατάστασις ἐπανήκει. Διὰ τοῦτο κοινῇ συναθροισθέντες ἀρχιερεῖς τε καὶ ἱερεῖς, ὅσοι μὴ ἑαυτοῖς (ἐῶ γὰρ εἰπεῖν ἄλλοις) ἀρέσκειν ἠγάπησαν, ἀλλὰ τῆς ἐκκλησίας τὴν εἰρήνην τοῦ στασιάζειν προετίμησαν, συνείδομεν, ἐπείπερ ἐκ τῶν γαμικῶν ἀφορμῶν τὰ σκάνδαλα τὴν γένεσιν ἔλαβε, ταῦτα διανακαθᾶραι, καὶ διασφαλίσασθαι τοῦ μηδαμῶς ἔτι διὰ τῆς αὐτῶν εἰς τὸν βίον προόδου μήτε τὴν ἐκκλησίαν ταράττειν μήτε τὴν ζωὴν τῶν οὕτω ζῆν ἑλομένων κατάκριτον καὶ κατεγνωσμένην ποιεῖν.

Καὶ λοιπὸν ἀποφαινόμεθα κοινῇ γνώμῃ καὶ κρίσει, ἀπό γε τοῦ παρόντος ἔτους, ὅ ἐστιν ἔτος ͵ςυκη', ἰνδικτιῶνος η', τέταρτον γάμον μηδενὶ τολμᾶσθαι, ἀλλ' εἶναι ἀπόβλητον παντελῶς, καὶ τὸν εἴ τις ἐπὶ τοιοῦτον ἐλθεῖν συνοικέσιον προθυμηθείη, πάσης ἀπεστερημένον εἶναι συνάξεως ἐκκλησιαστικῆς καὶ αὐτῆς τῆς πρὸς τὸν ἅγιον ναὸν εἰσόδου ἀλλότριον, μέχρις ἂν ἐπιμένοι τῷ συνοικεσίῳ. Τοῦτο μὲν

40 ἐκείνου] αὐτοῦ S ‖ τῆς ἐκκλησίας om. FS ‖ κρίσις] κλῆσις T ‖ γνώμην] συγγνώμην VT ‖ 41 τοῦ] τὸ FS ‖ ἔρχεσθαι F ‖ ἔτι] ἐπὶ S ‖ 42 καὶ om. HZ ‖ 42–43 παραγενήσεται H(?)Z ‖ 45 ἐξεφύη F ‖ τοῦ εἰρηνεύειν] post εἰρήνην pon. FS ‖ τὴν εἰρήνην VST ‖ 46 πρόφασις ἡ κωλύουσα colloc. S ‖ 46 κωλύσασα T ‖ 47 γενέτιδος S ‖ 48 καθισταμένης] γεγενημένης S γενομένης Z ‖ ἀποκαθίστασθαι FS ‖ 49 τὸ om. VT ‖ 50 προσγινομένης JGOMPFTZ: προσγενομένης WHL προσγεγενημένης S προγινομένης N ‖ 51 βιαιοτάτων OFSZ βιαιοτάτως H ‖ 52 παυσαμένης HZ ‖ 53 -θροισθέντες] hinc denuo U ‖ 54 εἰπεῖν] λέγειν SHZ ‖ 56 ἔλαβον FSTHZ ‖ 56–57 διακαθᾶραι FST ‖ 58 μήτε — ταράττειν om. T ‖ 60 λοιπὸν] γοῦν FS ‖ 61 ὅ] ὅπερ FS ‖ ἔτος JWUNMPVT: om. GOFSLHZ ‖ ἰνδικτιῶνος] def. X ‖ 62 μηδενὶ τολμᾶσθαι] μηδαμῶς τολμᾶσθαί τινι FS ‖ πανταχοῦ F πανταχῇ S ‖ τὸν] τῶν JM ‖ 63 συνοικέσιον ἐλθεῖν colloc. FS ‖ προθυμηθῇ S ‖ 64 ἐκκλησιαστικῆς συνάξεως colloc. F ‖ 65 ἐπιμένῃ T ‖ μὲν om. L

200 B

Church ordains its prevention, and that it shall not be allowed to take place again. Thus, now and henceforth, release from the prevailing scandals will be obtained by all who do not choose quarrel and strife above the peace of Christ; indeed, when the occasion that gave rise to the scandals has been removed, there is no reason for the peacefully minded not to live in peace. This is true in every situation: once the calamitous cause that produced the untoward events has been eliminated, the things that were adversely affected by it for a time are restored to their former normal state. Thus, when the body is affected by disease, health returns when the cause of the disease is gone; when the sea is troubled by the violence of winds, fair weather comes back after the storm is over. Therefore, we have gathered together archpriests and priests, all those who, rather than choosing to please themselves (not to speak of pleasing others), sought peace for the Church instead of strife, and, since the scandals originated in matters of marriage, we have decided on measures to clear them away and to provide safeguards that they will never again appear in our society either to trouble the Church or to make the lives of those who adopt such conduct subject to censure and condemnation.

So now we declare unanimously and by common consent that from this present year, which is the year 6428, in the eighth indiction, no one shall venture to contract a fourth marriage, but that it shall be utterly banned, and that anyone who should wish to enter into such a union shall be excluded from every religious congregation and even forbidden to enter the holy temple, as long as the union continues. This, in fact, is what the

200 B

γὰρ καὶ τοῖς πρὸ ἡμῶν ἁγίοις ἔδοξε πατράσι· καὶ ἡμεῖς δὲ τὴν γνώμην ἐνδηλοτέραν ποιοῦντες ὡς ἀλλότριον αὐτὸν τῆς Χριστιανικῆς πολιτείας ἀποκηρύττομεν.

Ἀλλ' οὕτω μὲν περὶ τοῦ τετάρτου γάμου. Ἵνα δὲ καὶ τὰ τῶν ἄλλων γάμων εὐσχημονέστερον τυπωθῇ καὶ τοῦ τῶν Χριστιανῶν βίου μὴ ἀνάξιον ἔχῃ τὴν προαγωγήν, καὶ περὶ τοῦ τρίτου ὁρίζομεν γάμου ὥστε μὴ ἁπλῶς μηδὲ ὡς ἔτυχεν ἐπιτελεῖσθαι αὐτόν. Καὶ γὰρ συγκεχώρηται μὲν ὡς ῥύπασμα τοῖς πατράσιν, οὔπω τότε καθὼς νῦν γινομένου τοῦ πράγματος ἀπηρυθριασμένως οὐδ' εἰς πλάτος ἐξηπλωμένου, ἀλλ' ὥσπερ εἴ τις ἐν οἴκῳ παραπεπτωκὸς ἐν γωνίᾳ παρίδοι πολλάκις κείμενον ῥύπασμα· νῦν δέ, ὅτι χώραν ἔλαβε παρρησίας καὶ ὡς οὐδὲν ἔχων εἰς ἀσχημοσύνην οὐδὲ ῥυπαίνων λογίζεται ἐκ τοῦ προβῆναι εἰς πληθυσμόν, καλῶς ἔδοξεν ἀνακαθαίρειν αὐτόν, ὥσπερ καὶ αἶσχος οὐκ ἐν γωνίᾳ παρερριμμένον, ἀλλ' ἐξηπλωμένον ἐπὶ τῆς οἰκίας, οὐδαμῶς ἐῶμεν, ἀλλὰ καθαίρομεν καὶ τὸ ἐκ τούτου ἀηδὲς ἀποβάλλομεν.

Καὶ τῇ ἀνθρωπίνῃ τοίνυν συνυπείκοντες ἀσθενείᾳ καὶ τῆς πρεπούσης εὐσχημοσύνης φροντίδα ποιούμενοι τῇ Χριστιανῶν ζωῇ, τοῦτο ἐπὶ τῶν τριγάμων παραφυλάττεσθαι διορίζομεν, ὥστε, εἴ τις πρὸς τεσσαρακοστὸν ἀναβεβηκὼς ἔτος καὶ μήτε τὴν φύσιν αἰδούμενος μήτε τῆς ὀφειλομένης Χριστιανοῖς εὐκόσμου ζωῆς φροντίδα ποιούμενος, ἀλλὰ μόνης τῆς ἐμπαθοῦς ἐπιθυμίας γινόμενος πρὸς τρίτον ἑαυτὸν ἐπιρρίπτοι γάμον, τοῦτον μετὰ πάσης ἀκριβείας καὶ παρατηρήσεως μέχρι πενταετίας ἀμέτοχον εἶναι τῆς τοῦ ἁγιασμοῦ μεταλήψεως καὶ μηδαμῶς ἐπ' αὐτῷ συντέμνεσθαι τὸν χρόνον. Ὃς

73: Basil., *Ep.* 199, can. 50, PG, 32, 732C4–5.

---

66 ἔδοξεν ἁγίοις colloc. N ἔδοξεν ἁγιωτάτοις FS ‖ 67 ἐνδηλοτέραν (vel -ω-) JGUMPV: ἐκδηλοτέραν (vel -ω-) WNOFSTLHZ ‖ τῆς om. T ‖ 68 πολιτείας] καταστάσεως T ‖ ἀνακηρύττομεν L ‖ 69 τοῦ om. V ‖ Ἵνα — 72 γάμου] καὶ περὶ τοῦ τρίτου δὲ (τρίτου γάμου F) τάδε διοριζόμεθα FS ‖ 70 γάμων] huc des. Z ‖ 71 τοῦ om. V ‖ 71–72 γάμου ὁρίζομεν colloc. M ‖ 72 ἐπιτελεῖσθαι] γίνεσθαι T ‖ γὰρ om. T ‖ 73–74 τοῦ πράγματος γινομένου καθὼς νῦν colloc. T ‖ 74 γενομένου V ‖ 75 παραπεπτωκῶς NVL ‖ 75–76 πολλάκις ῥύπασμα παρίδοι κείμενον colloc. F ‖ πολλάκις παρίδοι colloc. S ‖ 76 κείμενον om. VT ‖ ὅτε SH ‖ 77 ὡς om. V ‖ ἔχον TH ‖ οὐδὲ] μηδὲ S ‖ ῥυπαῖνον TH ‖ 78 καλῶς] ἔχειν add. H ‖ ἀνακαθᾶραι H ‖ 79 καὶ om. H ‖ ἀλλ' ἐξηπλωμένον om. H ‖ 83 πρεπούσης] προσηκούσης FST ‖ τῇ] τῇ τῶν H ‖ 84 ὁρίζομεν WTL ‖ εἴ τις om. S ‖ 85 μήτε] μηκέτι H ‖ 86 τοῖς ὀφειλομένοις V ‖ χριστιανῆς M τοῖς χριστιανοῖς S ‖ 87 ποιούμενος] τιθέμενος WF θέμενος S ‖ ἀλλὰ] ἀλλ' ἀπὸ VT ‖ τῆς om. P ‖ γενόμενος WVPF ‖ 88 ἐπιρρίπτει TL ἐπιτρέποι FS ‖ 89 ἁγιάσματος T ‖ 90 καὶ — χρόνον om. L

Holy Fathers before us have also decreed; and we, too, making their view more explicit, excommunicate him as alien from the Christian polity.

So much for the fourth marriage. However, in order that other marriages as well may follow a stricter rule and not take place in a way unworthy of the life of Christians, we also decree with regard to the third marriage that it shall not be concluded indiscriminately or arbitrarily. It is true that it was permitted by the Fathers as a "defilement," because at that time the thing was not perpetrated unblushingly, as it is now, and had not spread widely, but could be overlooked as in a house one overlooks some dirt that has fallen in a corner. But now that it has come to be openly recognized and is regarded as having nothing shameful or defiling, because examples have multiplied, we have deemed it right to cleanse it, just as, when something indecorous is not lying unnoticed in a corner, but is spread all over the house, we do not leave it there, but clean it out and rid ourselves of the distaste it causes.

Accordingly, showing indulgence for human weakness on the one hand, and concern for the decency that befits the Christian life on the other, we decree that the following shall be observed in cases of third marriages. If a man who has reached his fortieth year abandons himself, without respect for nature or concern for the sober life that becomes a Christian, to his passionate desire and rushes into a third marriage, he shall, with the strictest observance, be excluded from Holy Communion for five years, and under no circumstances shall the term be shortened; for one who

γὰρ μετὰ τεσσαρακοστὸν ἔτος τὸ ῥύπασμα ἐν τῇ τοῦ Χριστοῦ ἐκκλησίᾳ εἶναι καὶ λέγεσθαι ἠγάπησε, τίνα παρέξει πληροφορίαν τῆς περὶ τὸν βίον αὐτοῦ σπουδῆς, δι' ἣν ὁ χρόνος τῆς μεταλήψεως τῶν ἁγιασμάτων αὐτῷ συντμηθήσεται; Ἀλλὰ γὰρ καὶ μετὰ τὸ ἀξιωθῆναι τῆς ἀχράντου μεταλήψεως οὐκ ἔσται συγκεχωρημένον αὐτῷ ἐν ἄλλῳ καιρῷ τῇ μεταλήψει προσιέναι ἢ ἐν μόνῃ τῇ σωτηρίῳ τοῦ Χριστοῦ καὶ θεοῦ ἡμῶν Ἀναστάσει, διὰ τὴν ἐκ τῆς προηγουμένης ἐγκρατείας τῶν νηστειῶν ὅσον δυνατὸν ἀνακάθαρσιν. Ταῦτα δέ φαμεν, ὅταν μὴ τέκνα παρῇ ἐκ τῶν προτέρων γάμων τοῖς ἤδη μετὰ τὸ τεσσαρακοστὸν ἔτος τρίτην ἄγεσθαι προῃρημένοις γυναῖκα, ἐπεί, ἐὰν τέκνα παρῇ, ἀσυγχώρητος αὐτοῖς ἡ τριγαμία· λίαν γάρ ἐστιν ἄδικον τῶν μὲν χαρίζεσθαι τῇ ἐξώρῳ ἐπιθυμίᾳ, τοῖς δὲ παισὶ τῶν προτέρων γάμων μὴ προνοεῖσθαι τὸ ἀσφαλὲς καὶ τὸ ἄλυπον καὶ ἀτάραχον, καὶ ὅσα οἶδε τὸ ἀνθρώπινον καταλαμβάνειν ἐκ τῆς πολυσπόρου τεκνώσεως.

Καὶ εἴ τις δὲ τριακονταέτης ὢν καὶ τέκνα ἔχων ἐκ τῶν προλαβόντων γάμων τρίτῃ γυναικὶ συνάπτοιτο, καὶ οὗτος δὲ ἀσυγχωρήτως μέχρι τετάρτου ἔτους τῆς κοινωνίας τῶν ἁγιασμάτων ἀμέτοχος ἔστω, διότι δῆλός ἐστιν ἐξ οὐδενὸς ἑτέρου ἀλλ' ἢ ὑπ' ἀκρασίας κινούμενος καὶ τοῦ δοῦλος εἶναι σαρκικῆς ἐπιθυμίας ἐπὶ τὸν τοιοῦτον γάμον ἐλθεῖν. Καὶ μετὰ τὸ τυχεῖν δὲ τῆς μεταλήψεως τῶν μυστηρίων, τρὶς τοῦ ἐνιαυτοῦ μόνον ἀξιωθήσεται τῆς ἀπολαύσεως, ἅπαξ μὲν ἐν τῇ σωτηρίῳ τοῦ Χριστοῦ καὶ θεοῦ ἡμῶν Ἀναστάσει, δεύτερον δὲ ἐν τῇ Κοιμήσει τῆς ἀχράντου δεσποίνης ἡμῶν θεοτόκου, καὶ τρίτον ἐν τῇ Γενεθλίῳ ἡμέρᾳ τοῦ Χριστοῦ καὶ θεοῦ ἡμῶν, διὰ τὸ καὶ ἐν ταύταις προηγεῖσθαι νηστείαν καὶ τὸ ἐκ ταύτης ὄφελος. Εἰ δὲ παῖδες μὴ

---

92 καὶ εἶναι καὶ FS ‖ πληροφορίαν παρέξει colloc. H ‖ 94 αὐτοῦ V ‖ 98 ὅσον – ἀνακάθαρσιν] κάθαρσιν κατὰ τὸ δυνατὸν H ‖ 99 παρῆν V ‖ τῶν om. F ‖ τὸ om. LH ‖ 100 προειρημένοις GV ‖ 101 τῶν JGUMP: τὸν WNFSHL τῷ V ‖ 103 καὶ[1]] τε καὶ H ‖ τὸ[2] om. FH ‖ 107 συνάπτοιτο γυναικὶ colloc. FSL ‖ δὲ om. S ‖ 107–108 ἀσυγχώρητος VTH ‖ 108 μέχρι τοῦ T ‖ 109 ἔσται F ‖ ἑτέρου om. T ‖ ὑπ'] ἐξ J ‖ 111 καὶ om. F ‖ 112 ἀπολαύσεως] μετοχῆς S ‖ ἅπαξ μὲν om. S ‖ μὲν om. L ‖ 113 *Ambros. B 107 sup.*, fol. 122r mg. inf.; *Brit. Mus. Addit. 28822,* fol. 4v mg. sup.: ἐκ τοῦ κατὰ λατίνων ἀντιρρητικοῦ λόγου νικολάου πατριάρχου κωνσταντινουπόλεως περὶ τῆς νηστείας τῆς τελουμένης πρὸ τῆς ἑορτῆς τῆς ὑπεραγίας θεοτόκου: Ἔτι καὶ ἑτέρα παρ' ἡμῖν νηστεία προηγουμένη τῆς κοιμήσεως τῆς ὑπεραγίας θεοτόκου ἀπὸ τῆς πρώτης τοῦ αὐγούστου μηνὸς ἐναρχομένη, ἥτις ἐν τῇ περὶ τῆς ἑνώσεως ἁγία συνόδω μνημονεύεται (= *REB*, 28 [1970], 231, 20–23) ‖ δεύτερον δὲ] καὶ S ‖ δὲ om. F ‖ 114 τρίτον om. S ‖ 115 γενεθλίων J ‖ τοῦ χ(ριστο)ῦ καὶ JWGUNPVT: τοῦ κ(υρίο)υ καὶ M χ(ριστο)ῦ τοῦ FSLH ‖ ἡμῶν] ἰ(ησο)ῦ χ(ριστο)ῦ add. M ‖ καὶ[2] om. WTL

after his fortieth year is content for this defilement to exist in the Church of Christ and to be spoken of as such, what evidence can he give of moral earnestness, so that on this ground the term of his excommunication should be shortened? Indeed, even after he has been thought worthy to receive Holy Communion, he will not be allowed to do so except at the Feast of Salvation, the Resurrection of Christ our God, because he has then been purified, as far as possible, by the continence of the preceding days of Lent. We allow this, provided that those who marry a third wife, even after reaching forty, have no children from the previous marriages, for, if they do, the third marriage cannot be permitted; it is utterly unjust that we should indulge the untimely desire of these persons rather than safeguard the children of their earlier marriages from grief and turmoil and all the ills that beset mankind as a result of having children from different wives.

Even if a man of thirty, having children from his previous marriages, should wed a third wife, he shall without pardon be excluded from Holy Communion until the fourth year, since it is clear that it was from no other motive than incontinence and enslavement to carnal desire that he came to such a marriage; and even after he has been allowed to participate in the sacrament, he will be found worthy to partake of it only three times a year: once, at the Feast of Salvation, the Resurrection of Christ our God, a second time at the Dormition of our Immaculate Lady the Mother of God, and the third time on the Birthday of Christ our God, because of the fasts that have preceded these days also and the profit gained from them. In cases, however, where there are no children, since the desire for reproduc-

παρείησαν, ἐπειδὴ τὸ τεκνογονίας ἐπιθυμεῖν οὐκ ἀσύγγνωστον, τὸ τηνικαῦτα συγγνώμης ἀξιωθήσεται ὁ τοιοῦτος γάμος καὶ μόνῳ τῷ ἐξ ἀρχῆς καὶ μέχρι τοῦ νῦν κρατήσαντι ἐπιτιμίῳ θεραπευθήσεται.

Ταῦτα μὲν καὶ περὶ τοῦ τρίτου γάμου. Οὐ μὴν οὐδὲ τὸν δεύτερον οὐδὲ τὸν πρῶτον ἐκτὸς ἀσφαλείας ἐῶμεν, ἀλλὰ κἀκείνους ὁρίζομεν οὕτως συνίστασθαι ὥστε μηδεμίαν ἔχειν πονηρὰν αἰτίαν, ἢ ἐξ ἁρπαγῆς ἢ ἐκ προηγησαμένης λαθρίου φθορᾶς, ἀλλὰ νομίμως καὶ καθαρεύοντας τῶν τοιούτων μολυσμάτων καὶ πορνικῆς ἀκαθαρσίας. Εἴ τις οὖν τῶν εἰρημένων καταφρονήσας τύπων πρὸς γαμικὴν ὁμιλίαν πρώτην ἢ δευτέραν συνέλθοι, τοῦτον ἡ τοῦ Χριστοῦ ἐκκλησία, ἡ καθαρὰ καὶ μηδένα σπῖλον ἔχουσα ἢ ῥυτίδα, τοῖς σωτηρίοις ὑποβάλλουσα ἐτασμοῖς, οὐ πρὶν εἰς μετάληψιν τῶν θείων παραδέξεται μυστηρίων ἢ τὸν ὡρισμένον ἐπὶ τῇ πορνείᾳ χρόνον ἀκριβῶς αὐτοὺς ἐκπληρῶσαι (εἰ μὴ ἄρα ἡ τοῦ βίου ἀναγκαία κατεπείγοι ἀναχώρησις), τουτέστι, μέχρις ἂν τὸ ἕβδομον ἐκπληρωθῇ ἔτος. Ὁ δὲ τολμῶν ἱερεὺς παρὰ τὸν διατετυπωμένον ὅρον μεταλήψεως θείας τινὰ τούτων ἀξιῶσαι περὶ τὸν ἴδιον κινδυνεύσει βαθμόν, δηλονότι τοῦ ἀξιωθέντος παρὰ τὸν ὡρισμένον τύπον τῆς θείας κοινωνίας πάλιν εἰς τὸ ἀκοινώνητον περιϊσταμένου μέχρι τῆς συμπληρώσεως τοῦ ἑβδόμου ἔτους.

C. Appendix

Ἀλλὰ ταῦτα μέν, ὡς δεδήλωται, ὑπὸ τῶν πάλαι βασιλευσάντων ἐπράχθησαν. Νῦν δὲ τῇ τοῦ πατρὸς καὶ υἱοῦ καὶ ἁγίου πνεύματος εὐδοκίᾳ καὶ χάριτι καὶ ταῖς τῆς πανάγνου καὶ θεομήτορος καὶ τοῦ μεγάλου

---

200 B: 127: Ephes. 5:27.

---

117 τὸ[1] om. H τὸ τῆς V ‖ τὸ[2] om. T ‖ 118 ὁ] καὶ ὁ H ‖ 119 κρατήσαντι καὶ μέχρι τοῦ νῦν colloc. FST ‖ κρατήσαντι] καταντήσαντι H ‖ 120 τοῦ om. V ‖ 121 κἀκείνοις V ‖ 122 πονηρὰν om. H ‖ 123 ἢ[1] om. F ‖ λαθρίου JWGUNV: λαθραίου STL λάθρου M λαθραίας H ‖ νομίμους FH ‖ 125 τύπων om. T ‖ 126 ὁμιλίαν] συνάφειαν T ‖ 127 σωτηρίας S ‖ 129 ὡρισμένον] εἰρημένον T ‖ αὐτοὺς GUNMPFSLH: αὐτὸν J om. WVT ‖ 130 κατεπείγει S ‖ 131 τουτέστι om. FS ‖ post ἂν] δηλονότι add. FS ‖ ἐκπληρωθείη FS πληρωθ(ῇ) H ‖ 132 διατεταγμένον L τετυπωμένον H ‖ 132–133 καταξιῶσαι F ‖ 133 κινδυνεύει H ‖ 134 τόπον S ‖ τὸ] τὸν S ‖ 135 ἔτους] φυλαττομένου δηλονότι τοῦ ἐνιαυσιαίου ἐπιτιμίου ἐλθεῖν πάντως τινὰ ἐπὶ διγαμίαν, ἔστι νοῆσαι τοὺς π(ατέ)ρας τούτους ὁρίσαι add. T

200 C: N 203[v] O 126–127 M 116[v] P 40[v] F 317[v]–318[r] S 188[r-v] T 399[r] L 330[r] ‖ 1 ταῦτα] τὰ FS ‖ 2 πατρὸς] θ(εο)ῦ καὶ π(ατ)ρ(ὸ)ς εὐδοκία S ‖ καὶ[1]] καὶ τοῦ P καὶ τῇ τοῦ μονογενοῦς S ‖ καὶ[2]] καὶ τοῦ PS ‖ 2 ἁγίου — 3 χάριτι] εὐδοκία καὶ χάριτι καὶ τοῦ ἁγίου πν(εύματο)ς F ‖ 2 ἁγίου] καὶ ζωοποιοῦ add. S ‖ 3 καὶ[3] om. FS

tion is not unforgivable, such a marriage will be granted forgiveness, and it will be redressed only by the traditional penance that has been valid until now.

So much for the third marriage. We, however, do not leave even the second or the first without a safeguard, but we decree that these, too, be brought to pass in such a way that they have no evil cause, either abduction or previous secret corruption, but that they be contracted lawfully and free from such stains as these and from the impurity of fornication. If, then, any one should enter upon a first or second union in contempt of the aforesaid rules, the Church of God, the Pure One without a spot or wrinkle, will subject him to salutary trials and not admit him to participation in the Divine Sacrament until he has completed to the full the time decreed for fornication (unless, perchance, the inevitable end of this life should be close at hand), that is to say, until the completion of the seventh year. The priest who, in defiance of the decree laid down here, should presume to admit any one of these to Holy Communion, will be liable to be deprived of his rank, it being understood that the person admitted to Holy Communion in contravention of the rule here decreed shall be excommunicated anew until the completion of the seventh year.

C. Appendix

These things, as expounded, were enacted by the former emperors. Now, however, by the favor and grace of the Father and the Son and the Holy Spirit and by the intercession of the Most Pure Virgin and Mother of God and of the Great

ἀρχιστρατήγου πρεσβείαις τοὺς ἤδη πρὸ ἐνενήκοντα χρόνων ἕνεκεν τῆς προδηλωθείσης αἰτίας καὶ ἀφορμῆς ἀπορραγέντας ἱερεῖς καὶ μονάζοντας ἡ παγγάληνος βασιλεία τῶν θεοστεφῶν βασιλέων ἡμῶν Βασιλείου καὶ Κωνσταντίνου συνῆψέ τε καὶ συνήνωσε, καὶ μίαν καθολικὴν καὶ ἀποστολικὴν ἐκκλησίαν εἰργάσατο· ὅθεν χρεὼν ἀνακηρύττεσθαί τε καὶ μεγαλύνεσθαι τοὺς τοιοῦτον θεοφιλὲς καὶ ἀξιόλογον ἔργον πεπληρωκότας.

D. Acclamations

I

Πολλὰ τὰ ἔτη τῶν βασιλέων.

Ῥωμανοῦ, Χριστοφόρου, Κωνσταντίνου, Στεφάνου καὶ Κωνσταντίνου, μεγάλων βασιλέων καὶ αὐτοκρατόρων, πολλὰ τὰ ἔτη.

Μιχαὴλ τοῦ Πορφυρογεννήτου, πολλὰ ⟨τὰ ἔτη⟩.

Σοφίας καὶ Ἑλένης τῶν εὐσεβεστάτων αὐγουστῶν, πολλὰ τὰ ἔτη.

Λέοντος καὶ Ἀλεξάνδρου τῶν τὴν οὐράνιον βασιλείαν τῆς ἐπιγείου ἀλλαξαμένων, αἰωνία ἡ μνήμη.

Νικολάου τοῦ ἁγιωτάτου καὶ ἀοιδίμου πατριάρχου, αἰωνία ἡ μνήμη.

Στεφάνου τοῦ ἁγιωτάτου καὶ ἀοιδίμου πατριάρχου, αἰωνία ἡ μνήμη.

Τρύφωνος τοῦ ἁγιωτάτου καὶ οἰκουμενικοῦ πατριάρχου, πολλὰ τὰ ἔτη.

Θεοφυλάκτου τοῦ θεοφιλεστάτου ὑποδιακόνου καὶ συγκέλλου, πολλὰ ⟨τὰ ἔτη⟩.

II

Πολλὰ τὰ ἔτη τῶν βασιλέων.

Βασιλείου καὶ Κωνσταντίνου, Λέοντος καὶ Ἀλεξάνδρου, Χριστοφόρου καὶ Ῥωμανοῦ, Κωνσταντίνου, Ῥωμανοῦ καὶ Νικηφόρου, τῶν τὴν οὐράνιον βασιλείαν τῆς ἐπιγείου ἀλλαξαμένων, αἰωνία ἡ μνήμη.

Γερμανοῦ, Ταρασίου, Νικηφόρου καὶ Μεθοδίου, τῶν ἀοιδίμων καὶ μακαρίων πατριαρχῶν, αἰωνία ἡ μνήμη.

Ἰγνατίου, Φωτίου, Στεφάνου καὶ Ἀντωνίου, Νικολάου, Εὐθυμίου, Στεφάνου, Τρύφωνος καὶ Θεοφυλάκτου, τῶν ἁγιωτάτων καὶ ὀρθοδόξων πατριαρχῶν, αἰωνία ἡ μνήμη.

Πολυεύκτου τοῦ τρισμακαρίστου καὶ ὡς ἀληθῶς ἁγιωτάτου πατριάρχου, αἰωνία ἡ μνήμη.

---

4 χρόνων] ἐτῶν F ‖ 6 ἡμῶν βασιλέων colloc. FS ‖ 8 ὅθεν] καὶ add. S ‖ 9 τὸ τοιοῦτον L ‖ πεποιηκότας S

200 D I: J 267^{r} ‖ 5 αὐγούστων J

200 D II: W 70^{r}

Commander of the Heavenly Host, the Most Serene Majesty of our God-crowned Emperors Basil and Constantine has joined and united to us those priests and monks who for as many as ninety years had been separated from us by the aforesaid cause and occasion, and has made us one Catholic and Apostolic Church; so that it is meet to proclaim and magnify those who have achieved so godly and momentous a work.

D. Acclamations

I

Long live the Emperors!

Romanus, Christopher, Constantine, Stephen and Constantine, great Emperors and Sovereigns—long may they live!

Michael the Porphyrogennetus—long may he live!

Sophia and Helen, the most pious Augustas—long may they live!

Leo and Alexander, who have passed from the earthly to the heavenly Kingdom—eternal their memory!

Nicholas the most holy and illustrious Patriarch—eternal his memory!

Stephen the most holy and illustrious Patriarch—eternal his memory!

Tryphon the most holy Ecumenical Patriarch—long may he live!

Theophylact, the most pious Subdeacon and Syncellus—long may he live!

II

Long live the Emperors!

Basil and Constantine, Leo and Alexander, Christopher and Romanus, Constantine, Romanus and Nicephorus, who have passed from the earthly to the heavenly Kingdom—eternal their memory!

Germanus, Tarasius, Nicephorus and Methodius, the illustrious and blessed Patriarchs—eternal their memory!

Ignatius, Photius, Stephen and Anthony, Nicholas, Euthymius, Stephen, Tryphon and Theophylact, the most holy and Orthodox Patriarchs—eternal their memory!

Polyeuctus, the thrice-blessed and truly most holy Patriarch—eternal his memory!

III

Πολλὰ τὰ ἔτη τῶν βασιλέων.

Βασιλείου καὶ Κωνσταντίνου, τῶν ὀρθοδόξων ἡμῶν βασιλέων, πολλὰ τὰ ἔτη.

Θεοφανοῦς τῆς εὐσεβεστάτης αὐγούστης, πολλὰ τὰ ἔτη.

Νικολάου τοῦ ἁγιωτάτου καὶ οἰκουμενικοῦ πατριάρχου, πολλὰ τὰ ἔτη.

Βασιλείου καὶ Κωνσταντίνου, Λέοντος καὶ Ἀλεξάνδρου, Χριστοφόρου καὶ Ῥωμανοῦ, Κωνσταντίνου, Ῥωμανοῦ, Νικηφόρου καὶ Ἰωάννου, τῶν τὴν οὐράνιον βασιλείαν τῆς ἐπιγείου ἀλλαξαμένων, αἰωνία ἡ μνήμη.

Εὐδοκίας καὶ Θεοφανοῦς, Θεοδώρας καὶ Ἑλένης, τῶν εὐσεβεστάτων αὐγουστῶν, αἰωνία ἡ μνήμη.

Γερμανοῦ, Ταρασίου, Νικηφόρου καὶ Μεθοδίου, τῶν ἀοιδίμων καὶ μακαρίων πατριαρχῶν, αἰωνία ἡ μνήμη.

Ἰγνατίου, Φωτίου, Στεφάνου καὶ Ἀντωνίου, Νικολάου καὶ Εὐθυμίου, Στεφάνου, Τρύφωνος, Θεοφυλάκτου, Πολυεύκτου καὶ Ἀντωνίου, τῶν ὀρθοδόξων πατριαρχῶν, αἰωνία ἡ μνήμη.

IV

Πολλὰ τὰ ἔτη τῶν βασιλέων.

Τοῦ ὀρθοδόξου ἡμῶν βασιλέως, πολλὰ τὰ ἔτη.

Τοῦ ἁγιωτάτου καὶ οἰκουμενικοῦ πατριάρχου, πολλὰ τὰ ἔτη.

Βασιλείου καὶ Κωνσταντίνου, Λέοντος καὶ Ἀλεξάνδρου, Χριστοφόρου καὶ Ῥωμανοῦ, Κωνσταντίνου, Ῥωμανοῦ, Νικηφόρου, Ἰωάννου καὶ Βασιλείου, τῶν τὴν οὐράνιον βασιλείαν τῆς ἐπιγείου ἀλλαξαμένων, αἰωνία ἡ μνήμη.

Εὐδοκίας καὶ Θεοφανοῦς, Θεοδώρας καὶ Ἑλένης, Θεοφανοῦς καὶ Θεοδώρας, τῶν εὐσεβεστάτων αὐγουστῶν, αἰωνία ἡ μνήμη.

Γερμανοῦ, Ταρασίου, Νικηφόρου καὶ Μεθοδίου, τῶν ἀοιδίμων καὶ μακαρίων πατριαρχῶν, αἰωνία ἡ μνήμη.

Ἰγνατίου, Φωτίου, Στεφάνου καὶ Ἀντωνίου, Νικολάου καὶ Εὐθυμίου, Στεφάνου, Τρύφωνος, Θεοφυλάκτου, Πολυεύκτου, Ἀντωνίου, Νικολάου, Σισιννίου, Σεργίου καὶ Εὐσταθίου, τῶν ὀρθοδόξων πατριαρχῶν, αἰωνία ἡ μνήμη.

---

200 D III: V 120

200 D IV: N 203v–204r ‖ 13 πολυέκτου N

III

Long live the Emperors!

Basil and Constantine, our Orthodox Emperors—long may they live!

The most pious Augusta Theophano—long may she live!

Nicholas, the most holy and Ecumenical Patriarch—long may he live!

Basil and Constantine, Leo and Alexander, Christopher and Romanus, Constantine, Romanus, Nicephorus and John, who have passed from the earthly to the heavenly Kingdom—eternal their memory!

Eudocia and Theophano, Theodora and Helen, the most pious Augustas—eternal their memory!

Germanus, Tarasius, Nicephorus and Methodius, the illustrious and blessed Patriarchs—eternal their memory!

Ignatius, Photius, Stephen and Anthony, Nicholas and Euthymius, Stephen, Tryphon, Theophylact, Polyeuctus and Anthony, the Orthodox Patriarchs—eternal their memory!

IV

Long live the Emperors!

Our Orthodox Emperor—long may he live!

The most holy and Ecumenical Patriarch—long may he live!

Basil and Constantine, Leo and Alexander, Christopher and Romanus, Constantine, Romanus, Nicephorus, John and Basil, who have passed from the earthly to the heavenly Kingdom—eternal their memory!

Eudocia and Theophano, Theodora and Helen, Theophano and Theodora, the most pious Augustas—eternal their memory!

Germanus, Tarasius, Nicephorus and Methodius, the illustrious and blessed Patriarchs—eternal their memory!

Ignatius, Photius, Stephen and Anthony, Nicholas and Euthymius, Stephen, Tryphon, Theophylact, Polyeuctus, Anthony, Nicholas, Sisinnius, Sergius and Eustathius, the Orthodox Patriarchs—eternal their memory!

V

Πολλὰ τὰ ἔτη τῶν βασιλέων· καὶ λέγει τὸν κατὰ τὸν καιρὸν αὐτὸν βασιλεύοντα, καὶ πάλιν ἄρχεται·

Βασιλείου καὶ Κωνσταντίνου, Λέοντος καὶ Ἀλεξάνδρου, Χριστοφόρου καὶ Ῥωμανοῦ, Κωνσταντίνου, Ῥωμανοῦ, Νικηφόρου, Ἰωάννου, Βασιλείου, Κωνσταντίνου, Ῥωμανοῦ καὶ Μιχαήλ, τῶν τὴν οὐράνιον βασιλείαν τῆς ἐπιγείου ἀλλαξαμένων, αἰωνία ἡ μνήμη.

Εὐδοκίας καὶ Θεοφανοῦς, Θεοδώρας, Ἑλένης καὶ Θεοφανοῦς, τῶν εὐσεβεστάτων αὐγουστῶν, αἰωνία ἡ μνήμη.

Χριστοφόρου, Θεοδώρου, Ἀγαπίου, Ἰωάννου, Νικολάου, Ἡλιοῦ καὶ Θεοδώρου, τῶν ἁγιωτάτων πατριαρχῶν, αἰωνία ἡ μνήμη.

Γερμανοῦ, Ταρασίου, Νικηφόρου καὶ Μεθοδίου, τῶν ἀοιδίμων καὶ μακαρίων πατριαρχῶν, αἰωνία ἡ μνήμη.

Ἰγνατίου καὶ Φωτίου, Στεφάνου καὶ Ἀντωνίου, Νικολάου καὶ Εὐθυμίου, Στεφάνου, Τρύφωνος καὶ Θεοφυλάκτου, Πολυεύκτου καὶ Ἀντωνίου, Νικολάου, Σισιννίου, Σεργίου, Εὐσταθίου καὶ Ἀλεξίου, τῶν ὀρθοδόξων πατριαρχῶν Κωνσταντινουπόλεως, αἰωνία ἡ μνήμη.

VI

Πολλὰ τὰ ἔτη τῶν βασιλέων.

Κωνσταντίνου καὶ Θεοδώρας, τῶν ὀρθοδόξων ἡμῶν βασιλέων, πολλὰ τὰ ἔτη.

Βασιλείου καὶ Κωνσταντίνου, Λέοντος καὶ Ἀλεξάνδρου, Χριστοφόρου καὶ Ῥωμανοῦ, Κωνσταντίνου, Ῥωμανοῦ, Νικηφόρου καὶ Ἰωάννου, Βασιλείου, Κωνσταντίνου, Ῥωμανοῦ καὶ Μιχαήλ, τῶν τὴν οὐράνιον βασιλείαν τῆς ἐπιγείου ἀλλαξαμένων, αἰωνία ἡ μνήμη.

Εὐδοκίας καὶ Θεοφανοῦς, Θεοδώρας, Ἑλένης, Θεοφανοῦς καὶ Ζωῆς, τῶν εὐσεβεστάτων αὐγουστῶν, αἰωνία ἡ μνήμη.

Σωφρονίου τοῦ ἁγιωτάτου ἡμῶν πατριάρχου, πολλὰ τὰ ἔτη.

Χριστοφόρου, Θεοδώρου, Ἀγαπίου καὶ Ἰωάννου, Νικολάου, Ἡλιοῦ, Θεοδώρου καὶ Βασιλείου, τῶν ἁγιωτάτων πατριαρχῶν Ἀντιοχείας, αἰωνία ἡ μνήμη.

Γερμανοῦ, Ταρασίου, Νικηφόρου καὶ Μεθοδίου, τῶν ἀοιδίμων καὶ μακαρίων πατριαρχῶν, αἰωνία ἡ μνήμη.

Ἰγνατίου, Φωτίου, Στεφάνου καὶ Ἀντωνίου, Νικολάου καὶ Εὐθυμίου, Στεφάνου, Τρύφωνος καὶ Θεοφυλάκτου, Πολυεύκτου καὶ Ἀντωνίου, Νικολάου, Σισιννίου, Σεργίου, Εὐσταθίου καὶ Ἀλεξίου, τῶν ὀρθοδόξων πατριαρχῶν Κωνσταντινουπόλεως, αἰωνία ἡ μνήμη.

Ἡ ἁγία τριὰς αὐτοὺς ἐδόξασεν.

---

200 D V: G 232^{v} ‖ 8 εὐβεστάτων G ‖ 9 Ἰωάννου mg. add. G

200 D VI: U 16^{v}–19^{v} ‖ 14 ταρασσίου Θ

V

Long live the Emperors! (Then, after mentioning the reigning Emperor, he recommences:)

Basil and Constantine, Leo and Alexander, Christopher and Romanus, Constantine, Romanus, Nicephorus, John, Basil, Constantine, Romanus and Michael, who have passed from the earthly to the heavenly Kingdom—eternal their memory!

Eudocia and Theophano, Theodora, Helen and Theophano, the most pious Augustas—eternal their memory!

Christopher, Theodore, Agapius, John, Nicholas, Elias and Theodore, the most holy Patriarchs—eternal their memory!

Germanus, Tarasius, Nicephorus and Methodius, the illustrious and blessed Patriarchs—eternal their memory!

Ignatius and Photius, Stephen and Anthony, Nicholas and Euthymius, Stephen, Tryphon and Theophylact, Polyeuctus and Anthony, Nicholas, Sisinnius, Sergius, Eustathius and Alexius, the Orthodox Patriarchs of Constantinople—eternal their memory!

VI

Long live the Emperors!

Constantine and Theodora, our Orthodox Emperors—long may they live!

Basil and Constantine, Leo and Alexander, Christopher and Romanus, Constantine, Romanus, Nicephorus and John, Basil, Constantine, Romanus and Michael, who have passed from the earthly to the heavenly Kingdom—eternal their memory!

Eudocia and Theophano, Theodora, Helen, Theophano and Zoe, the most pious Augustas—eternal their memory!

Sophronius, our most holy Patriarch—long may he live!

Christopher, Theodore, Agapius and John, Nicholas, Elias, Theodore and Basil, the most holy Patriarchs of Antioch—eternal their memory!

Germanus, Tarasius, Nicephorus and Methodius, the illustrious and blessed Patriarchs—eternal their memory!

Ignatius, Photius, Stephen and Anthony, Nicholas and Euthymius, Stephen, Tryphon and Theophylact, Polyeuctus and Anthony, Nicholas, Sisinnius, Sergius, Eustathius and Alexius, the Orthodox Patriarchs of Constantinople—eternal their memory!

The Holy Trinity has glorified them.

VII

Πολλὰ τὰ ἔτη τῶν βασιλέων.

Βασιλείου, Κωνσταντίνου, Λέοντος καὶ Ἀλεξάνδρου, Χριστοφόρου, Ῥωμανοῦ, Κωνσταντίνου, Ῥωμανοῦ, Νικηφόρου καὶ Ἰωάννου, ⟨Βασιλείου⟩ καὶ Κωνσταντίνου, Ῥωμανοῦ καὶ Μιχαήλ, τῶν τὴν οὐράνιον βασιλείαν τῆς ἐπιγείου ἀλλαξαμένων, αἰωνία ἡ μνήμη.

Εὐδοκίας καὶ Θεοφανοῦς, Θεοδώρας καὶ Ἑλένης, Θεοφανοῦς καὶ Θεοδώρας, τῶν εὐσεβεστάτων αὐγουστῶν, αἰωνία ἡ μνήμη.

Ζωῆς τῆς εὐσεβεστάτης αὐγούστης καὶ τρισμακαρίστου, αἰωνία ἡ μνήμη.

Γερμανοῦ, Ταρασίου, Νικηφόρου καὶ Μεθοδίου, τῶν ἀοιδίμων καὶ μακαρίων πατριαρχῶν, αἰωνία ἡ μνήμη.

Ἰγνατίου, Φωτίου, Στεφάνου καὶ Ἀντωνίου, Νικολάου, Εὐθυμίου, Στεφάνου, Τρύφωνος, Θεοφυλάκτου, Πολυεύκτου, Ἀντωνίου καὶ Νικολάου καὶ Σισιννίου, Σεργίου, Εὐσταθίου καὶ Ἀλεξίου, τῶν ὀρθοδόξων πατριαρχῶν, αἰωνία ἡ μνήμη.

VIII

Πολλὰ τὰ ἔτη τῶν βασιλέων· καὶ εὐθὺς ἡ συνήθης φήμη τῶν βασιλέων καὶ τοῦ ἀρχιερέως.

Κωνσταντίνου τοῦ ὀρθοδόξου ἡμῶν βασιλέως, αἰωνία ἡ μνήμη.

Εὐδοκίας τῆς ὀρθοδόξου ἡμῶν βασιλίσσης, αἰωνία ἡ μνήμη.

Κωνσταντίνου τοῦ ἁγιωτάτου καὶ οἰκουμενικοῦ πατριάρχου, αἰωνία ἡ μνήμη.

Βασιλείου καὶ Κωνσταντίνου, Λέοντος καὶ Ἀλεξάνδρου, Χριστοφόρου καὶ Ῥωμανοῦ, Κωνσταντίνου, Ῥωμανοῦ, Νικηφόρου καὶ Ἰωάννου, Βασιλείου καὶ Κωνσταντίνου, Ῥωμανοῦ, Μιχαὴλ καὶ Κωνσταντίνου, Μιχαὴλ καὶ Ἰσαακίου, τῶν τὴν οὐράνιον βασιλείαν τῆς ἐπιγείου ἀλλαξαμένων, αἰωνία ἡ μνήμη.

---

200 D VII: P 40ᵛ–41ʳ Q 39–40 ‖ 3 Κωνσταντίνου] bis P ‖ Βασιλείου addidi ‖ 4 καὶ[1] om. P ‖ post Μιχαήλ] κωνσταντ(ί)ν(ου)· μιχαὴλ· ἰσαακίου· κωνσταν-τ(ί)ν(ου)· ῥωμανοῦ· μιχαὴλ· νικηφόρου· καὶ ἀλεξίου mg. superiore add. Q ‖ 7 post Θεοδώρας] ζωῆς· θεοδώρας· αἰκατερίνης· εὐδοκίας· μαρίας καὶ εἰρήνης mg. add. Q ‖ 13 καὶ om. Q ‖ 14 post Ἀλεξίου] μιχαὴλ· κωνσταντ(ί)ν(ου)· ἰω(άννου)· κοσμᾶ· εὐστρατίου· καὶ νικολάου mg. add. Q

200 D VIII: R 387ᵛ–388ʳ Y 270ᵛ–271ʳ ‖ 1 ἡ – 2 ἀρχιερέως R: τοὺς βασιλεῖς πάντας· εἶτ(α) τὸν π(ατ)ριάρχ(ην) καὶ τὸν μ(ητ)ροπολίτην· καὶ πάλιν ὕστερον. πολλὰ τὰ ἔτη τῶν βασιλέων Y ‖ 4 ἡμῶν om. Y ‖ 6, 11, 13 post μνήμη] γ̄ add. Y ‖ 8 κωνσταντίνου καὶ Y ‖ 9 καὶ[2] – Μιχαὴλ[2] om. Y

VII

Long live the Emperors!

Basil, Constantine, Leo and Alexander, Christopher, Romanus, Constantine, Romanus, Nicephorus and John, ⟨Basil⟩ and Constantine, Romanus and Michael, who have passed from the earthly to the heavenly Kingdom–eternal their memory!

Eudocia and Theophano, Theodora and Helen, Theophano and Theodora, the most pious Augustas–eternal their memory!

Zoe, the most pious and thrice-blessed Augusta–eternal her memory!

Germanus, Tarasius, Nicephorus and Methodius, the illustrious and blessed Patriarchs–eternal their memory!

Ignatius, Photius, Stephen and Anthony, Nicholas, Euthymius, Stephen, Tryphon, Theophylact, Polyeuctus, Anthony and Nicholas and Sisinnius, Sergius, Eustathius and Alexius, the Orthodox Patriarchs–eternal their memory!

VIII

Long live the Emperors! (Next, the usual acclamation of the Emperors and the Archpriest.)

Constantine, our Orthodox Emperor–eternal his memory!

Eudocia, our Orthodox Empress–eternal her memory!

Constantine, the most holy and Ecumenical Patriarch–eternal his memory!

Basil and Constantine, Leo and Alexander, Christopher and Romanus, Constantine and Romanus, Nicephorus and John, Basil and Constantine, Romanus, Michael and Constantine, Michael and Isaac, who have passed from the earthly to the heavenly Kingdom–eternal their memory!

Εὐδοκίας καὶ Θεοφανοῦς, Θεοδώρας καὶ Ἑλένης, Θεοφανοῦς καὶ Θεοδώρας, τῶν εὐσεβεστάτων αὐγουστῶν, αἰωνία ἡ μνήμη.

Ζωῆς, Θεοδώρας καὶ Αἰκατερίνης, τῶν εὐσεβεστάτων αὐγουστῶν, αἰωνία ἡ μνήμη.

Γερμανοῦ, Ταρασίου, Νικηφόρου καὶ Μεθοδίου τῶν ἀοιδίμων καὶ μακαρίων πατριαρχῶν, αἰωνία ἡ μνήμη.

Ἰγνατίου, Φωτίου, Στεφάνου καὶ Ἀντωνίου, Νικολάου καὶ Εὐθυμίου, Στεφάνου, Τρύφωνος, Θεοφυλάκτου, Πολυεύκτου, Ἀντωνίου, Νικολάου καὶ Σισιννίου, Σεργίου, Εὐσταθίου, Ἀλεξίου καὶ Μιχαὴλ τῶν ὀρθοδόξων πατριαρχῶν, αἰωνία ἡ μνήμη.

IX

Πολλὰ τὰ ἔτη τῶν βασιλέων.

Βασιλείου, Κωνσταντίνου, Λέοντος καὶ Ἀλεξάνδρου, Χριστοφόρου, Ῥωμανοῦ, Κωνσταντίνου, Ῥωμανοῦ, Νικηφόρου καὶ Ἰωάννου, Βασιλείου καὶ Κωνσταντίνου, Ῥωμανοῦ καὶ Μιχαήλ, Κωνσταντίνου, Μιχαήλ, Ἰσαακίου, Κωνσταντίνου, Ῥωμανοῦ καὶ Μιχαήλ, τῶν τὴν οὐράνιον βασιλείαν τῆς ἐπιγείου ἀλλαξαμένων, αἰωνία ἡ μνήμη.

Εὐδοκίας καὶ Θεοφανοῦς, Θεοδώρας καὶ Ἑλένης, Θεοφανοῦς καὶ Θεοδώρας, Ζωῆς καὶ Θεοδώρας, Αἰκατερίνης, Εὐδοκίας, τῶν εὐσεβεστάτων αὐγουστῶν, αἰωνία ἡ μνήμη.

Γερμανοῦ, Ταρασίου, Νικηφόρου καὶ Μεθοδίου, τῶν ἀοιδίμων καὶ μακαρίων πατριαρχῶν, αἰωνία ἡ μνήμη.

Ἰγνατίου, Φωτίου καὶ Ἀντωνίου, Νικολάου καὶ Εὐθυμίου, Στεφάνου, Τρύφωνος, Θεοφυλάκτου, Πολυεύκτου, Ἀντωνίου, Νικολάου, Σισιννίου, Σεργίου, Εὐσταθίου, Ἀλεξίου, Μιχαήλ, Κωνσταντίνου, τῶν ὀρθοδόξων πατριαρχῶν, αἰωνία ἡ μνήμη.

X

Πολλὰ τὰ ἔτη τῶν βασιλέων.

Βασιλείου, Κωνσταντίνου, Λέοντος καὶ Ἀλεξάνδρου, Χριστοφόρου, Ῥωμανοῦ, Κωνσταντίνου, Ῥωμανοῦ, Νικηφόρου, Ἰωάννου, Βασιλείου καὶ Κωνσταντίνου, Ῥωμανοῦ καὶ Μιχαήλ, Κωνσταντίνου, Μιχαήλ, Ἰσαακίου,

---

14 ζωῆς καὶ Y ‖ 15, 17 ἡ μνήμη γ̄ Y: om. R ‖ 16–17 καὶ μακαρίων om. Y ‖ 19 καὶ om. Y ‖ 21 post μνήμη] αἰωνία ἡ μνήμ(η). αἰων(ία) ἡ μνήμ(η)· γ̄ add. Y

200 D IX: O 128 ‖ 7 θεοφανῶ (bis) O ‖ 9 αὐγούστων O ‖ 13 σισινίου O ‖ 14 Κωνσταντίνου] add. Ἰωάννου?

200 D X: X 89[r-v]

Eudocia and Theophano, Theodora and Helen, Theophano and Theodora, the most pious Augustas—eternal their memory!

Zoe and Theodora and Aecaterina, the most pious Augustas—eternal their memory!

Germanus, Tarasius, Nicephorus and Methodius, the illustrious Patriarchs—eternal their memory!

Ignatius, Photios, Stephen and Anthony, Nicholas and Euthymius, Stephen, Tryphon, Theophylact, Polyeuctus, Anthony, Nicholas and Sisinnius, Sergius, Eustathius, Alexius and Michael, the Orthodox Patriarchs—eternal their memory!

IX

Long live the Emperors!

Basil, Constantine, Leo and Alexander, Christopher, Romanus, Constantine, Romanus, Nicephorus and John, Basil and Constantine, Romanus and Michael, Constantine, Michael, Isaac, Constantine, Romanus and Michael, who have passed from the earthly to the heavenly Kingdom—eternal their memory!

Eudocia and Theophano, Theodora and Helen, Theophano and Theodora, Zoe and Theodora, Aecaterina, Eudocia, the most pious Augustas—eternal their memory!

Germanus, Tarasius, Nicephorus and Methodius, the illustrious and blessed Patriarchs—eternal their memory!

Ignatius, Photius and Anthony, Nicholas and Euthymius, Stephen, Tryphon, Theophylact, Polyeuctus, Anthony, Nicholas, Sisinnius, Sergius, Eustathius, Alexius, Michael, Constantine, the Orthodox Patriarchs—eternal their memory!

X

Long live the Emperors!

Basil, Constantine, Leo and Alexander, Christopher, Romanus, Constantine, Romanus, Nicephorus, John, Basil and Constantine, Romanus and Michael, Constantine, Michael, Isaac, Constantine, Romanus, Michael, Nicephorus and Isaac,

Κωνσταντίνου, Ῥωμανοῦ, Μιχαήλ, Νικηφόρου καὶ Ἰσαακίου, τῶν τὴν οὐράνιον βασιλείαν τῆς ἐπιγείου ἀλλαξαμένων, αἰωνία ἡ μνήμη.

Εὐδοκίας καὶ Θεοφανοῦς, Θεοδώρας καὶ Ἑλένης, Θεοφανοῦς καὶ Θεοδώρας, Ζωῆς, Θεοδώρας, Ἑκατερίνης καὶ Εὐδοκίας, τῶν εὐσεβεστάτων αὐγουστῶν, αἰωνία ἡ μνήμη.

Γερμανοῦ, Ταρασίου, Νικηφόρου καὶ Μεθοδίου, τῶν ἀοιδίμων καὶ μακαρίων πατριαρχῶν, αἰωνία ἡ μνήμη.

Ἰγνατίου, Φωτίου, Στεφάνου καὶ Ἀντωνίου, Νικολάου καὶ Εὐθυμίου, Στεφάνου, Τρύφωνος καὶ Θεοφυλάκτου, Πολυεύκτου, Ἀντωνίου, Νικολάου, Σισιννίου, Σεργίου, Εὐσταθίου, Ἀλεξίου, Μιχαήλ, Κωνσταντίνου, Ἰωάννου, Κοσμᾶ καὶ Εὐστρατίου, τῶν ὀρθοδόξων πατριαρχῶν, αἰωνία ἡ μνήμη.

XI

Πολλὰ τὰ ἔτη τῶν βασιλέων.
Ὁ δεῖνα τοῦ ὀρθοδόξου ἡμῶν βασιλέως.
Ὁ δεῖνα τῆς ὀρθοδόξου ἡμῶν βασιλίσσης.
Ὁ δεῖνα τοῦ ἁγιωτάτου καὶ οἰκουμενικοῦ.
Ὁ δεῖνα τοῦ εὐτυχεστάτου καίσαρος.

Βασιλείου καὶ Κωνσταντίνου, Λέοντος καὶ Ἀλεξάνδρου, Χριστοφόρου καὶ Ῥωμανοῦ, Κωνσταντίνου, Ῥωμανοῦ, Νικηφόρου καὶ Ἰωάννου, Βασιλείου ⟨καὶ Κωνσταντίνου, Ῥωμανοῦ καὶ Μιχαήλ, Κωνσταντίνου, Μιχαήλ, Ἰσαακίου, Κωνσταντίνου, Ῥωμανοῦ, Ἀνδρονίκου, Μιχαήλ, Νικηφόρου καὶ Ἰσαακίου, τῶν τὴν οὐράνιον βασιλείαν τῆς ἐπιγείου ἀλλαξαμένων, αἰωνία ἡ μνήμη.

Εὐδοκίας καὶ Θεοφανοῦς, Θεοδώρας καὶ Ἑλένης, Θεοφανοῦς, Θεοδώρας, Ζωῆς, Θεοδώρας, Αἰκατερίνης, Εὐδοκίας καὶ Μαρίας, τῶν εὐσεβεστάτων αὐγουστῶν, αἰωνία ἡ μνήμη.

Γερμανοῦ, Ταρασίου, Νικηφόρου καὶ Μεθοδίου, τῶν ἀοιδίμων πατριαρχῶν, αἰωνία ἡ μνήμη.

Ἰγνατίου, Φωτίου, Στεφάνου καὶ Ἀντωνίου, Νικολάου καὶ Εὐθυμίου, Στεφάνου, Τρύφωνος, Θεοφυλάκτου, Πολυεύκτου, Ἀντωνίου, Νικολάου, Σισιννίου, Σεργίου, Εὐσταθίου, Ἀλεξίου, Μιχαήλ, Κωνσταντίνου, Ἰωάννου, Κοσμᾶ, Εὐστρατίου, τῶν ὀρθοδόξων πατριαρχῶν, αἰωνία.

Χριστοφόρου, Θεοδώρου, Ἀγαπίου καὶ Ἰωάννου, Νικολάου καὶ Ἡλιοῦ, Θεοδώρου, Βασιλείου, Πέτρου, Θεοδοσίου καὶ Νικηφόρου καὶ Ἰωάννου, τῶν ἀοιδίμων πατριαρχῶν Ἀντιοχείας, αἰωνία ἡ μνήμη.⟩

---

7 θεοφανῶ (bis) X

200 D XI: K 335^{r} ‖ 8 καὶ^{1} – 23 μνήμη] deperdita in K supplevi ex *Synod. Orthod.*, K 334^{v}–335^{r} ‖ 14 αὐγούστων K ‖ 19 εὐσταθίου ἀλεξίου ins. K^{2} ‖ 22 καὶ ἰω(άννου) ins. K^{2}

who have passed from the earthly to the heavenly Kingdom–eternal their memory!

Eudocia and Theophano, Theodora and Helen, Theophano and Theodora, Zoe, Theodora, Ecaterina and Eudocia, the most pious Augustas–eternal their memory!

Germanus, Tarasius, Nicephorus and Methodius, the illustrious and blessed Patriarchs–eternal their memory!

Ignatius, Photius, Stephen and Anthony, Nicholas and Euthymius, Stephen, Tryphon and Theophylact, Polyeuctus, Anthony, Nicholas, Sisinnius, Sergius, Eustathius, Alexius, Michael, Constantine, John, Cosmas and Eustratius, the Orthodox Patriarchs–eternal their memory!

XI

Long live the Emperors!

N. our Orthodox Emperor.

N. our Orthodox Empress.

N. the most holy and Ecumenical ⟨Patriarch⟩.

N. the most fortunate Caesar.

Basil and Constantine, Leo and Alexander, Christopher and Romanus, Constantine, Romanus, Nicephorus and John, Basil ⟨and Constantine, Romanus and Michael, Constantine, Michael, Isaac, Constantine, Romanus, Andronicus, Michael, Nicephorus and Isaac, who have passed from the earthly to the heavenly Kingdom–eternal their memory!

Eudocia and Theophano, Theodora and Helen, Theophano, Theodora, Zoe, Theodora, Aecaterina, Eudocia and Mary, the most pious Augustas–eternal their memory!

Germanus, Tarasius, Nicephorus and Methodius, the illustrious Patriarchs–eternal their memory!

Ignatius, Photius, Stephen and Anthony, Nicholas and Euthymius, Stephen, Tryphon, Theophylact, Polyeuctus, Anthony, Nicholas, Sisinnius, Sergius, Eustathius, Alexius, Michael, Constantine, John, Cosmas, Eustratius, the Orthodox Patriarchs–eternal their memory!

Christopher, Theodore, Agapius and John, Nicholas and Elias, Theodore, Basil, Peter, Theodosius and Nicephorus and John, the illustrious Patriarchs of Antioch–eternal their memory!⟩

XII

Πολλὰ τὰ ἔτη τῶν βασιλέων.
Τοῦ ὀρθοδόξου ἡμῶν βασιλέως.
Τῆς ὀρθοδόξου ἡμῶν αὐγούστης.
Τοῦ ἁγιωτάτου καὶ οἰκουμενικοῦ πατριάρχου.
Τοῦ εὐτυχεστάτου καίσαρος.

Βασιλείου, Κωνσταντίνου, Λέοντος, Ἀλεξάνδρου, Χριστοφόρου, Ῥωμανοῦ, ⟨Κωνσταντίνου, Ῥωμανοῦ,⟩ Νικηφόρου, Ἰωάννου, Βασιλείου, Κωνσταντίνου, Ῥωμανοῦ, Μιχαήλ, ⟨Κωνσταντίνου, Μιχαήλ,⟩ Ἰσαακίου, Κωνσταντίνου, Ῥωμανοῦ, Ἀνδρονίκου, Μιχαήλ, Νικηφόρου, Ἰσαακίου καὶ Ἀλεξίου, τῶν τὴν οὐράνιον βασιλείαν τῆς ἐπιγείου ἀνταλλαξαμένων, αἰωνία ἡ μνήμη.

Εὐδοκίας, Θεοφανοῦς, Θεοδώρας, Ἑλένης, Θεοφανοῦς, Θεοδώρας, Ζωῆς, Θεοδώρας, Αἰκατερίνης, Εὐδοκίας, Μαρίας, Εἰρήνης καὶ Εἰρήνης, τῶν εὐσεβεστάτων αὐγουστῶν, αἰωνία ἡ μνήμη.

Γερμανοῦ, Ταρασίου, Νικηφόρου καὶ Μεθοδίου, τῶν ἀοιδίμων πατριαρχῶν, αἰωνία ἡ μνήμη.

Ἰγνατίου, Φωτίου, Στεφάνου, Ἀντωνίου, Νικολάου, Εὐθυμίου, Στεφάνου, Τρύφωνος, Θεοφυλάκτου, Πολυεύκτου, Ἀντωνίου, Νικολάου, Σισιννίου, Σεργίου, Εὐσταθίου, Ἀλεξίου, Μιχαήλ, Κωνσταντίνου, Ἰωάννου, Κοσμᾶ, Εὐστρατίου, Νικολάου καὶ Ἰωάννου, τῶν ὀρθοδόξων πατριαρχῶν, αἰωνία ἡ μνήμη.

E. Anathemas

Ἅπαντα τὰ κατὰ τῶν ἁγίων πατριαρχῶν Γερμανοῦ, Ταρασίου, Νικηφόρου καὶ Μεθοδίου γραφέντα ἢ λαληθέντα, ἀνάθεμα.

Ἅπαντα τὰ κατὰ τῶν ἁγίων πατριαρχῶν Ἰγνατίου, Φωτίου, Στεφάνου, Ἀντωνίου καὶ Νικολάου γραφέντα ἢ λαληθέντα, ἀνάθεμα.

Ἅπαντα τὰ παρὰ τὴν ἐκκλησιαστικὴν παράδοσιν καὶ τὴν διδασκαλίαν καὶ ὑποτύπωσιν τῶν ἁγίων καὶ ἀοιδίμων πατέρων καινοτομηθέντα καὶ πραχθέντα ἢ μετὰ τοῦτο πραχθησόμενα, ἀνάθεμα.

Τοῖς συκοφαντοῦσι τὴν ἁγίαν ἐκκλησίαν ὅτι τετραγαμίαν ἐδέξατο, χάριν τῆς εὐδοκίᾳ θεοῦ γεγενημένης οἰκονομίας καὶ τῆς

---

200 E: 1–7: *Synod. Orthod.*, 114–16 (p. 53).

---

200 D XII: S 188^{v} ‖ 7 Κωνσταντίνου, Ῥωμανοῦ addidi ‖ 8 Κωνσταντίνου, Μιχαήλ addidi ‖ 13 αἰκατερίνης S ‖ 18–19 σισινίου S

200 E: J 267^{r-v} W 70^{r-v} G 232^{v}–233^{r} U 19^{v}–22^{v} N 204^{r-v} O 128 P 41^{r} V 120–121 F 318^{r} S188^{v}–189^{r} ‖ 1 Γερμανοῦ – 2 Μεθοδίου om. N ‖ 2 ἢ] καὶ GFS ‖ 3–4 om. NV ‖ 3 ση(μείωσαι) ὁ τὰ παρὰ τοῦ νικήτα τοῦ καὶ δα(υὶ)δ κατὰ φωτίου καὶ τῶν ἄλλων πατριαρχῶν γραφέντα δεχόμενος· ὅτι ἡ τοῦ θ(εο)ῦ ἐκκλησία ταῦτα οὐ προσίεται· [εἰ] δὲ καὶ σὺ ταῦτα ἀκούεις οὐ φθονοῦμεν σοι· ἀλλ' ἐλεοῦμεν. *Vindob. Hist. gr. 70,* fol. 89^{v} mg. ‖ 4 καὶ στεφάνου J ‖ καὶ Νικολάου] νικολάου καὶ στεφάνου J ‖ ἢ] καὶ F ‖ 9 γενομένης VS

XII

Long live the Emperors!
Our Orthodox Emperor.
Our Orthodox Augusta.
The most holy and Ecumenical Patriarch.
The most fortunate Caesar.

Basil, Constantine, Leo, Alexander, Christopher, Romanus, ⟨Constantine, Romanus,⟩ Nicephorus, John, Basil, Constantine, Romanus, Michael, ⟨Constantine, Michael,⟩ Isaac, Constantine, Romanus, Andronicus, Michael, Nicephorus, Isaac and Alexius, who have passed from the earthly to the heavenly Kingdom—eternal their memory!

Eudocia, Theophano, Theodora, Helen, Theophano, Theodora, Zoe, Theodora, Aecaterina, Eudocia, Mary, Irene and Irene, the most pious Augustas—eternal their memory!

Germanus, Tarasius, Nicephorus and Methodius, the illustrious Patriarchs—eternal their memory!

Ignatius, Photius, Stephen, Anthony, Nicholas, Euthymius, Stephen, Tryphon, Theophylact, Polyeuctus, Anthony, Nicholas, Sisinnius, Sergius, Eustathius, Alexius, Michael, Constantine, John, Cosmas, Eustratius, Nicholas and John, the Orthodox Patriarchs—eternal their memory!

E. Anathemas

All that has been written or spoken against the holy Patriarchs Germanus, Tarasius, Nicephorus, and Methodius—anathema!

All that has been written or spoken against the holy Patriarchs Ignatius, Photius, Stephen, Anthony, and Nicholas—anathema!

All innovations that have been made and all actions that have been undertaken, or will henceforth be undertaken, contrary to the ecclesiastical tradition and the doctrine and instruction of Holy and Illustrious Fathers—anathema!

Those who falsely accuse the Holy Church of having approved the fourth marriage, on the ground of the dispensation that with God's favor

προσλήψεως καὶ ἑνώσεως τῶν ἀδελφῶν ἡμῶν οὓς ἡ τῶν προλαβόντων σκανδάλων αἰτία ἐχώριζεν, ἀνάθεμα.

Τοῖς τολμῶσι λέγειν ὅτι ἡ ἐκκλησία τὸ καθαρὸν καὶ ἄχραντον οὐ σῴζει τῆς ἁγιστείας αὐτῆς, ἀλλὰ μολυσμόν τινα προσετρίψατο διὰ τὴν χάριτι θεοῦ γενομένην σύναψιν τῶν τέκνων, οὓς διεμέρισε μὲν τὸ ἤδη προγεγονὸς σκάνδαλον, συνῆψε δὲ ἡ τούτου παρὰ πάντων ὁμοῦ ἀθέτησις καὶ ἀποκήρυξις, ἀνάθεμα.

Τοῖς ἐν καταφρονήσει τιθεμένοις τοὺς ἱεροὺς καὶ θείους κανόνας τῶν μακαρίων πατέρων ἡμῶν, οἳ καὶ τὴν ἁγίαν ἐκκλησίαν ὑπερείδουσι καὶ ὅλην τὴν Χριστιανικὴν πολιτείαν κοσμοῦντες πρὸς θείαν ὁδηγοῦσιν εὐλάβειαν, ἀνάθεμα.

Τούτων οὕτως διωρισμένων πρὸς ἀσφάλειαν τῆς ἁγίας ἐκκλησίας καὶ τοῦ ἀμέτοχον εἶναι τὸ εὐσεβὲς τῶν Χριστιανῶν πλήρωμα τῶν ἐξ ἀθεμίτων γάμων ῥύπων, δεόμεθα τῆς σῆς ἀγαθότητος, Χριστὲ ὁ θεὸς ἡμῶν, καὶ ἔτι καὶ διὰ παντὸς πᾶν σκάνδαλον, πᾶσαν διαμερισμοῦ αἰτίαν τῆς σῆς ἐξελαύνειν ἐκκλησίας καὶ συντηρεῖν αὐτῇ τὴν εἰρηναίαν κατάστασιν, πρεσβείαις τῆς δεσποίνης ἡμῶν καὶ ἀχράντου μητρός σου, τῶν πανιέρων μαθητῶν σου καὶ ἀποστόλων, δι' ὧν ἐν πάσῃ τῇ οἰκουμένῃ τὴν σὴν κατεφύτευσας εἰρήνην, καὶ πάντων οἷς ἐξ αἰῶνος εὐαρεστούμενος ὤφθης ἁγίοις, ἀμήν.

201

Νικολάου πατριάρχου τοῦ παλαιοῦ, περὶ τοῦ τὰς πατριαρχικὰς ἐπιστολὰς ἀμισθὶ δίδοσθαι τοῖς αἰτοῦσιν, ὡς γέγραπται ἐν τῷ χαρτοφυλακείῳ

Χαλεπὸν μέν, πάθος σαρκὸς χρόνῳ τὸ †πάθος† λαβὸν ἐκμοχλεῦσαι, χαλεπώτερον δέ, χρονικῇ παρόδῳ βεβαιωθὲν ἔθος ἀπο-

---

10 προλήψεως GU ‖ 11 ἐχώριζεν] διΐστα S ‖ 13 ἁγιαστίας J ‖ 14 σύναξιν GU ‖ οὓς] ἃ F ‖ 15 τούτων F ‖ 17–18 κανόνας καὶ θείους colloc. S ‖ 18 μακαρίων] καὶ θείων add. S ‖ 19 κοσμοῦντας S ‖ 20 ποδηγοῦσιν FS ‖ 21 ἁγίας] θείας F om. S ‖ 22 πλήρωμα τῶν χριστιανῶν colloc. V ‖ 24 καὶ[2] om. PVS ‖ 26 δεσποί-] mut. des. U ‖ 27 σου[1]] καὶ θεοτόκου add. S ‖ 29 ἁγίων F

201: S 190^{v}–191^{r} Q 524–525 n 306^{r-v} s 355^{r-v} d 678^{v}–679^{r} et 707^{r-v} w 174^{v} ‖ 4 χρόνῳ — λαβὸν] χρόνιον ἤδη γενόμενον w ‖ πάθος] πάχος S, sed praestat κράτος vel sim.

has been granted and on the ground of the reception of, and union with, our brothers whom the cause of the former scandals kept separated from us–anathema!

Those who presume to say that the Church does not preserve her holiness pure and immaculate but has incurred a stain when through God's grace she united herself with her children who were severed by the scandal that took place in the past, and were joined to her by its unanimous rejection and prohibition–anathema!

Those who hold in contempt the sacred and divine canons of our blessed Fathers, which not only sustain the Holy Church, but also grace the entire Christian community and guide it toward godly piety–anathema!

This having thus been decreed for the security of the Holy Church and in order that the pious congregation or Christians may be free from the defilements of illicit marriages, we beseech Thy goodness, Christ our God, henceforward and forever to ban all scandal, all cause of division from Thy Church and to preserve its peaceful estate, by the intercession of our Lady, Thy Immaculate Mother, Thy all-holy disciples and apostles, through whom Thou hast planted Thy peace in all the world, and of all the saints to whom Thou hast shown Thy pleasure from the beginning of days, amen.

201

The Patriarch Nicholas the Ancient: that the Patriarchal Letters should be Made Available Free on Request, according to the Text Preserved in the Archives

It is difficult to dislodge a bodily ailment when it has acquired strength by a long lapse of time, but it is even more difficult to abolish a

201

σκευάσασθαι· ἄμφω γὰρ πρὸς ἕξιν τινὰ μεταστοιχειοῦνται, πρᾶγμα μονιμώτερον καὶ ῥᾳδίως ἥκιστα δυνάμενον μεθαρμόζεσθαι. Ἀλλ' εἰ καὶ ταῦθ' οὕτω τῷ ὄντι δοκεῖ, ῥᾷον παλαιὰν συνήθειαν τὸ φαῦλον πρόδηλον ἔχουσαν τοῦ εὐαγοῦς τοῦδε τόπου ἐξεφορήσαμεν, τὸ ἀκαπήλευτον αὐτῷ μνηστευσάμενοι.

Καὶ γὰρ ὁ τῶν τῇδε τὴν φυλακὴν ἐμπεπιστευμένος, ὃν ὀστιάριον ἡ Ῥωμαίων γλῶσσα καλεῖ, τοὺς πατριαρχικὰς αἰτουμένους ἐπιστολὰς μισθόν, ὡς οὐκ ὤφειλεν, ἀπήτει τῆς παραλήψεως· καὶ ἦν τὸ πρᾶγμα λίαν ἐφύβριστόν τε καὶ καταγέλαστον, οὐ μόνον θεὸν παροργίζον, ἀλλὰ καὶ τὸν σεμνὸν τόπον ἐξατιμοῦν καὶ αὐτὸ τὸ τῆς ἱερωσύνης ἐκφαυλίζον αἰδέσιμον. Ἀλλ' ἡμεῖς γε τὴν τοῦ ὀστιαρίου σκῆψιν ἐκφυλλοφοροῦντες, τούτῳ μὲν ῥόγαν ἐτήσιον δίδοσθαι ἐτάξαμεν, τὴν πονηρὰν δὲ συνήθειαν λήθῃ βαθείᾳ καὶ ἀιδίῳ ὑπερορίᾳ παρεπεμψάμεθα. Ἣν μηδαμῶς χώραν ἔτι ἔχειν ἐν ἁγίῳ διοριζόμενοι πνεύματι, ἐντελλόμεθα τοῖς τε κατὰ καιροὺς χαρτοφύλαξι καὶ τοῖς ἀμφ' αὐτοὺς νοταρίοις ἄθραυστον τὸν παρόντα τύπον διατηρεῖν καὶ τούτου ἐπιμελεῖσθαι ἀεί, ὡς μὴ ῥᾳστώνῃ τινὶ καὶ ὀλιγωρίᾳ (ὃ δὴ καὶ ὑπολαμβάνειν, μήτι γε πράττειν, ἐφάμαρτον) κἂν τὸ βραχύτατον παρατρέπεσθαι.

Εἰ δὲ παρόπται τινὲς τοῦ τοσούτου ἀγαθοῦ ἐκ μεγάλης περὶ τὰ θεῖα φωραθεῖεν καταφρονήσεως, τοῦτον μὲν γνώμη φιλόθεος πρὸς τὴν ἀξιέπαινον ἐπανάξει εὐγένειαν, αὐτοὶ δ' εὖ ἴστωσαν ὡς δίκας θεῷ δώσουσι νῦν τε καὶ ὁπηνίκα οὐ τὰ μείζω μόνον τῶν ἁμαρτημάτων, ἀλλὰ καὶ αὐτά γε τὰ μέτρια πυρὶ ταλαντεύεται καὶ διακρίνεται. Ὡς γὰρ τὰ θεῖα τῆς ἀξιολόγου καθεστήκασιν ἀντιδόσεως ἄξια, οὕτω καὶ τὰ τῆς ἐναντίας μοίρας τὴν ἰσοπαλῆ τοῖς ἔργοις παρέχεται ἀμοιβήν.

---

6 post πρᾶγμα] γινόμενα add. w ‖ 8 post δοκεῖ] ἀλλ' ἡμεῖς γε add. w ‖ 11 τῶν τῇδε SQn: τήνδε sd τοῦδε w ‖ 13 ὤφελεν w ‖ 15 αὐτό γε Qn ‖ 16 γε om. s ‖ τοῦ om. w ‖ 17 ἐκφυλλοφοροῦντες s: -φυλο- Qdnw ἐκφυλοφρονοῦντες S ‖ τοῦτο Qn ‖ 19 ἔχειν ἔτι colloc. dw ‖ διοριζόμενοι SQn: -μεθα sdw ‖ 20 ἐντελλόμεθα SQn: -όμενοι sdw ‖ 23 μήτοι w ‖ 24 περιτρέπεσθαι sdw ‖ 26 τοῦτο Qn ‖ 30 καθεστᾶσιν Qn ‖ ἄξια] αἴτια Qn

201
custom sanctioned by the passage of time; both transform themselves into a sort of settled condition that tends to be permanent and is by no means easy to redress. Yet though this appears to be true indeed, we have found it easy to rid this sacred place of an old but manifestly blameworthy custom, and thus to gain for it freedom from all commercialism.

Its keeper, who bears the Latin title of *ostiarius,* used to demand fees from those who requested patriarchal letters, in payment for the copy, a thing he should not have done; the practice was utterly outrageous and preposterous, one that besides rousing God's wrath was also an insult to this venerable place and compromised the very dignity of the priesthood. In order to preclude any pretext on the part of the *ostiarius,* however, we have fixed an annual salary for him and have consigned this evil practice to utter oblivion and everlasting banishment. Decreeing in the name of the Holy Spirit that henceforth it shall in no way be tolerated, we enjoin upon those who shall successively hold the office of *chartophylax* and upon the scribes at their disposal to maintain the present regulation and to see to it at all times that no indifference or negligence (an eventuality which it is sinful even to envisage, let alone to bring about) shall lead to the smallest infringement.

If, out of profound contempt for the sacred, some should be found guilty of ignoring a rule so beneficial, pious intent will restore this regulation to the rank of high respect which it deserves; the offenders, however, should be aware that God's punishment awaits them, both now and at the time when not only the greater sins but even the lesser ones are tried and judged by fire. For even as godly deportment deserves a just reward, so its opposite entails a retribution proportionate to the deed.

202. Decree on the Great Habit

Ὁ ἁγιώτατος οἰκουμενικὸς πατριάρχης Κωνσταντινουπόλεως Νικόλαος, ὁ ὑπὸ τῆς βασιλείας Λέοντος τοῦ φιλοσόφου καὶ μέχρι τῆς βασιλείας Ῥωμανοῦ τοῦ γέροντος, μετὰ τῆς αὐτοῦ ἁγίας ἐξεῖπε συνόδου περὶ τῶν ἀποκειραμένων μεγαλοσχήμων ὅτι

«Ἡ χάρις χάριν οὐκ ἐκδιώκει, ἀλλὰ καὶ ἁγιάζει μᾶλλον καὶ συνιστᾷ καὶ φωτίζει· διὸ καὶ τοὺς ἀποκειρομένους μεγαλοσχήμους οὐ χρὴ ἀπείργειν τῆς θείας λειτουργίας, κἂν καί τις ἴσως κανὼν εὑρεθῇ ἀπείργων αὐτούς· ἁμαρτία γὰρ καὶ μόνη ἀπείργει τῆς θείας λειτουργίας καὶ οὐχὶ τοῦ μεγάλου σχήματος ὁ ἁγιασμός.»

203

Κανὼν θρηνητικὸς τῆς ὑπεραγίας θεοτόκου ἐν τῇ σταυρώσει τοῦ κυρίου ἡμῶν Ἰησοῦ Χριστοῦ καὶ θεοῦ, ποίημα Νικολάου πατριάρχου Κωνσταντινουπόλεως

ᾠδὴ α'. ἦχος πλ. β'. «Ὡς ἐν ἠπείρῳ»
Ἀναρτηθέντα ὡς εἶδεν | ἐπὶ σταυροῦ
τὸν υἱὸν καὶ κύριον
ἡ παρθένος καὶ ἁγνή,
τρυχομένη ἔκλαιεν πικρῶς
μεθ' ἑτέρων γυναικῶν | καὶ «Οἴμοι» ἔλεγεν.

«Βλέπω σε, φίλτατον τέκνον | καὶ ποθεινόν,
ἐν σταυρῷ κρεμάμενον,
καὶ τιτρώσκομαι πικρῶς
τὴν καρδίαν,» ἔφη ἡ ἁγνή,
«ἀλλὰ δός μοι, ἀγαθέ, | λόγον τῇ δούλῃ σου.

203: 10: Ioann. 19:25.

202: b 132^{v} t 61^{r} h 307^{r} ‖ 1 οἰκουμενικὸς om. t ‖ 3–4 συνόδου ἐξεῖπε colloc. h ‖ 4 ἀποκειρομένων b ‖ 5 ἡ om. t ‖ 6 ἀποκειραμένους h ‖ μεγαλοσχήμους] ἀρχιερεῖς add. h ‖ 7 ἴσως om. h ‖ 8 θείας om. t

203: Π 12^{r}–15^{v} ‖ 10 οἴμμοι (semper) Π

202. Decree on the Great Habit

The Most Holy Patriarch of Constantinople, Nicholas (from the reign of Leo the Philosopher until the reign of Romanus the Ancient) with his Holy Synod declared as follows concerning the tonsured who wear the great habit:

"Grace does not expel Grace, rather it bestows even greater sanctity, firmness, and enlightenment. Therefore, those of the tonsure who wear the great habit must not be excluded from the Divine Liturgy, even if perhaps a canon so excluding them should be found; for only sin can exclude from the Divine Liturgy, not the sanctity of the great habit."

203

A Canon on the Lament of the Most Holy Mother of God at the Crucifixion of our Lord and God Jesus Christ: a Poem by Nicholas Patriarch of Constantinople

Ode 1. First plagal mode. *"Hōs en ēpeirō"*

When she saw her Son and Lord hanging on the cross, the Pure Virgin, rent by sorrow, wept bitterly with other women, and said "Alas!

"I see you, my dearest beloved Son, hanging on a cross, and my heart is grievously wounded," the Pure One spoke; "but in your goodness give me, your servant, a reason.

90

«Γνώμῃ ἰδίᾳ, υἱέ μου | καὶ ποιητά,»
ἡ παρθένος ἔλεγεν,
παρεστῶσα τῷ σταυρῷ
σὺν ἠγαπημένῳ μαθητῇ,
«ὑποφέρεις τὸν δεινὸν | ἐν ξύλῳ θάνατον.

«Νῦν τὴν ἐμὴν προσδοκίαν | καὶ τὴν χαρὰν
καὶ τὴν ἀγαλλίασιν,
τὸν υἱόν μου καὶ θεόν,
ἐστερήθην, οἴμοι, καὶ ἀλγῶ
τὴν καρδίαν,» ἡ ἁγνὴ | ἔλεγεν κλαίουσα.

ᾠδὴ γ΄. «Οὐκ ἔστιν ἅγιος»
Διὰ τὸν φόβον τὸν πολὺν | Ἰουδαίων ὁ Πέτρος
ἀπεκρύβη καὶ πάντες | ἀπέφυγον οἱ πιστοί,
καταλιπόντες Χριστόν·
ἡ παρθένος | θρηνῳδοῦσα ἔλεγεν·

«Ἐπὶ τῷ ξένῳ σου τοκετῷ | καὶ φρικτῷ σου, υἱέ μου,
ὑπὲρ πάσας μητέρας | ἐμεγαλύνθην ἐγώ·
ἀλλ' οἴμοι, νῦν σε ὁρῶ
ἐπὶ ξύλου, | φλέγονται τὰ σπλάγχνα μου.

«Ζητῶ τὸ σπλάγχνον τὸ ἐμὸν | ἐν ἀγκάλαις, αἷς πρώην
ὥσπερ βρέφος κατεῖχον, | ἀπὸ τοῦ ξύλου λαβεῖν,»
ἐφθέγγετο ἡ ἁγνή,
«ἀλλ' οὐδείς μοι, | οἴμοι, τοῦτο δίδωσιν.

«Ἰδοὺ τὸ φῶς μου τὸ γλυκύ, | ἡ ἐλπίς, ἡ ζωή μου,
ὁ υἱὸς καὶ θεός μου, | ἐσβέσθη ἐν τῷ σταυρῷ
καὶ φλέγομαι δι' αὐτό,»
ἡ παρθένος | ἔλεγεν σταλάζουσα.

18–19: Ioann. 19:26. ‖ 27: cf. Ioann. 20:19. ‖ 28: cf. Matth. 26:56; Marc. 14:50.

33 ὁρῶ Mai: ὁρᾷ Π ‖ 39 γλυκύ Mai: -ύν Π

203

"Of your own free will, my Son and Creator," the Virgin said, standing by the cross with the beloved disciple, "you suffer the terrible death on the rood.

"Now I am bereft of my hope, my joy, and my pride, of my Son and God, alas! and it hurts my heart," the Pure One spoke weeping.

Ode 3. *"Ouk estin hagios"*

Because of their great fear of the Jews, Peter hid and all the faithful fled, forsaking Christ; the Virgin, wailing, spoke:

"By your wondrous and awesome birth, my Son, I was glorified above all mothers; but alas! now I see you on a cross, and my bowels burn.

"I want to take my Son down from the cross in my arms, in which once I held you as a baby," the Pure One spoke, "but no one, alas! grants me this.

"Behold: my sweet light, my hope, my life, my Son, and my God, was extinguished on the cross, and I am seared with grief because of it," the Virgin said, shedding tears.

203

ᾠδὴ δ΄. «Χριστός μου δύναμις»
«Ἥλιε ἄδυτε, | θεὲ προάναρχε,
ποιητὰ τῶν ἁπάντων,
δημιουργὲ | τῶν κτισμάτων κύριε,
πῶς φέρεις πάθος ἐν σταυρῷ;»
ἡ ἁγνὴ κλαίουσα ἔλεγεν.

Θρηνοῦσα ἔλεγεν | ἡ ἀπειρόγαμος
τῷ εὐσχήμονι· «Σπεῦσον,
ὦ Ἰωσήφ, | τῷ Πιλάτῳ πρόσελθε
καὶ ἐξαίτησον καθελεῖν
ἐκ τοῦ ξύλου τὸν διδάσκαλον.»

Ἰδὼν τὴν ἄχραντον | πικρῶς δακρύουσαν
Ἰωσὴφ ἐταράχθη·
θρηνῳδῶν | τῷ Πιλάτῳ πρόσεισι,
«Δός μοι» βοῶν μετὰ κλαυθμοῦ
«νῦν τὸ σῶμα τοῦ κυρίου μου.»

«Κατεστιγμένον σε | ὁρῶ καὶ ἄδοξον
καὶ γυμνὸν ἐπὶ ξύλου
τέκνον ἐμόν, | καὶ τὰ σπλάγχνα φλέγομαι,»
ὀδυρομένη μητρικῶς
ἡ παρθένος ἀπεφθέγγετο.

ᾠδὴ ε΄. «Τῷ θείῳ φέγγει σου»
Κατατρυχόμενος ὁ Ἰωσὴφ
καὶ καταπληττόμενος ὁμοῦ
σὺν Νικοδήμῳ κατήγαγεν
τὸ τοῦ διδασκάλου ἄχραντον σκήνωμα,
θρηνοῦντες καὶ ὑμνοῦντες | τοῦτον ὡς κύριον.

50: Marc. 14:43. ‖ 56–58: Matth. 27:57–58; Marc. 15:43–45; Luc. 23:50–52; Ioann. 20:38.

---

52 ἐξαίτησον Mai: ἐξαιτήσου Π

203

Ode 4. *"Christos mou dynamis"*

"Never-setting Sun, God before all eternity, Maker of the Universe, Creator and Lord of your creatures, how can you bear to suffer on a cross?" the Pure One said, weeping.

Lamenting, she who knew no man said to the honorable Joseph: "Hasten, Joseph, go to Pilate and ask him leave to take down your Teacher from the cross."

When he saw the Immaculate One weeping bitterly, Joseph was troubled; lamenting, he approached Pilate and cried out with tears: "Give me at last the body of my Lord!"

"I see you pierced with wounds and humiliated and naked upon the rood, my Child, and my bowels burn"–thus, wailing as a mother does, the Virgin spoke.

Ode 5. *"Tō theiō phengei sou"*

Joseph, worn out by sorrow, and awed at the same time, took down with Nicodemus his Teacher's immaculate body, both of them mourning for him and singing his praises as their Lord.

Λαβοῦσα τοῦτον μετὰ κλαυθμοῦ
  μήτηρ ἡ ἀπείρανδρος ἁγνὴ
καὶ περιθεῖσα τοῖς γόνασι,
  βρέχουσα τοῖς δάκρυσι κατεφίλει αὐτόν,
πικρῶς ὀδυρομένη | καὶ ἀλαλάζουσα.

«Μόνην ἐλπίδα σὲ καὶ ζωήν,
  δέσποτα, υἱέ μου καὶ θεέ,
καὶ ὀφθαλμῶν φῶς ἡ δούλη σου
  εἶχον· νῦν δέ, οἴμοι, ἀποστερεῖς σου,
γλυκύτατόν μου τέκνον | καὶ ποθεινότατον.

«Ὀδύναι, θλίψεις καὶ στεναγμοὶ
  εὗροσάν με, οἴμοι,» ἡ ἁγνὴ
πικρῶς θρηνοῦσα ἐφθέγγετο,
  «βλέπουσά σε, τέκνον μου ποθεινότατον,
γυμνόν, ἀπερριμμένον, | ἐσμυρνισμένον, νεκρόν.»

ᾠδὴ ς΄. «Τοῦ βίου τὴν θάλασσαν»
«Νεκρόν σε, φιλάνθρωπε, | τὸν ζωώσαντα νεκροὺς
  κρατῶν δεινῶς τιτρώσκομαι
τὰ σπλάγχνα, καὶ σὺν σοὶ θέλω τοῦ θανεῖν,»
  ἡ πάναγνος ἔλεγεν·
«οὐ γὰρ φέρω σε ἄπνουν | καὶ νεκρὸν καθορᾶν.

«Ξενίζομαι βλέπουσα, | ὑπεράγαθε θεὲ
  καὶ πανοικτίρμον κύριε,
ἄδοξον, ἄπνουν, ἄμορφον καὶ γυμνόν,
  καὶ κλαίω κρατοῦσά σε,
ὡς οὐκ ἤλπιζον, οἴμοι, | κατιδεῖν σε, υἱέ.

73: cf. Luc. 7:38. ‖ 84: Ioann. 20:39.

---

78 ἀποστερεῖς Mai: -εῖν Π ‖ 84 ἀπερρημένον Π: -γμένον scr. Mai ‖ 87 fort. κρατῶ· δεινῶς ‖ 92 πανοικτίρμον] sic Π

203

The pure Mother, who knew no man, receiving him with weeping and laying him on her knees, washed him with her tears and kissed him, crying bitterly and wailing.

"You were to your servant her only hope and her life, O Master, O my Son and my God, and you were the light of her eyes; but now, alas! you allow me to lose you, my sweetest and most beloved Child!

"Sorrows, troubles, and sighs have overtaken me, alas!" the Pure One cried lamenting bitterly, "now that I see you, my dearly beloved Son, naked, cast out, embalmed, dead."

Ode 6. *"Tou biou tēn thalassan"*

"As I hold you dead, Merciful One, you who brought the dead to life, my heart is terribly wounded, and I wish to die with you," the most Pure One spoke, "for I cannot bear seeing you lifeless, dead.

"I am bewildered at seeing you, God beyond all goodness, Lord all-merciful, inglorious, lifeless, shapeless, and naked, and I weep, holding you as I never, alas! expected to see you, my Son.

203

«Οὐ λέγεις τῇ δούλῃ σου | λόγον, λόγε τοῦ θεοῦ,
οὐ κατοικτείρεις, δέσποτα,
τὴν σὲ τεκοῦσαν,» ἔλεγεν ἡ ἁγνὴ
θρηνοῦσα καὶ κλαίουσα
καὶ φιλοῦσα τὸ σῶμα | τὸ πανάχραντον.

«Λογίζομαι, δέσποτα, | οὐκέτι ***
λαλιάν σου ἀκούσομαι
οὐδὲ τὸ κάλλος βλέψω σου τῆς μορφῆς
ὡς πρώην ἡ δούλη σου·
καὶ γὰρ ἔδυς, υἱέ μου, | ἐξ ἐμῶν ὀφθαλμῶν.»

ᾠδὴ ζ΄. «Δροσοβόλον μὲν τήν»
«Πῶς, υἱέ μου καὶ θεέ, τὰ εὐαγγέλια
ἃ Γαβριὴλ μοι ἔλεγεν,
βασιλέα σε καὶ υἱὸν ὑψίστου καὶ θεὸν
ἐκάλει καὶ νῦν σε θεωρῶ,
φῶς μου γλυκύτατον, γυμνόν, | κατεστιγμένον, νεκρόν;

«Ῥυόμενος δεινῶν με συμπαράλαβε
μεθ' ἑαυτοῦ, υἱὲ καὶ θεέ·
συγκατέλθω σοι ἐν τῷ ᾅδῃ, δέσποτα, κἀγώ·
μὴ λίπῃς με μόνην ἔτι ζῆν,
καὶ γὰρ οὐ φέρω ⟨μὴ⟩ ὁρᾶν | σὲ τὸ γλυκύτατον φῶς.»

Σὺν ταῖς ἄλλαις μυροφόροις ἐπωδύρετο
ἡ ἄμεμπτος πικρότατα
κομιζόμενον ἐν τῷ τάφῳ βλέπουσα Χριστόν,
καὶ ἔλεγεν «Οἴμοι, τί ὁρῶ;
ποῦ νῦν ὑπάγεις, υἱέ, | καὶ μόνην λείπεις ἐμέ;»

Ἀθυμοῦσα καὶ θρηνοῦσα ἡ πανάμωμος
ταῖς μυροφόροις ἔλεγεν·
Συνθρηνήσατε σὺν ἐμοὶ καὶ κλαύσατε πικρῶς·
ἰδοὺ γὰρ τὸ φῶς μου τὸ γλυκὺ
καὶ ὁ διδάσκαλος ὑμῶν | τάφῳ παραδίδοται.»

107–110: Luc. 1:31–33. ‖ 117: cf. Luc. 23:56–24:1.

---

101 supple ex. gr. ⟨ἀπὸ τοῦ νῦν⟩ ‖ 116 μὴ addidi ‖ σε Π ‖ 121 λίπεις Π ἔλιπες Mai

203
"You do not speak a word to your servant, Word of God, you have no pity, Master, on her who bore you," the Pure One said, lamenting and weeping and kissing the body free from the stain of all sin.

"I think, Master, that I shall never again hear your voice nor see the beauty of your form, as I, your servant, did before; for you have disappeared, my Son, out of my eyes."

Ode 7. *"Drosobolon men tēn"*

"How could, my Son and my God, the joyful message which Gabriel brought to me call you a King and a Son of the Most High and a God? and how do I see you now, my sweetest light, naked, pierced with wounds, dead?

"Rescue me from my misery and take me with you, my Son and my God; let me, too, descend to hell with you, Master; do not leave me to live on alone, for I cannot bear not to see you, my sweetest light."

With the other bearers of unguents the blameless One lamented most bitterly, as she saw Christ carried into the tomb, and she said: "Alas, what do I see! Where are you going now, my Son, leaving me behind lonely?"

Despondent and mourning the Virgin without any blemish spoke to the bearers of unguents: "Lament with me and weep bitterly, for behold, my sweet light who is your Teacher is committed to the grave."

203

ᾠδὴ η΄. «Ἐκ φλογὸς τοῖς ὁσίοις»
Τὴν παρθένον θρηνοῦσαν | ὁ Ἰωσὴφ θεωρῶν
κατετρύχετο ὅλως | καὶ ἀνεβόα πικρῶς·
«Πῶς σε, ὦ θεέ μου, νῦν κηδεύσω ὁ δοῦλός σου,
ποίαις δὲ σινδόσιν | είλήσω σου τὸ σῶμα;»

Ὑπὲρ νοῦν ὑπερβαίνει | τὸ ξένον θέαμα·
ὁ βαστάζων τὴν κτίσιν | πᾶσαν ὁ κύριος,
τοῦτον Ἰωσὴφ ὡς νεκρὸν ἐν χερσὶν ἑαυτοῦ
σὺν τῷ Νικοδήμῳ | βαστάζει καὶ κηδεύει.

«Φοβερὸν καὶ φρικῶδες | βλέπω μυστήριον,»
ἡ παρθένος ἐβόα· | «υἱέ ***,
πῶς ἐν εὐτελεῖ μνημείῳ κατατίθεσαι,
ὁ νεκροὺς προστάξει | ἐγείρας ἐκ μνημάτων;

«Οὐ τοῦ τάφου σου, τέκνον, | νῦν ἐγερθήσομαι,
οὐ τὰ δάκρυα παύσω | ῥαίνειν ἡ δούλη σου,
ἕως οὗ κἀγὼ συγκατέλθω ἐν ᾅδῃ·
φέρειν γὰρ οὐ σθένω | τὴν στέρησίν σου, φῶς μου.»

ᾠδὴ θ΄. «Θεὸν ἀνθρώποις ἰδεῖν»
«Χαρὰ οὐδ' ὅλως ἐμοὶ προσψαύσειεν
ἀπὸ τοῦ νῦν» ἐβόα θρηνῳδοῦσα ἡ ἄμεμπτος·
«τὸ γὰρ φῶς τῆς χαρᾶς μου ἐν μνήματι
ἔδυσεν· ἀλλ' οὐ λίπω | τοῦτο μονώτατον·
ἐνθάδε τεθνήξομαι κἀγώ, καὶ συνθανοῦμαι αὐτῷ.

«Ψυχῆς τὸ ἄλγος νῦν θεράπευσον,
τέκνον ἐμόν,» ἡ πάναγνος ἐβόα δακρύουσα,
«καὶ ἀνάστηθι, παῦσον τοὺς πόνους μου
καὶ ⟨τὰς⟩ πικράς μου θλίψεις· | δύνασαι, δέσποτα·
ὅσα γὰρ σὺ θέλεις, καὶ ποιεῖς, εἰ καὶ ἐτάφης ἑκών.»

131: Marc. 15:46. ‖ 133–135: Ioann. 19:40–42. ‖ 139: Ioann. 11:38–44.

---

128 θρηνοῦσαν Mai: -σα Π ‖ 131 εἰλίσω Π ‖ 137 supple ex. gr. ⟨μου καὶ θεέ⟩ ‖ 153 τὰς addidi ‖ 154 θέλεις Mai: -ης Π

203

Ode 8. *"Ek phlogos tois hosiois"*

When Joseph saw the Virgin mourning, he was all grief-smitten and cried out bitterly: "How, O my God, shall I, your servant, now bury you, and in what shrouds shall I wrap your body?"

The strange sight passes understanding: the Lord who carries all creation is carried as a dead body in the arms of Joseph and Nicodemus, and is laid in the grave.

"Terrible and awesome is the mystery I see," the Virgin cried; "my Son ⟨and my God,⟩ how can you be laid in a lowly tomb, you that by the word of your command raised the dead from their graves?

"I shall no more rise up from your grave, my child, nor shall I, your servant, cease the flood of my tears, until I too have descended to hell; for I cannot bear the loss of you, my light."

Ode 9. *"Theon anthrōpois idein"*

No joy whatever could touch me henceforth," the Blameless One cried, lamenting: "for the light of my joy has set in the grave; but I cannot leave it all alone; here I shall also die, and I shall die with him.

"Now heal the pain of my soul, my Child," the Pure One cried out weeping, "and rise, end my sorrows and my bitter trials; you can do so, Master, for whatever you will, you do, even though you consented to be buried."

«Ὦ πῶς διέλαθέν σε ἡ ἄβυσσος,»
τῇ ἁγνῇ ἔφη ὁ κύριος, «⟨τῶν κριμάτων μου;⟩
Τὸ πλάσμα μου σῶσαι βουλόμενος
θνῆξαι κατεδεξάμην· | ἀλλ' ἀναστήσομαι
καὶ μεγαλυνῶ ὡς θεός, ἐν οὐρανῷ καὶ ἐν γῇ.»

«Ὑμνῶ τὸ εὔσπλαγχνόν σου, φιλάνθρωπε,
προσκυνῶ τὸ πλοῦτος τοῦ ἐλέους σου, δέσποτα·
τὸ γὰρ πλάσμα σου σῶσαι βουλόμενος
ὡς θεὸς κατεδέξω,» | ἔφη ἡ ἄχραντος·
«ἀλλ' ἐν τῇ ἐγέρσει σου, σῶτερ, πάντας ἐλέησον.»

204. Canon to St. Gregory the Illuminator and Rhipsimia

Ὁ κανών

ᾠδὴ α'. ἦχος πλ. δ'. «Ἄισωμεν τῷ κυρίῳ»
Σήμερον ἡ φωσφόρος
τοῦ καλοῦ ποιμένος | ἐξανέτειλε
Γρηγορίου ἡ μνήμη,
ἣν οἱ πίστει τιμῶντες φαιδρύνονται.

Κατεδίωξε, πάτερ,
ὁ ἐχθρὸς πορείαν | τῶν ἀγώνων σου·
ἀλλ' ἐπαναστραφείσης
κατεσχέθη αὐτοῦ τῆς διώξεως.

Ὢ τῆς παντοδυνάμου
Ἰησοῦ θεέ μου, | ἀσθενείας σου·
τοὺς διώκτας προσάγει
λατρευτὰς ἐν τῷ πάσχειν Γρηγόριος.

155–156: cf. Ps. 35:7. ‖ 158–159: Cosmas, *can. in Magnum Sabbatum* (Christ-Paranikas, 196–201), od. 9 str. 3. ‖ 161: cf. Rom. 9:23.
204: 4: Ioann. 10:11.

---

156 τῶν κριμάτων μου ex. gr. supplevi ‖ 159 μεγαλυνῶ Mai: μεγαλύνω Π μεγαλύνω σε Cosmas, can. in Magnum Sabbatum, od. 9, str. 3
204: Λ 217v–220v Θ 78r–81v Δ 82r–84v ‖ initia hirmorum secundum Δ dedi ‖ 1 νικολά(ου) πατρ(ιάρχου) mg. Λ ‖ 6 πιστοὶ ΛΘ ‖ 10 κατεσχέθη αὐτοῦ Δ: κατησχύνθη αὐτῷ ΛΘ ‖ 12 ἀσθενείας Λ: εὐσθενείας Δ δυναστείας Θ

"I praise your compassion, Friend of Mankind, I adore the wealth of your mercy, Master: wanting to save your creation you accepted to die as God," the Immaculate One said; "but in your Resurrection, Savior, have pity upon us all."

"Ah, how you have failed to fathom," the Lord spoke to the Pure One, "the depth ⟨of my judgments⟩! In order to save my creation I accepted to die; but I shall rise again and do great deeds as God, in heaven and on earth."

204. Canon to St. Gregory the Illuminator and Rhipsimia

The Canon

Ode 1. First plagal mode. *"Asōmen tō Kyriō"*

Today has dawned the shining memory of Gregory the good shepherd, which those who revere it in faith celebrate joyfully.

The enemy, Father, pursued you on the road of your struggles; but the pursuit was reversed, and he was captured.

Oh your almighty weakness, Jesus my God! Gregory in his suffering brings the persecutors to you as worshipers.

Ἄχραντε θεοτόκε,
ἡ σεσαρκωμένον | τὸν ἀΐδιον
καὶ ὑπέρθεον λόγον
ὑπὲρ φύσιν τεκοῦσα, ὑμνοῦμέν σε.

ᾠδὴ γ'. «Σὺ εἶ τὸ στερέωμα»
Σκῆνος τὸ φθειρόμενον
τοῖς καταξαίνουσιν, ἔνδοξε,
παραδιδοὺς | τὸ τῆς ἀφθαρσίας
ἀντεκτήσω διαίτημα.

Ἤμβλυνεν, Γρηγόριε,
τῶν ἀσεβῶν ἀκμὴν ἔνστασις
ἡ εὐσεβής, | ἣν ὡς πανοπλίαν
περιφέρων ἠγώνισαι.

Ἔρως ὁ πανάχραντος
σῆς ὡραιότητος εἵλκυσε
σοί, Ἰησοῦ, | θήλεος τὴν φύσιν
ἠρνημένην ἀσθένειαν.

Δὸς ἡμῖν βοήθειαν
ταῖς ἱκεσίαις σου, πάναγνε,
τὰς προσβολὰς | ἀποκρουομένη
τῶν δεινῶν περιστάσεων.

ᾠδὴ δ'. «Εἰσακήκοα, κύριε»
Τῷ σῷ λύθρῳ τοῦ αἵματος
τῷ τοῦ μαρτυρίου, πάτερ Γρηγόριε,
ἀντὶ μέλανος χρησάμενος
τοῦ Χριστοῦ τὰ δόγματα διεχάραξας.

21: cf. *Acta Greg. Illum.* (ed. G. Garitte, *Documents pour l'étude du livre d'Agathange* [Roma, 1946], 23–116), 25, 15–16. ‖ 26: Ephes. 6:11. ‖ 37–40: cf. *Acta Greg.* (supra), 26, 10–12.

---

18 τεκοῦσα ΘΔ: καὶ λόγον Λ ‖ 23 διάδημα ΛΘ ‖ 29 σῆς] τῆς Θ ‖ 30 θήλεως ΘΔ ‖ 31 ἠρνημένον Θ

204

Immaculate Mother of God, you that bore the eternal and supremely divine Word incarnate in a way beyond nature, we praise you!

Ode 3. *"Sy ei to stereōma"*

When you abandoned your perishable tabernacle to the torturers, Glorious One, you received instead the abode of imperishability.

The sword edge of the impious was blunted, Gregory, by your pious resistance, which you wore as a suit of armor in your fight.

The blameless love of your beauty, Jesus, drew to you feminine nature, which belied its own weakness.

Give us help through your entreaties, most Pure One, warding off the assaults of fearful temptations.

Ode 4. *"Eisakēkoa, Kyrie"*

Using as ink the blood shed in your martyrdom, Father Gregory, you wrote out the teachings of Christ.

204

Τῷ πυρὶ τῆς ἀγάπης σου,
  Ἰησοῦ φιλάνθρωπε, ἐκκαιόμενος
κατεσβέννυεν τὴν φλόγωσιν
  τῶν δεινῶν βασάνων ὁ Γρηγόριος.

Λογισμῶν φέρων ἔκστασιν
  σοῦ τοῦ ποιητοῦ τῆς δόξης ὁ τύραννος
διαμείβει καὶ τὴν μόρφωσιν
  ἀλογίας εἴδει συμμορφούμενος.

Ἱλασμὸν ἡμῖν δώρησαι
  τῶν ἀγνοημάτων ὡς ἀναμάρτητος·
καὶ εἰρήνευσον τὸν κόσμον σου,
  ὁ θεός, πρεσβείαις τῆς τεκούσης σε.

ᾠδὴ ε΄. «Ὀρθρίζοντες βοῶμεν»
Ναὸς ὡς χρηματίσας,
Γρηγόριε, | τῆς τριάδος
  εἰδώλων κατέστρεψας
  τὰ ἐναγῆ τεμενίσματα.

Τὸ αἷμά σου, νυμφίε,
τὸ ἄχραντον | ἀρραβῶνα
  γυναῖκες δεξάμεναι
  σοὶ τὸ οἰκεῖον ἀντέδωκαν.

Σπονδὰς τῆς ἀσεβείας
κατέπαυσας, | ἱεράρχα,
  θυσία γενόμενος
  τῷ ζωοδότῃ καὶ θύματι.

45–48: ibid., 48, 7–16. ‖ 46–48: cf. Rom. 1:23. ‖ 54–57: *Acta Greg.* (supra), 75, 6–80, 10.

41–44 post 48 pon. Λ ‖ 45 ἔνστασιν ΛΘ ‖ 48 ἔδει Θ ‖ 55 γρηγόρε τὴν τριάδα Θ ‖ 57 τεμενίσματα] τεμένη μακάριε Θ ‖ 58–59 νυμφίε τὸ ἄχραντον ΛΘ: τὸ ἄχραντον κύριε Δ ‖ 60–61 δεξάμεναι — οἰκεῖον ΛΘ: ἐδέξαντο καὶ τὸ αὐτῶν σοὶ Δ

204

Burning with the fire of your love, Merciful Jesus, Gregory quenched the flame of the horrible tortures.

The oppressor, bereft of his mind, changed even the image of the glory of you, his Maker, to conform to the shape of brutishness.

Grant us forgiveness of our errors, as you are free from sin; and give peace to your world, O God, by the intercession of your Mother.

Ode 5. *"Orthrizontes boōmen"*

Being yourself a temple, Gregory, of the Trinity, you overthrew the unholy sanctuaries of the idols.

Your innocent blood, Bridegroom, was received as a pledge by women, who gave you theirs in return.

You set an end to the libations of impiety, Holy Bishop, by becoming a sacrifice to the Giver of Life and Sacrificial Victim.

Μαρία, θεοτόκε
ἀνύμφευτε, | τὰς ἐλπίδας
τῶν ἐχθρῶν ματαίωσον
καὶ τοὺς ὑμνοῦντάς σε εὔφρανον.

ᾠδὴ ϛ΄. «Χιτῶνά μοι παράσχου»
Ὡς ἴχνη ἀγαπήσας, ἀθλητά,
τοῦ ξύλῳ προσπήξαντος
ἡμῶν τὸ ἁμάρτημα
ἀνηρτήθης ἐν τῷ ξύλῳ ἐκμιμήσει αὐτοῦ.

Βασάνων ἐν ποικίλοις ἐτασμοῖς
τὸν σὸν ἐξετέλεσας
ἀγῶνα, Γρηγόριε·
ἀλλὰ στέφει πολυπλόκῳ νῦν κεκόσμησαι.

Τὸ κλέος τῶν παρθένων τὸ σεπτόν,
Ῥιψιμία ἔνδοξε,
τοῖς θείοις ἀγῶσί σου
κατεσέμνυνας τὸ γένος τὸ τοῦ θήλεος.

Ναόν σε τοῦ θεοῦ καὶ κιβωτὸν
καὶ παστάδα ἔμψυχον
καὶ πύλην οὐράνιον,
θεοτόκε, οἱ πιστοὶ καταγγέλλομεν.

ᾠδὴ ζ΄. «Οἱ ἐκ τῆς Ἰουδαίας»
Ὠχυρωμένος τῇ πίστει
μηχαναῖς τῶν βασάνων | ὤφθης ἀνάλωτος,
τηρήσας ἀμειώτως
τὸν πλοῦτον τὸν τῆς δόξης
Ἰησοῦ τῷ δεσπόζοντι·
ὁ τῶν πατέρων ἡμῶν θεός, εὐλογητὸς ⟨εἶ⟩.

72–73: Coloss. 2:14. ‖ 74: *Acta Greg.*, 26, 21–29. ‖ 91: Rom. 9:23; Coloss. 1:27. ‖ 93: Dan. 3:52.

---

71 ἀγαπήσας Δ: ποθήσας ΛΘ ‖ 72 ξύλου Θ ‖ 74 ἐκμιμήσει ΛΘ: ἐν μιμήσει Δ ‖ 79 παρθένων: ἀν(θρώπ)ων ΛΘ ‖ 82 τὸ[2] om. Δ ‖ θήλεως ΘΔ ‖ 91 τὸν τῆς δόξης] τῆς δόξης σου Θ

204

Mary, unbrided Mother of God, frustrate the hopes of our enemies and give joy to those who sing your praises.

Ode 6. *"Chitōna moi paraschou"*

Because you chose, Martyr, to follow in the steps of Him Who nailed our sin to the cross, you were hung on the cross after His example.

Tried by manifold tortures you finished your fight, Gregory, but now you are graced by a multiple crown.

Venerable glory of virgins, Celebrated Rhipsimia, by your divine struggles you have honored womankind.

A temple of God and an ark, a living bridal chamber, a gate of heaven, we, your faithful, proclaim you, Mother of God.

Ode 7. *"Hoi ek tēs Ioudaias"*

Fortified by your faith, you were found impregnable to the engines of torture, preserving undiminished the riches of his glory for Jesus your Lord. God of our fathers, blessed art Thou!

Οἱ βυθῷ ἀσεβείας
  διαιτώμενοι θῆρες | φρέαρ ὁρίζουσι
διαίτημα θηρῶν σοι·
ἐκδέχεται δὲ οἶκος
  τοῦ φωτός σε κραυγάζοντα
«ὁ τῶν πατέρων ⟨ἡμῶν θεός, εὐλογητὸς εἶ⟩.»

Ἡ σεμνὴ Ῥιψιμία
  τοῦ φωτὸς ὁπλισθεῖσα | σὺν τοῖς συνάθλοις αὐτῆς
τὴν θείαν πανοπλίαν,
τὸν ἄρχοντα τοῦ σκότους
  τροπουμένη ἐκραύγαζεν
«ὁ τῶν πατέρων ἡμῶν θεός, εὐλογητὸς ⟨εἶ⟩.»

Παρθενικῆς ἐκ νηδύος
  σαρκωθεὶς ἐπεφάνης | εἰς σωτηρίαν ἡμῶν·
διό σου τὴν μητέρα
εἰδότες θεοτόκον
  εὐχαρίστως κραυγάζομεν
«ὁ τῶν πατέρων ⟨ἡμῶν θεός, εὐλογητὸς εἶ⟩.»

ᾠδὴ η'. «Τὸν βασιλέα τῶν»
Τῆς καρτερίας σου τῷ στερρῷ
  ἀνατρέπων | προσβολὰς τυράννου ἀνεβόας
  «Χριστὸν ὑπερυψοῦτε | εἰς πάντας ⟨τοὺς αἰῶνας⟩.»

Τὴν κεκρυμμένην ποθῶν ζωὴν
  ἐνεδύσω | τοῦ Χριστοῦ τὴν νέκρωσιν δοξάζων
  τοῦτον ὡς δεσπότην | εἰς πάντας τοὺς αἰῶνας.

94–96: *Acta Greg.* (supra), 30, 5–31, 3. ‖ 101–102: Rom. 13:12. ‖ 115: cf. Dan. 3:57, etc. ‖ 116: Coloss. 3:3. ‖ 117: Rom. 13:14; 2 Cor. 4:10.

---

95 ὁρίζουσι ΛΘ: ὀρύσσουσι Δ ‖ 98 σε] σοι Λ ‖ 100 σεπτὴ Λ ‖ 101 immo ταῖς, cf. *Acta Greg.* (supra), 45, 1–46, 2 ‖ 114 τοῦ τυράννου ἐβόας ΛΘ ‖ 115 κ(ύριο)ν ὑμνεῖτε καὶ ὑπερ Λ κ(ύριο)ν ὑμνεῖτε καὶ πρ(΄) Θ ‖ 116 πόθω Δ ‖ 118 κ(ύριο)ν ὑμνεῖτε· καὶ ὑπερ Λ καὶ ὑπερυψῶν τὸν χ(ριστὸ)ν εἰς τοὺς αἰῶν(ας) Θ

204

The beasts dwelling in the depth of impiety consign you to a pit, a dwelling of wild beasts; but you are received in the House of Light, crying out: "God of our fathers, blessed art Thou!"

Chaste Rhipsimia with her companions, wearing the divine armor of light, put the Prince of Darkness to rout with the cry: "God of our fathers, blessed art Thou!"

Incarnated from a virgin womb you manifested yourself for our salvation; therefore, acknowledging your mother as the Mother of God, we cry out in gratitude: "God of our fathers, blessed art Thou!"

Ode 8. *"Ton basilea tōn"*

By your firm constancy you foiled the attacks of the oppressor, shouting: "Exalted be Christ for ever and ever!"

Longing for the hidden life, you put on the dying of Christ, glorifying him as your Master for ever and ever.

204

Τῇ ἀσθενείᾳ σου, Ἰησοῦ,
  ἀνδρωθεῖσα | γυναικεία φύσις σε δοξάζει
  τὸν ἀγωνοθέτην | εἰς πάντας τοὺς αἰῶνας.

Φωτιστικήν σε καὶ χρυσαυγῆ
  τὸ σκηνῶσαν | ἐν σοὶ φῶς ἀπρόσιτον, παρθένε,
  ἔδειξε λαμπάδα | εἰς πάντας τοὺς αἰῶνας.

ᾠδὴ θ΄. «Κυρίως θεοτόκον»
Ἠλλάξω τῶν μαστίγων
ἄνεσιν τὴν θείαν
  καὶ ἀτιμίας τιμὴν τὴν ἀίδιον,
  ἱερομάρτυς, ἀφθάρτῳ | στέφει στεφόμενος.

Φρουρὰ ἡ τῶν τυράννων,
μάρτυς, σοὶ ἀνοίγει
  τῆς οὐρανῶν βασιλείας τὴν εἴσοδον,
  ἐν ᾗ συγχαίρων ἀγγέλοις | θεῷ παρίστασαι.

Θεόφρον Ῥιψιμία,
ἄνθος σωφροσύνης,
  τροπαιοφόρος γενοῦ τῶν παθῶν ἡμῶν,
  ὡς ἐτροπώσω τυράννου | τὴν ἐπανάστασιν.

Ὡραῖος, θεοτόκε,
ἔφυ ὁ καρπός σου,
  οὐχὶ φθορᾶς τοῖς μετέχουσι πρόξενος,
  ἀλλὰ ζωῆς τοῖς ἐν πίστει | σὲ μεγαλύνουσι.

123: 1 Tim. 6:16. ‖ 138–140: cf. Gen. 3:6.

---

119 ἀσθενεία ΛΔ: δυναστεία Θ ‖ 120 ἀνδρειωθεῖσα ΛΔ ‖ 130 φρουρὰ ΛΔ: φθορὰ Θ ‖ 133 ἐν ᾗ ΘΔ: ἐνοῖς Λ ‖ 141 μακαρίζουσιν Δ

204

Womanhood, made manly by your weakness, Jesus, glorifies you, the judge in the contest, for ever and ever.

The inaccessible Light that dwelt in you, Virgin, made you a luminous lamp, shining like gold, for ever and ever.

Ode 9. *"Kyriōs theotokon"*

You passed from whiplashes to divine repose and from dishonor to eternal honor, Martyr and Priest, crowned with an imperishable crown.

The guard of the oppressors opens for you, Martyr, the entrance to the kingdom of heaven, where you rejoice with the angels, standing before God.

Godly Rhipsimia, flower of modesty, triumph over our passions, as you defeated the oppressor's assault.

Pleasant, O Mother of God, was your fruit, not bringing perdition on those who partake of it, but life to those who in true faith glorify you.

205. Stichera to Peter and Paul

Στιχηρά, ἦχος δ'. Νικολάου πατριάρχου

Ὁ στόματι οὐρανίῳ | τὰ ἐπὶ γῆς οὐρανώσας
Πέτρος σήμερον ὑμνείσθω | νῦν ἀναστρέψας·
δρόμον γὰρ ὡραίων ποδῶν
πορείαν | πρὸς τὴν ἄνω ἀποπτὰς
κάτωθεν ἀνέδραμεν | πρὸς τὸν κατελθόντα
τοῦ ζωγρῆσαι αὐτόν,
καὶ χεῖρας ἐξήπλωσεν | ζώνην μαρτυρίου | εἰς τὸ ζώσασθαι
κατ' ἴχνος ἑπόμενος | τῷ διδασκάλῳ, | ὃν ἠγνόησεν πρίν·
καὶ τῆς σαγήνης | προσφέρων τὴν ἄγραν
ὄψον τῇ θείᾳ τραπέζῃ λαμβάνει
μισθὸν τὸν θρόνον τοῦ θεοῦ
κρίσιν τε τὴν πάνδημον.

Ὁ ἥλιος τῶν δογμάτων | ὁ τοῦ φωτὸς ἀπορροίας
πληρωθεὶς διωκομένου | ἀνευφημείσθω·
Παῦλος ἐκλογῆς
τὸ σκεῦος, | δι' οὗ μύρα τῆς ζωῆς
πέρατα ὠσφράνθησαν | κάρου ἀπιστίας
ἀνασχόντα δεινῆς·
τὸ στόμα τὸ ἥδιστον, | ὅθεν τῆς ἀγάπης | βλύζει ἄβυσσος,
ἐξ οὗ τὸν πολύτιμον | σωρεύει κόσμος | μαργαρίτην στοργῆς·
νῦν τῶν ἐσόπτρων, | μαθητά, λυθέντων
καὶ τῶν σαρκίνων παραπετασμάτων,
προσεντυγχάνεις θεῷ,
οὗ φορεῖς τὰ στίγματα.

205: 2: cf. Matth. 16:15–19; 18:18. ‖ 3: cf. Luc. 22:32. ‖ 4: Rom. 10:15; Is. 52:7. ‖ 7: cf. Luc. 5:10; 2 Tim. 2:26. ‖ 8: Ioann. 21:18–19. ‖ 9: Ioann. 21:19–22. ‖ Matth. 26:69–75; Marc. 14:66–72; Luc. 22:54–62; Ioann. 18:25–27. ‖ 10–11: cf. Ioann. 21:4–13. ‖ 12–13: Matth. 19:27–28. ‖ 14–15: Act. 9:3–9. ‖ 16–17: Act. 9:15. ‖ 20: 1 Cor. 13. ‖ 21: Matth. 13:46. ‖ 22: 1 Cor. 13:12. ‖ 25: Gal. 6:17.

205: Σ 2^{v}–3^{r} ‖ 11 λαμβάνη Σ ‖ 16 desid. 3 syllabae ‖ 24 προσεντυγχάνης Σ

205

205. Stichera to Peter and Paul

Stichera, fourth mode. By Nicholas the Patriarch.

He who by his heavenly word changed things on earth to things in heaven, Peter, must be sung today, since it is now that he has returned home: he ran the course of the beautiful feet, he took his upward flight, and from here below he ascended to the One who came down to catch him. He stretched forth his hands to be girded with the girdle of martyrdom, following in the footsteps of his Teacher, whom he had denied before; and offering the catch of his net for a dish on the Divine Table, he received in return the throne of God and judgment upon all nations.

The Sun of the Faith, imbued with the radiance of the Light he persecuted, must be celebrated in song: Paul, the chosen vessel, through whom came to the ends of the earth the fragrance of the ointments of life, waking them up from the torpor of deadly unbelief; that mouth so sweet, the fountain of the deep waters of love, from which the world gathers the precious pearls of tenderness. Now, Disciple of Christ, the mirrors taken away and the veils of the body, you meet God face to face, of whose wounds you bear the marks.

206

Ἕτερος κανὼν παρακλητικὸς εἰς τὸν ἅγιον Νικόλαον ἐν τοῖς θεοτοκίοις «Νικολάου»

ᾠδὴ α΄. ἦχος πλ. β΄. «Κύματι θαλάσσης»
Πάτερ θεοφόρε, | πατέρων ἀκρότης,
σοφὲ Νικόλαε,
μὴ ὑπερίδῃς με | καταφυγόντα τῇ σκέπῃ
τὸν ἀνάξιον καὶ ἄθλιον | τῆς σεπτῆς πρεσβείας σου
τυχεῖν με τῆς αἰτήσεως.

Ἅρπασον χειρῶν με | ἀδίκων ἀνθρώπων,
πάτερ Νικόλαε,
καὶ διαφύλαξον, | ὅτι ἰδοὺ ὥσπερ κύνες
ὠρυόμενοι ζητοῦσί με | ἀπολέσαι, ἅγιε·
ἐλέησον τὸν δοῦλόν σου.

Μή με ἀποστρέψῃς | θλιβόμενον, πάτερ,
τῆς ἀντιλήψεως
τῆς σῆς τὸν ἄσωτον· | μὴ ἐκκακήσῃς ἀκούων
τῆς φωνῆς τῆς ἀναξίας μου· | ὅσα θέλεις δύνασαι,
ἐπίσκεψαί με, ἅγιε.

Νεῦσον, παναγία, | ἁγία ἁγίων,
παρθένε δέσποινα,
Χριστιανῶν ἡ ἐλπίς, | τῇ ἀναξίᾳ δεήσει
τοῦ οἰκέτου σου· εἰσάκουσον, | ἀσθενοῦντα ἴασαι
καὶ σῶσόν με τὸν δείλαιον.

ᾠδὴ γ΄. «Σὲ τὸν ἐπὶ ὑδάτων»
Ἀσθενοῦντά με, πάτερ, | ἀνάστησον
ἀπεγνωσμένον ὄντα·
ὡς ὁ Χριστὸς τὴν παῖδα | τοῦ Ἰαΐρου ἀνέστησεν,
οὕτως κἀμὲ τὸν δοῦλόν σου, | πατέρων ἄριστε,
σῶσον, ἅγιε Νικόλαε.

206: 16: Luc. 15:13. ‖ 27: Marc. 5:22–43; Luc. 8:41–56.

206: Ξ 133^{r}–134^{r} Γ 22^{r}–24^{v} Φ 92^{v}–96^{v} ‖ initia hirmorum secundum Ξ dedi ‖ 1 ἕτερος κανὼν εἰς τὸν ὅσιον π(ατέ)ρα ἡμῶν νικόλαον Γ Κανὼν παρακλητικὸς τοῦ ὁσ(ίου) π(ατ)ρ(ὸ)ς ἡμῶν νικολ(άου) Φ ‖ 7 τῆς σεπτῆς Ξ: τῇ θερμῇ ΓΦ ‖ πρεσβεία Γ ‖ 8 τύχιμοι τῆς ἰάσεως Γ ‖ 9–13 post 18 pon. Γ ‖ 9 ἐξάρπασων Φ ‖ 10–11 καὶ διαφύλαξον πάτερ νικόλαε colloc. Γ ‖ 10 πάτερ] σοφέ Φ ‖ 11 ἰδοῦ ὅτι colloc. Φ ‖ 16 ἐγκακήσεις Φ ‖ 21 ἡ – 22 εἰσάκουσον om. Γ ‖ 22 ἐπάκουσον Φ ‖ ἀσθενοῦντα ἴασαι Ξ: ἀσθενῆ ἀνάστησον ΓΦ ‖ 23 δείλαιον Ξ: δοῦλόν σου ΓΦ ‖ 27–28 vss. 37–38 hic habent, vss. 26–28 loco vss. 36–38 pon. ΓΦ ‖ 27 ὡς – παῖδα om. Φ ‖ τοῦ] τῆς Γ ‖ ἰαείρου Ξ

206

Another Supplicatory Canon to Saint Nicholas
In the theotokia the acrostic *"Nikolaou"*

Ode 1. Second plagal mode. *"Kymati thalassēs"*

Father inspired, most exalted of fathers, wise Nicholas, do not forsake me, as I take refuge, unworthy and miserable, in the shelter of your venerable intercession, that I may obtain my request.

Snatch me from the hands of unjust men, Father Nicholas, and protect me, for behold, like howling dogs they seek to destroy me, o holy one; take pity on your servant.

Do not turn me away in my distress, Father, from your help, me the prodigal; do not weary of listening to my unworthy voice; whatever you want, you can do: take care of me, holy one.

Lend your ear, All-holy One, Holy of Holy Ones, Virgin Lady, Hope of Christians, to the unworthy prayer of your servant; hear me, cure my sickness, and save me in my misery.

Ode 3. *"Se ton epi hydatōn"*

From my sickness, Father, raise me, for whom there is no hope; as Christ raised up the daughter of Jairus, so save me, your servant also, kindest of fathers, holy Nicholas.

206

Ἰδοὺ ἐπέστη ἡ ὥρα, | ψυχὴ ταπεινή,
τοῦ βίου μετελθεῖν σε·
ἰδοὺ τὸ τέλος ἦλθεν, | ἰδοὺ τὰς χεῖρας ἐκτείνασα
εἰς οὐρανὸν καὶ ὄμματα | «μὴ ὑπερίδῃς με»
κράξον «ἅγιε Νικόλαε.»

Ἐλέησόν με, βοῶ σοι, | πανάγιε,
ἀπογνωσθέντα ὅλως
ὑπὸ τῶν συγγενῶν μου, | ὑπὸ οἰκείων καὶ φίλων μου·
αὐτὸς μὴ ὑπερίδῃς με | δεινῶς στενάζοντα
«σῶσον, ἅγιε Νικόλαε.»

Ἴασαί με, θεοτόκε, | ἡ πάντων πιστῶν
ἐλπὶς καὶ προστασία,
ἡ βοηθὸς καὶ σκέπη | τῶν θλιβομένων, ἀνάστησον
τῇ ἀσθενείᾳ κείμενον | ἐμὲ τὸν δοῦλόν σου·
πέλεις γὰρ ἀπελπισμένων ἐλπίς.

ᾠδὴ δʹ. «Τὴν ἐν σταυρῷ σου»
Ὁλολαμπὴς ὑπάρχων, ἅγιε,
σκοτισθέντα με | ὑπὸ τῆς ἀθυμίας
καταύγασόν με, δέομαι, | φώτισον, σοφέ·
παρρησίαν γὰρ ἔχεις πρὸς τὸν φιλάνθρωπον.

Οἱ τὴν ψυχὴν ἐπηρεάζοντες
ἐπληθύνθησαν | ζητοῦντες ἀπολέσαι
τὸν δοῦλόν σου, πανάγιε, | γλῶσσαι δολεραί·
τὰς βουλὰς αὐτῶν θραῦσον κἀμὲ ἐλέησον.

Ἐπὶ τῆς κλίνης κατακείμενον
καὶ βαρούμενον | ὑπὸ τῆς ἀθυμίας
τῷ λόγῳ σου, Νικόλαε, | ἅγιε θεοῦ,
ἐξανάστησον ὥσπερ τὸν παρειμένον Χριστός.

49: 1 Ioann. 3:21. ‖ 52: cf. Ps. 51:6; 108:2; 119:2; 3. ‖ 57: Matth. 9:1–8; Marc. 2:1–12; Luc. 5:17–26.

---

32 τὸ om. Φ ‖ ἦλθεν Ξ: ἦξεν Γ εἶξεν Φ ‖ ἐκτείνασα Ξ ἐκτίνω σοι Γ ἐκτήνω συχνὸς Φ ‖ 33 οὐ(ρα)νοῦς Φ ‖ 34 κράξον Ξ: κράζων ΓΦ ‖ 36–38 vss. 26–28 hic hab. ΓΦ ‖ 37 οἰκείων Ξ: ἰδίων ΓΦ ‖ 40 με om. Ξ ‖ θεοτόκε] παρθένε Φ ‖ 43 δοῦλόν σου] ἄσωτον Γ ‖ 44 ἀπελπισμένων] sic ΞΓΦ (item in 82) ‖ 46 ὑπάρχων ἅγιε Ξ: ὢν (ὂν Φ) σὺ πανάγιε ΓΦ ‖ 47 με] δεινῶς Ξ ‖ 48 φώτισον σοφέ Ξ: τὸν ἠμιθανῆ Γ -ῆν Φ ‖ 50 ἐπηρεάζοντες Ξ: μου ἐκπειράζοντες Γ μου περεάζωντες Φ ‖ 51 ἐπληθύνθησαν] νῦν add. Γ(Φ) ‖ 52 πανάγιε] νικόλαε Φ ‖ δολεραὶ] πονηρας (sic) Φ ‖ 54 κατακείμενος ΞΓ ‖ 55 βαρούμενος ΞΓ ‖ ἀθυμίας] ἁμαρτείας Φ ‖ 56 τῷ — Νικόλαε] καταύγασόν με δέομαι Γ

Behold, the hour has come, my lowly soul, for you to pass from this life; behold, the end has come; now, lifting up your arms and eyes to heaven, cry out: "Do not forsake me, holy Nicholas!"

Have pity on me, as I cry out to you, all-holy one, now that all hope for me has been abandoned by my kinsmen, my companions, and my friends; do not forsake me, as I sigh pitifully: "Save me, holy Nicholas!"

Heal me, Mother of God, hope and support of all the faithful, helper and shelter of the oppressed, raise me up, your servant laid low by sickness; for you are the hope of the hopeless.

Ode 4. *"Tēn en staurō sou"*

You that are all splendor, holy one, shine upon me, I pray, who am enveloped by the darkness of despondency, enlighten me, wise one; for God the Merciful lends you his ear.

Those who harass my soul have multiplied, seeking to destroy your servant, most holy one, with their treacherous tongues; shatter their counsels and take pity on me.

As I lie on my bed, weighed down by despair, raise me up by your word, Nicholas, saint of God, as Christ raised the one that was sick of the palsy.

206

Κυριοτόκε ἀπειρόγαμε,
μὴ ἐάσῃς με | εἰς τέλος ἀπολέσθαι·
ἀνάστησόν με, δέσποινα, | τὸν ἡμιθανῆ
κατακείμενον ἄφωνον καὶ δακρύοντα.

ᾠδὴ ε΄. «Θεοφανείας σου, Χριστέ»
Τῶν θλιβομένων βοηθὸς
ἐπικληθεὶς ἐξ ὀνόματος ὤφθης,
καὶ ἐρρύσω, ἅγιε Νικόλαε,
τοὺς τρεῖς στρατηλάτας τοὺς μέλλοντας
ἀναιτίους διὰ νυκτὸς | ἀναιρεθῆναι τούτους
ὑπὸ τοῦ ἐπάρχου·
ἐλέησον καὶ ἐμὲ ταῖς ἱκεσίαις σου.

Νεκρὰν ἐγείρας Ταβιθὰ
θλίψεις πολλὰς καταπαύει ὁ Πέτρος·
ὁ δὲ Παῦλος Εὔτυχον ἐζώωσεν
κρημνισθέντα, πάτερ Νικόλαε·
διὸ σπεῦσον, ὅτι ἰδοὺ | ἀπεγνωσμένος εἰμὶ
ἐκ παντὸς ἀνθρώπου·
ἀνάστησον, δυσωπῶ σε, παναοίδιμε.

Ἐλέησόν με, ὁ θεός,
τὸν κείμενον ἐπὶ κλίνης ὀδύνης
ἱκεσίαις τοῦ οὐρανοφάντορος
Νικολάου τοῦ σοῦ θεράποντος,
ὅτι κεῖμαι καὶ δυσπετῶ | ἀπορραγεὶς τὸ σῶμα
καὶ ἀπελπισμένος·
ἐπάκουσον, ἀγαθέ, καὶ ἐξανάστησον.

Οὐδεὶς προστρέχων ἐπὶ σοί,
πανύμνητε θεοτόκε παρθένε,
ὁλοψύχως, κενὸς ἐκπορεύεται,
ἀλλ᾽ εὐθὺς λαμβάνει τὸ αἴτημα·
οὕτως, δέσποινα, καὶ ἐμὲ | μὴ ἀποστρέψῃς κενὸν
τῆς σῆς βοηθείας,
ἀλλ᾽ ἕξω χάριν καὶ φῶς καὶ ἀγαλλίαμα.

63–68: G. Anrich, *Hagios Nikolaos,* I (Lipsiae, 1913), 67–77 et 129, 9–130, 18. ‖ 70–71: Act. 9:40–41. ‖ 72–73: Act. 20:9–12. ‖ 78: Ps. 40:4.

---

60 δέσποινα] δέομαι Γ(Φ) ‖ 61 ἄφον Φ ‖ 68 ὑπάρχου Ξ ‖ 70 ταβηθὰν Γ: -ᾶ Φ ‖ 73 πάτερ] ἅγιε Φ ‖ 79 ἱεροφάντωρος Γ(Φ) ‖ 81 δυσωπῶ Γ ‖ 82 ἀπεγνωσμένος ΓΦ ‖ 83 ἀγαθὲ καὶ ἐξανάστησον Ξ: καὶ ἐμὲ (ἐμοῦ Φ) ταῖς ἱκε- σίαις σου ΓΦ ‖ 86 καὶ κενὸς Γ(Φ) ‖ πορεύεται Γ ‖ 90 ἕξω] εὕρω Γ

206

Mother of God, untouched by man, do not let me perish forever; raise me up, Our Lady, as I lie half dead, speechless and weeping.

Ode 5. *"Theophaneias sou, Christe"*

You appeared when called by name, a helper of the oppressed, and you saved, holy Nicholas, the three commanders, when the moment was near for them to be innocently slain at night by the prefect; take pity also on me through your entreaties.

When Peter raised up dead Tabitha, he assuaged the sorrows of many; Paul restored life to Eutychus after his headlong fall, Father Nicholas; therefore hasten, for behold! I have been given up for dead by every man; raise me, I beseech you, most glorious one.

Have mercy upon me, O God, as I lie on my bed of languishing, through the entreaties of the revealer of heaven, Nicholas, thy servant; for I lie in misery, my body torn, bereft of hope; listen to me, Good Lord, and raise me again.

No one that took refuge with you with all his heart, ever-praised virgin Mother of God, goes away empty-handed, but forthwith he receives what he asked; thus, Our Lady, do not turn me away deprived of your help, but let me find grace and light and rejoicing.

206

ᾠδὴ ς΄. «Συνεσχέθη, ἀλλ᾽ οὐ κατεσχέθη»
Ἁγιάζεις | καὶ καταφωτίζεις,
  πάτερ, τὰς ψυχὰς τῶν βροτῶν·
σοῦ γὰρ τὸ εἶδος φέρει
  φωτισμὸν καὶ φωταυγῆ ἀκτῖνα
  καὶ καταυγάζει | ὁ ναός σου ἅπαντας
τοὺς προστρέχοντας καὶ δυσωποῦντας
  καὶ ἀνυμνοῦντάς σε, ἅγιε τοῦ θεοῦ·
  δέξαι καὶ ἡμᾶς παρακαλοῦντάς σε.

Σοὶ προσπίπτω | δάκρυσιν ὁ τάλας,
  ἅγιε Νικόλαε,
ὅτι ἰδοὺ ἐκλείπω
  καὶ ἐτάκη ὡς κηρὸς τὸ σῶμα
  καὶ ἡ ψυχή μου | πλήρης ἡ κατώδυνος·
ἐπικάμφθητί μου τῇ δεήσει
  καὶ ἐξανάστησον, ἅγιε τοῦ θεοῦ,
  ὥσπερ ὁ Χριστὸς τὸν τετραήμερον.

Οἱ ἀδίκως | μέλλοντες τεθνάναι
  εὗρόν σε λιμένα ζωῆς·
λιμὴν ὁ σὸς ναὸς γὰρ
  καὶ ἀντίληψις τοῖς ἐν ἀνάγκαις·
  διὸ προσπίπτω, | ἅγιε Νικόλαε,
παρακλήθητι καὶ μὴ ἀπώσῃ,
  ὅτι ἐξέλιπεν ὅλη μου ἡ ἰσχύς·
  τύχω διὰ σοῦ τῆς προσδοκίας μου.

Λευκανθῆναι, | δέσποινα, αἰτοῦμαι
  τὴν ἐσκοτισμένην ψυχήν·
ἠμαυρωμένος γάρ μου
  καὶ ὁ βίος καὶ ὁ χρόνος ἐστίν·
  δεδοξασμένη, | ἅγνισόν με, πάναγνε,
καὶ ἀνάστησόν με, θεοτόκε,
  καὶ τοῦ φωτός με υἱὸν ἔργασαι, ὅτι φῶς
  ἔτεκες Χριστόν, διό με φώτισον.

103: Ps. 21:15. ‖ 104: cf. Iob 7:4. ‖ 107: Ioann. 11:33–44. ‖ 114: Ps. 70:9. ‖ 122: Luc. 16:8; Ioann. 12:36; 1 Thess. 5:5.

---

93 βροτῶν Ξ: πιστῶν ΓΦ ‖ 94 φέροι Γ ‖ 95 ἀκτῖνας Γ(Φ) ‖ 98 ἀνυμνοῦντα Γ ‖ 99 παρακαλοῦντα Γ ‖ 102 ἰδοὺ om. Γ ‖ 103 ἐτάκην Γ(Φ) ‖ σῶμα] πν(εῦμ)α Γ ‖ 104 ἡ^{2} Wk: εἰ Ξ ἦν Γ ἣν Φ ‖ 106 ἀνάστησον Γ ‖ 109 εὕρου Φ ‖ 110 λιμὴν γὰρ ὁ ναός σου ΓΦ ‖ 111 τοῖς ἐν ἀνάγκαις] τῶν ἐπανισταμένων Ξ ‖ 112 προσπίπτω] σοι add. ΓΦ ‖ 115 διάσαι (= διὰ σὲ) Φ ‖ 117 μου ψυχὴν ΓΦ ‖ 119 καὶ^{1} om. Φ ‖ 120 post δεδοξασμένη] σεμὴ (= σεμνὴ?) Γ ‖ ἅγνισόν με, πάναγνε] σῶσον με πανάχραντε Φ ‖ 121 με] ὦ Γ ‖ 123 Χριστόν] ἁγνὴ Γ ‖ διού Φ

206

Ode 6. *"Syneschethē, all' ou kateschethē"*

You sanctify and illuminate, Father, the souls of mortals; for your appearance brings illumination and radiant brightness, and your temple sheds light upon all who flee to you and implore you and celebrate you, Saint of God; receive us also as your supplicants.

I throw myself at your feet in tears, a miserable wretch, holy Nicholas, for behold, I am failing, my body has melted like wax, and my soul is full of woe; stoop down to my prayer and raise me up, Saint of God, as Christ raised Lazarus on the fourth day.

Those about to die unjustly found you a haven of life; yes, your temple is a haven and a refuge for those in distress; therefore I implore you, holy Nicholas, listen to my prayer and do not reject me, for all my strength has failed; let me obtain my desire through you.

Let my darkened soul, I pray you, Our Lady, be made white, for tarnished are my life and my age; Glorious One, All-pure One, purify me, raise me up, Mother of God, and make me a child of light, for you bore the Light that is Christ; therefore enlighten me.

ᾠδὴ ζ'. «Ἄφραστον θαῦμα»
Ὢ ξένον θαῦμα· | τοῦ ἐν πενίᾳ ὑπάρχοντος
ὡς ἐρρύσω ὕλης ἀπεχθοῦς
κόρια σεμνά, | μέλλοντα εἰς βάραθρον
τῆς ἀτιμίας | εἰσδῦναι οὐκ ἐάσας·
τῷ χρυσῷ γὰρ αὐτὰ | ἔσωσας, πάτερ.

Πάσης πικρίας | ἐπερχομένης ἐκλύτρωσαι,
ἱεράρχα, τὸν ἁμαρτωλόν,
ἀνθρώπων δεινῶν | καὶ θανατηφόρου ὁρμῆς
καὶ ἀδικίας | καὶ πάσης καταιγίδος,
εἰρηνεύσας τὸν νοῦν | καὶ τὴν ζωήν μου.

Ἐπὶ τὸ βάθος | τῆς εὐσπλαγχνίας κατέφυγα
καὶ τὸ ὕψος τῶν σῶν δωρεῶν·
ἀνάστησόν με, | ἅγιε Νικόλαε,
ἵνα κραυγάζω | ῥυσθεὶς ἐκ τῶν κακῶν μου
«λυτρωτὰ ὁ θεός, | εὐλογητὸς εἶ.»

Ἁγνὴ παρθένε, | ἴδε τὴν θλίψιν τοῦ σώματος
καὶ γενοῦ μοι ῥῶσις ἀγαθή·
ἰδοὺ τὰ ὀστᾶ | πάντα συνετρίβησαν
καὶ οἱ νεφροί μου· | ἀνάστησον κραυγάζειν
«λυτρωτὰ ὁ θεός, | εὐλογητὸς εἶ.»

ᾠδὴ η'. «Ἔκστηθι φρίττων»
Σπεῦσον κατάλαβε ταχύ,
πάτερ Νικόλαε, | ὅτι σπεύδει κατ' ἐμοῦ
ἡ ψῆφος τοῦ θανάτου μέλλουσα | καταδικάσαι με
ὥσπερ τὴν συκῆν τὴν ξηρανθεῖσαν·
καὶ ἔκτεινόν μοι χεῖρα | καὶ ἀνάστησον τάχος,
ἵνα σε δοξάζω | εἰς πάντας τοὺς αἰῶνας.

125–29: Anrich, *Hagios Nikolaos,* I, 118, 10–123, 6. ‖ 142: cf. Ps. 21:15. ‖ 149: Marc. 11:13; 20; Matth. 21:19. ‖ 150: cf. Act. 3:7; 9:41.

---

125 τοὺς . . . ὑπάρχοντας Γ ‖ 127 μέλλοντας Φ ‖ βάραθρα ΓΦ ‖ 128 ἀτιμίας] ἀπωλείας Γ ‖ εἰσδοῦναι Φ ‖ 129 αὐτὰς ΓΦ ‖ 130 πιρίας Φ ‖ με λύτρωσαι Γ(Φ) ‖ 133 καὶ ἀδικίας] τῶν ἀδικούντων Φ ‖ ἀδικίας] ἁμαρτίας Γ ‖ 134 εἰρηνεῦσαι Γ ‖ νοῦν] μου add. Γ ‖ 135 σῆς Φ ‖ 136 δωρεῶν] οἰκτιρμῶν Γ ‖ 141 ἀγαθή] ἐναργῆ Φ ‖ 142 ἴδε Γ ‖ 143 κραυγάζειν Ξ: με κράζειν Φ με ψάλλειν Γ ‖ 146 κατάβαλε Γ ‖ 150 καὶ[1]] ἀλλ' Γ ‖ καὶ[2] — τάχος] βοηθείας παμμάκαρ Φ ‖ τάχος] ψάλλειν Γ ‖ 151 σὲ Φ

206

Ode 7. *"Aphraston thauma"*

Oh, the astounding miracle, how you rescued from loathsome mire the poor man's chaste daughters, not allowing them to sink down into the gulf of shame; with your gold you saved them, Father.

Deliver me, a sinner, from all the hardship that assails me, holy Bishop, from treacherous men and deadly assault and injustice and all turmoil, granting peace to my mind and my life.

I take refuge in the profundity of your mercy and in the sublimity of your gifts; raise me up, holy Nicholas, so that I may cry out, delivered from my ills: "God our Liberator, blessed art Thou!"

Pure Virgin, look upon the affliction of my body and be to me a goodly source of strength; see, my bones and my kidneys are all crushed; raise me up, so that I may cry: "God, our Liberator, blessed art Thou!"

Ode 8. *"Ekstēthi phrittōn"*

Hasten, come to me soon, Father Nicholas, for without delay the sentence of death will be pronounced on me as on the fig tree that withered; stretch out your hand to me and raise me up fast, so that I may glorify you for ever and ever.

206

Τῆς χαλεπῆς με συμφορᾶς
νῦν ἐξανάστησον, | ἐπιστάτα ἀγαθέ·
ἰδοὺ γὰρ τὰ μὲν χείλη ἔπτυξα, | ὧδε κἀκεῖσε συχνῶς
ὄμματα καὶ χεῖρας περιστρέφων·
οὐδεὶς δὲ βοηθῆσαι | ἢ ἐγεῖραι ἢ σῶσαι
πλήν σου, ἱεράρχα, | διὸ ἐπίσκεψαί με.

Τίς σοι προσέδραμεν ποτέ,
τίς σε ἐκάλεσεν | ἐξ ὀνόματος, σοφέ,
βοήσας «ἅγιε Νικόλαε,» | καὶ οὐκ εὐθὺς βοηθὸς
ἐγένου τοῖς σὲ προσκαλουμένοις;
κἀμὲ μὴ ἀποστρέψῃς, | ἀλλὰ τύχω ὁ τάλας
τῆς ἐλπιζομένης | ψυχικῆς σωτηρίας.

Ὅλος ὑπάρχω ῥυπαρός,
ὅλος αἰσχρός εἰμι | καὶ οὐ βλέπω σου τὸ φῶς·
ἁγία θεοτόκε, φώτισον | τὴν ταπεινήν μου ψυχὴν
καὶ δώρησαι καιρὸν μετανοίας,
αἰνεῖν τε καὶ δοξάζειν, | παναγία παρθένε,
σὲ καὶ τὸν υἱόν σου | πρεσβείαις τοῦ ὁσίου.

ᾠδὴ θ'. «Μὴ ἐποδύρου μοι, μῆτερ»
Συνημιλλήθης ἀγγέλοις, | τῆς ἁγίας τριάδος
ὁμιλητὴς καὶ θεατὴς | ὑπάρχων ὡς Μωσῆς,
ἐκ προνοίας θείας | ἱερουργὸς χειρισθείς·
παρρησίαν ὡς ἔχων, | σοφέ, πρὸς τὸν θεὸν
μὴ ἐλλίπῃς πρεσβεύειν | ὑπὲρ τῶν δούλων σου.

Οἱ καταφεύγοντες πίστει | ἐν τῷ οἴκῳ σου, πάτερ,
τῶν θλιβερῶν καὶ λυπηρῶν | λυτροῦνται παρευθύ·
μὴ ἀπώσῃ κἀμέ, | τῶν ὀρφανῶν ὁ πατήρ,
ἀλλὰ δέξαι καὶ ῥῦσαι | ἀνθρώπων πονηρῶν,
ἱεράρχα, καὶ σῶσόν | με τὸν ἀνάξιον.

171–175: Anrich, 123, 7–127, 8. ‖ 172: Deut. 34:10; Num. 12:8. ‖ 174: 1 Ioann. 3:21. ‖ 178: Ps. 67:5.

---

153 ἐπιστάτα] εὐεργέτα ΓΦ ‖ 155 περιστρέφω ΓΦ ‖ 159 σοφέ] ποτὲ Γ ‖ 161 προσκαλούμενος Ξ παρακαλοῦσιν ΓΦ ‖ 162 ἀποστρέψῃς Ξ: -εις Φ ἀπορρίψῃς Γ ‖ 163 τῆς ἐλπιζομένης] τοῖς ἐπικειμένοις Φ ‖ 167 δώρησαί μοι Γ(Φ) ‖ 168 τε] σε Γ(Φ) ‖ 173 ἱερουργὸς] γὰρ add. Γ ‖ 174 ὡς] γὰρ Φ ‖ 175 ἐλλείπῃς Γ ἐλλύπεις Φ ‖ πρεσβεύον Φ ‖ τοὺς δούλους Φ ‖ 177 λυτροῦται Γ(Φ) ‖ παρ' εὐθὺς Γ(Φ) ‖ 178 ἀπώσῃ] ἐάσῃς Γ

From my cruel misfortune now lift me up, good Master; for behold, I have shaped my lips, turning hither and thither again and again my eyes and my arms; but there is no one to help me or lift me up or save me, except you, holy Bishop; therefore visit me.

Who has ever taken refuge with you, who has called you by your name, wise one, crying out "Holy Nicholas!" and you did not forthwith become a helper for those who invoked you? Do not reject me either, but let me, wretch that I am, find the salvation of my soul for which I hope.

I am all soiled, I am all ugly, and I do not see your light; Holy Mother of God, enlighten my lowly soul and grant me time for repentance, to praise and glorify, Most Holy Virgin, you and your Son, by the intercession of the Saint.

Ode 9. *"Mē epodyrou moi, mēter"*

You vied with the angels, speaking, like Moses, face to face with the Holy Trinity, ordained priest by Divine Providence. Since you, wise one, can speak freely to God, do not cease from interceding for your servants.

Those who in faith take refuge in your house, Father, are freed forthwith from oppression and grief; do not reject me, father of orphans, but let me in and rescue me from evil men, holy Bishop, and save me, unworthy though I am.

Δέξαι τὸν αἶνον καὶ δίδου | ἀμοιβὴν τῇ ψυχῇ μου
καὶ τῆς μελλούσης κρίσεως | διάσωσον, σοφέ·
μὴ στερήσης, αἰτοῦμαι, | τοῦ χοροῦ τῶν πιστῶν,
χαριστήριον δέ μου | προσδέχου τὴν εὐχήν,
ἵνα τύχω ἐλέους, | πάτερ Νικόλαε.

Ὑπερασπίζῃ σπουδαίως, | παναγία παρθένε,
τῶν γηγενῶν καὶ διασῴζεις | νόσων ψυχικῶν·
διὸ δὴ καὶ ἐμὲ | παρακαλοῦντά σε
συμφορῶν καὶ κινδύνων | καὶ βλάβης τοῦ ἐχθροῦ
ἐλευθέρωσον μόνη, | θεοχαρίτωτε.

207

Κανὼν εὐχαριστήριος εἰς τὴν ὑπεραγίαν θεοτόκον οὗ ἡ ἀκροστιχὶς «Ἡ βασιλὶς τὰ σῶστρα σοὶ τῇ παρθένῳ» ἐν δὲ τοῖς θεοτοκίοις «Νικολάου»

ᾠδὴ α΄. ἦχος δ΄. «Ἀνοίξω τὸ στόμα μου»
Ἠιρέτισας, ἄχραντε, | λαὸν καὶ πόλιν βασίλειον
οἰκεῖν ὡς βασίλισσα | καὶ βασιλεύειν αὐτῆς·
ἣν ἁλώσεως | βαρβάρων ἀνωτέραν
φυλάττοις γεραίρουσαν | τὰ μεγαλεῖά σου.

Βαβαὶ τῶν ἀπείρων σου | περὶ τὸν κλῆρόν σου, πάναγνε,
θαυμάτων, πῶς ἄτρωτον, | ἀκαταπόντιστον
διετήρησας | αὐτὸν ὡς ἐν πελάγει
βαρβάρων κυκλούμενον | ταῖς ἀντιπνεύσεσιν.

Ἀιδέτω σοι, δέσποινα, | Δαυὶδ ὁ θεῖος προπάτωρ σου
φωνὴν τὴν χαρμόσυνον, | «Θύγατερ, ἄκουσον,
ἐπικλίνασα | τὸ οὖς ἐπὶ λαόν σου,
ἐτήσιον ᾄδοντα | σοὶ χαριστήριον.»

207: 7–8: cf. Ioseph, *can. in sabbato Acathisti* (Christ-Paranikas, 247–52), od. 9 str. 1. ‖ 13–14: Theophanes, *can. in Annunt.* (Christ-Paranikas, 236–42), od. 1 str. 1. ‖ 14–15: Ps. 44:11.

---

181 τὸν] τὴν Γ ‖ 183 στερήσεις ΞΓ ‖ αἰτοῦμαι] αἰτῶ καὶ Γ ἑτὸν Φ ‖ 184 χαριστήριον δέ μου] παρρησίαν ὡς ἔχων Γ ‖ εὐχὴν] ᾠδὴν Γ(Φ) ‖ 185 πάτερ Νικόλαε] καὶ μεγαλύνω σε Γ(Φ) ‖ 186 ὑπερασπίζης Γ ‖ 187 νόσω Γ ‖ ψυχικῶν] χαλεπῶν ΓΦ ‖ 188 δὴ] νῦν Φ ‖ 189 βλάβης τοῦ ἐχθροῦ] νόσων χαλεπῶν Γ ‖ 190 ἐλευθέρωσον] ἐξανάστησον Γ

207: Ψ 263r–268r ε 123–124 ‖ initia hirmorum secundum ε dedi ‖ 1 ἕτερος κανὼν εἰς τὴν αὐτὴν ἑορτὴν Ψ ‖ 8 φυλάττεις Ψ

Receive my praise and grant my soul a gift in return: preserve me from the judgment to come, wise Nicholas. Do not exclude me, I pray, from the choir of the faithful, but accept my prayer of thanksgiving so that I may find mercy, Father Nicholas.

You are the steadfast defender, Most Holy Virgin, of the earthborn, protecting them from the ills of the soul. Therefore free me also, as I call to you, from misfortunes and dangers and the enemy's harm, as you alone can, who have found favor with God.

207

A Canon of Thanksgiving to the Most Holy Mother of God with the acrostic *Hē basilis ta sōstra soi tē parthenō* and in the theotokia *"Nikolaou"*

Ode 1. Fourth mode. *"Anoixō to stoma mou"*

You have chosen, Immaculate Virgin, a royal people and city, to reside there as its queen and to reign over it; safeguard it from capture by the barbarians, as it celebrates your great deeds.

Oh! your infinite miracles performed for your heritage, All-pure One, how you preserved it unscathed, unsubmerged, as in a sea of barbarians, surrounded by adverse winds!

Let David, your divine forefather, sing to you, Our Lady, the joyful words: "Hearken, o daughter, inclining your ear to your people, who sing to you their yearly hymn of thanksgiving."

Συνέσεισας, δέσποινα, | καὶ συνετάραξας θάλασσαν
καὶ ἄρδην ἐπόντωσας | στόλον μισόχριστον,
Σκύθην ὄλεθρον, | καθάπερ τοὺς τῆς Ἄγαρ·
λαὸς σεσωσμένος δὲ | ᾄδει τὰ θαύματα.

Νομὴν πολυχρόνιον | κατατρεχόντων σῆς πόλεως,
παρθένε, ἀνέστειλας | τῶν ἐκ τῆς Ἄγαρ δεινῶν,
ἐπιτρίψασα | τὸ στράτευμα τὸ τούτων
καὶ τέλος βυθίσασα | οἴκαδε φεύγοντας.

ᾠδὴ γʹ. «Τοὺς σοὺς ὑμνολόγους»
Ἰδοὺ τῶν ἐθνῶν ἐν πονηρίᾳ
τὰ ὕδατα ἤχησαν, ἁγνή,
τῇ πόλει σου τὸν ὄλεθρον
αὐτῶν ἐν κραταιότητι·
ἀλλ' ἐμφανῶς τῇ ῥώμῃ σου
παρὰ τὸν ᾅδην διεσπάρησαν.

Λαὸν περιούσιον, παρθένε,
καὶ ἅγιον ἔθνος σοι σαφῶς
καὶ θεῖον ἱεράτευμα
βασίλειον ἐξαίρετον
τὴν βασιλίδα δέδωκεν
ὁ σὸς υἱὸς εἰς περιποίησιν.

Ἰσόρροπον κίνησιν οἱ Πέρσαι
τοῖς Σκύθαις ἐνθέμενοι τῇ σφῶν
καρδίᾳ δίκην λαίλαπος
καὶ καταιγίδος, ἄχραντε,
τῇ σῇ πόλει προσέρρηξαν·
ἀλλ' ὡσεὶ χνοῦν αὐτοὺς ἐλίκμησας.

Ἰάθη τὸ σύντριμμα, παρθένε,
τῆς σῆς θυγατρός, καὶ συντριβὴν
ἀλάστωρ ὁ καὶ βλάσφημος
ὀξέως καθυπέμεινεν·
ἵππον γὰρ καταβέβληκας
καὶ ἀναβάτην ἐνδικώτατα.

17: cf. Ps. 59:2. ‖ 27–29: Ps. 45:4. ‖ 31: Ps. 140:7. ‖ 32–37: 1 Petr. 2:9. ‖ 32: Tit. 2:14; cf. Exod. 23:22; Deut. 14:2. ‖ 38–42: *Util. narr.*, PG, 106, 1336C1–37B3. ‖ 43: Is. 17:13. ‖ 44: Is. 30:26; Ier. 3:22. ‖ 44–45: cf. Ier. 8.21; Lament. 2.11; 3.48; 4.10. ‖ 48–49: Exod. 15:1.

---

18 ἐπόντωσας Ψ ‖ 22 δεινῆς Ψ ‖ 29 αὐτὴν Ψ ‖ 40 καρδίαν Ψ ‖ 41 καταιγίδες Ψ ‖ 45 καὶ] ὡς Ψ

207

You shook, Our Lady, and disturbed the sea and utterly destroyed the fleet of Christ's enemies, the murderous Scythian as well as the sons of Hagar, and your rescued people sings your miracles.

You checked, O Virgin, the raiding of Hagar's terrible sons, who year after year assaulted your city, by crushing their army and finally submerging them in the depths of the sea, as they fled home.

Ode 3. *"Tous sous hymnologous"*

Behold, the waters of the nations roared in fury, O Pure One, roared ruin for your city by their violence; but your strength manifested itself to scatter them in hell.

As a peculiar people, Virgin, a holy nation, a divine priesthood, royal and elect, your Son clearly gave you the Queen of Cities to preserve her.

The Persians, having planned an attack as heavy as that of the Scythians, rushed upon your city, Immaculate One, like a whirlwind and a hurricane, but you winnowed them like chaff.

Your daughter's affliction, Virgin, was healed, and it was the blasphemous wretch who soon was shattered; for justly you threw down the horse and its rider.

ᾠδὴ δʹ. «Τὴν ἀνεξιχνίαστον»
Σήμερον παράδοξα εἶδεν, ἁγνή,
πόλις ἡ ἐξάρχουσα πόλεων·
σοῦ τῆς παρθένου | στρατηγούσης κατ᾽ ἐχθρῶν
παρ᾽ ἑκατέραν ἤπειρον
πάχος ὡσεὶ γῆς διερράγησαν.

Τί σοι ἀνταπόδομα, μῆτερ θεοῦ,
νῦν ἀνταποδοίημεν ἄξιον,
ἀχρεῖοι δοῦλοι, | ἀντὶ πάντων ὧν ἡμᾶς,
ἁγνή, προσευηργέτησας;
ὅθεν ἐκ ψυχῆς σε γεραίρομεν.

Ἄγαρ οἱ ἀπόγονοι, οἷς συστοιχεῖ
πόλις ἡ δουλεύουσα, δέσποινα,
λήξει τῇ κάτω, | προσβαλόντες ὡς σκηπτὸς
τῇ ἐλευθέρᾳ πόλει σου
λίθος οἷα πόντῳ κατέδυσαν.

Σύμβολα, πανάμωμε, τῆς σῆς μορφῆς
ἐν εἰκονικοῖς ἐκτυπώμασιν
ὁ ἱεράρχης | καὶ ἡ σύμπασα πληθὺς
ἱκετικῶς κατέχοντες
νίκην κατ᾽ ἐχθρῶν ἀνεστήσαντο.

Κόσμου σε βασίλισσαν ἡ βασιλὶς
πόλεων πασῶν βασιλεύουσαν
καίπερ εἰδυῖα, | ὅμως δέσποιναν αὐτῆς
ἐξόχως σε πλουτήσασα
μένει πολεμίοις ἀνάλωτος.

ᾠδὴ εʹ. « Ἐξέστη τὰ σύμπαντα»
Ὠράθη τὸ λόγιον | αἰσίως περατούμενον·
εἷς γὰρ κατεδίωξε χιλίους
καὶ δύο αὖθις | μετεκινήσαντο
ὅλας μυριάδας εἰς φυγήν,
δύναμιν φραξάμενοι | τῆς παρθένου τὴν ἄμαχον.

55: Ps. 140:7. ‖ 56–57: cf. Ps. 115:3. ‖ 58: Luc. 17:10. ‖ 61–64: Gal. 4:24–26. ‖ 66–70: *Util. narr.*, PG, 106, 1337D2–9. ‖ 78–80: Deut. 32:20; *Util. narr.*, PG, 106, 1344D2–3.

---

59 προσευεργέτησας Ψ ‖ 60 ὅθεν] ὅπως Ψ ‖ γεραίρωμεν Ψ ‖ 72 βασιλεύουσα ε ‖ 74 πλουτήσας ε

207

Ode 4. *"Tēn anexichniaston"*

Today, O Pure One, the city that rules the cities, has seen miraculous events: when you, the Virgin, took command against the enemies, along the coasts of both continents they crumbled like a clod of earth.

What worthy gift, Mother of God, can we render to you now, we unprofitable servants, for all the benefits which you have bestowed on us, Pure One? For them, we honor you with all our hearts.

The offspring of Hagar, symbolizing the city in bondage to the world here below, O Our Lady, struck at your free city with hurricane force, but was sunk in the sea like a stone.

The holy bishop and all the crowd, holding as supplicants the symbols of your form, Blameless One, represented in images, raised the banner of victory over the enemies.

Though the Queen of Cities, which rules all cities, knows you as Queen of the World, yet having you in a special sense as its mistress, it remains impregnable to enemies.

Ode 5. *"Exestē ta sympanta"*

The divine word was seen fulfilled auspiciously: one chased a thousand, and again two put tens of thousands to flight, having taken as their armor the invincible power of the Virgin.

207

Συνέκοψεν ἄγγελος | ὡς ἐν ἐκστάσει πρότερον
τοῦ Σεναχηρεὶμ τὰς μυριάδας
φρυαξαμένου | κατὰ τοῦ ζῶντος θεοῦ·
νῦν δὲ τὰς ἀπείρους τῶν ἐθνῶν
ὑφ' ἓν ἐθανάτωσε | μυριάδας ἡ δέσποινα.

Τηκόμενοι πάθεσι | τοῖς ἀνηκέστοις βάρβαροι
πάντες ἐπιθέμενοι τῷ κλήρῳ
τῷ σῷ, παρθένε, | λιμῷ καὶ βρώσει πτηνῶν
καὶ ἐκδειματούμενοι φρικτῶς
ἔμαθον οἷς ἔπαθον | ὡς εἰς σὲ κατεφρόνησαν.

Ὅτε δὴ ὁ ὕψιστος | τὰ ἔθνη διεμέριζεν,
ὡς ἐπιτροπεύοιντο ἀγγέλοις,
αἵματι θείῳ | οὓς ἐξηγόρασε,
σχοίνισμα μερίδος τῇ μητρὶ
πόλιν ὑπεξείλετο, | ἣν φυλάττοις ἀπόρθητον.

ᾠδὴ ϛ'. «Τὴν θείαν ταύτην»
Ῥομφαίαν, ὅπλον καὶ πόλεμον
ἐχθρῶν ἐπεμβαινόντων, θεόνυμφε,
τῇ κληρουχίᾳ σου | κενὰ καὶ ἄπρακτα ἤλεγξας,
ὡς πολιοῦχος ταύτης | ὑπερασπίσασα.

Ἀδίκως ἐπιστρατεύσασα
Περσὶς τῇ βασιλίδι τῶν πόλεων
δουλείαν ἔνδικον | κατεδικάσθη τῷ ἄνακτι,
ὑπερμαχούσης τούτῳ | τῆς θεομήτορος.

Σωροὺς ἐξέβρασε θάλασσα,
καθάπερ Αἰγυπτίους τὸ πρότερον,
Ἀγαρηνῶν τοὺς νεκρούς, | οὓς θεηλάτως ἐβύθισεν
ἐπιθεμένους κλήρῳ | τῆς θεομήτορος.

Ὁ σοὶ τὴν πόλιν δειμάμενος
ἀνάκτορον, παρθένε, περίπυστον
ἄναξ ἀγάλλεται, | ταύτην ἀμφέπουσαν βλέπων σε
καὶ τὸν ψιλῶς καλοῦντα | ἐχθρὸν συντρίψασαν.

82–83: 4 Regn. 19:35; Is. 37:36. ‖ 87–91: *Util. narr.*, PG, 106, 1349A8–15. ‖ 92–95: Deut. 32:8–9. ‖ 106–109: *Util. narr.*, PG, 106, 1349B2–C6. ‖ 106–107: cf. Exod. 14:30. ‖ 113: *Util. narr.*, PG, 106, 1348C8–12.

---

91 εἰς σὲ] ἐν σοὶ Ψ ‖ 92 ὁ ὕψιστος ὅτε δὴ colloc. Ψ ‖ 96 φυλάττει Ψ ‖ 104 ἔκδικον Ψ ‖ 105 τούτου Ψ ‖ 106 ἐξέβρασσε Ψ ‖ 113 τὸν] τὰ Ψ ‖ συντρίψασαν Wk: -σα ε συνέτριψας Ψ

207 Once an angel, as in panic fear, smote the tens of thousands of Sennacherib, who had boasted against the living God; now, Our Lady has put to death numberless tens of thousands of gentiles all at once.

All the barbarians who assailed your heritage, O Virgin, consumed by incurable ills, by hunger and carrion birds, and haunted by horror, learned through experience that it was you they had scorned.

When the Most High divided the nations to have angels for their guardians, he set aside as the lot of his Mother's inheritance the city of those he had bought with his divine blood: we pray you, safeguard it from destruction.

Ode 6. *"Tēn theian tautēn"*

Sword, armor, and warfare of the enemies who trespassed upon your inheritance, Bride of God, were proven idle and worthless by you, who defended it as its Patroness.

When Persia unjustly attacked the Queen of Cities, it was justly condemned to slavery by the Emperor, whose champion was the Mother of God.

The sea washed up masses of bodies, as formerly those of the Egyptians: the dead of the Agarenes, which it had swallowed by divine justice, as they invaded the inheritance of the Mother of God.

The Prince who built the City as an illustrious palace for you, Pure One, rejoices seeing how you heed it and have shattered the enemy, who calls you merely by your name.

Λαὸς καὶ πόλις φιλόχριστος,
ῥυσθέντες φοβερᾶς καταπόσεως
ὑπερμαχούσης σου, | νῦν χαριστήριον πάννυχον
ἐν ἀκαθίστῳ στάσει | τελεῖ δοξάζων σε.

ᾠδὴ ζ′. «Οὐκ ἐλάτρευσαν»
Ἱκετήριόν σοι δέησιν προσάγομεν
οἱ σεσωσμένοι φρικτῆς | αἰχμαλωσίας, ἁγνή,
ῥυσθῆναι δεόμενοι | καὶ ἀοράτων ἐχθρῶν,
ὧν ὁ πόλεμος | οὐκ ἐν σαρκὶ καὶ αἵματι,
τῷ νοῒ δὲ ἀντιπίπτει.

Τόξα πάντα συνετρίβη καὶ ἠσθένησε
τῶν δυνατῶν ἐν αὐτοῖς· | οἱ ἀσθενεῖς δὲ σαφῶς
ἰσχύν τε καὶ δύναμιν | περιεζώσαντο
ὡς τὴν ἄμαχον | πεπλουτηκότες δύναμιν
πεποιθήσει σου, παρθένε.

Ἡ παλίμφημος ἀπέσβη καὶ ἠφάνιστο
γλῶσσα τοῦ κήρυκος | τῆς μυσαρᾶς τελετῆς·
ἐξ ὕψους γὰρ ἔρριπτο | πτῶμα ἐξαίσιον,
μὴ κραυγάζων σοι | «Εὐλογημένος, δέσποινα,
ὁ καρπὸς τῆς σῆς κοιλίας.»

Ἀνοιγέσθωσαν αἱ πύλαι σου, βασίλισσα
πασῶν τῶν πόλεων | καὶ προερχέσθωσαν | ἐν ἐλευθέρῳ ποδὶ
οἱ πρώην σου δέσμιοι | καὶ ἐγκατάκλειστοι·
ὁ τοῦ παίοντος | καὶ γὰρ ζυγὸς συντέτριπται
στρατηγούσης τῆς παρθένου.

ᾠδὴ η′. «Παῖδας εὐαγεῖς»
Πέρσαι τε καὶ Μῆδοι | καὶ τῶν Οὔννων
τὰ ἔχθιστα φῦλα συνελάλησαν·
«Δεῦτε καὶ κατάσχωμεν | κλῆρον τὸν ἀπόλεκτον,
ἐν γὰρ αὐτοῖς οὐδείς ἐστιν | ὁ βασιλεύων τὰ νῦν·»
ἠλέγχθησαν δὲ φρύαγμα μόνον,
πάντας γὰρ ἐξῆρεν | ὡς χλόην ἡ παρθένος.

114–117: cf. *Util. narr.*, PG, 106, 1345B3–4. ‖ 122: Ephes. 6:12. ‖ 124: cf. Ps. 36:15; 45:9. ‖ 129–131: *Util. narr.*, PG, 106, 1348C12–D2. ‖ 132–133: Luc. 1:42. ‖ 137: Is. 14:29. ‖ 140–143: cf. *Util. narr.*, PG, 106, 1336C6–1337A6.

---

122 αἵματι] πν(εύματ)ι Ψ ‖ 135 πασῶν τῶν πόλεων] delenda metri causa ‖ 137 συντέτριπτο Ψ ‖ 143 αὐτὴ Ψ

207

A Christ-loving people and city, saved from terrible destruction by your protection, now perform a thanksgiving hymn, standing, unseated, all night long.

Ode 7. *"Ouk elatreusan"*

We offer up a suppliant prayer to you, Pure One, we who were saved from dreadful captivity, asking you to be saved also from invisible enemies, who wage war not against flesh and blood, but against the mind.

All the bows of the mighty were broken and failed; but the failing were seen to gird themselves with strength and power, because they possessed invincible power by their faith in you, Virgin.

The ill-omened voice of the herald of the unholy rite was muffled and stifled; for he was thrown down from on high in a headlong fall, because he did not cry out to you: "Blessed, Our Lady, is the fruit of your womb."

Let your gates be opened, Queen of all Cities, and let your former prisoners and besieged come forth free; for the yoke of him who smote you is broken, the Virgin leading our armies.

Ode 8. *"Paidas euageis"*

Persians and Medians and the most hateful tribes of the Huns conspired together: "Come let us seize the elect inheritance, for there is no one among them to rule them now." But all this proved idle boasting, for the Virgin uprooted them all like grass.

Ἄνασσά σοι πόλις, | θεοτόκε,
παρ' ἧς ἡ εὐσέβεια κρατύνεται,
πάννυχον ἐτήσιον | ᾄδει τὸ κατόρθωμα
καὶ ἑορτάζει χαίρουσα | τῆς βασιλίδος σαφῶς
τὰ ῥύσια καὶ σῶστρα, παρθένε,
ἀνυμνολογοῦσα | τὸν τόκον σου τὸν ξένον.

Ῥήγνυται τὰ σκάφη | τῶν ἀθέων,
ἀλλήλοις ἐν συσσεισμῷ καὶ καταιγίδι φρικτῇ
βίᾳ προσαράξαντα, | ἄλλα τε βεβύθισται,
πάντα δ' ὑφ' ἓν ἀπόλωλε | καὶ ἐξηφάνισται·
θρηνεῖ δὲ καὶ ὁ φύλαρχος βλέπων
ἔργον γενομένους | καὶ τοὺς λοιποὺς μαχαίρας.

Ὄλωλε τὰ ἔθνη | παραδόξως,
σῇ κληρονομίᾳ ἐπιθέμενα·
ἔθεντο τὸ στόμα γὰρ | ὕψος πρὸς οὐράνιον
καὶ τὴν αὐτῶν ὑβρίστριαν | γλῶσσαν διήγαγον
εἰς γῆν μεγαλαυχοῦσαν, παρθένε,
ὥσπερ ὁ Ῥαψάκης, | σὺν ᾧ καὶ διεφθάρη.

ᾠδὴ θ'. «Ὡς ἐμψύχῳ θεοῦ»
Θαυμαστή σου ἐστὶν ἡ σκηνή,
παλάτιον τοῦ πάντων βασιλέως·
πνεῦμα γὰρ ἐν σοὶ ἐπισκιάσαν, | θεοτόκε,
φρικτὸν κατεσκεύασέ σε θάλαμον,
νῦν δὲ ἡ πόλις σοῦ αὕτη κλῆρος·
ἀλλὰ σῴζοις ταύτην | ἐχθρῶν βαρβάρων ἀσινῆ.

Ἐνεδρεύονται, θεοτόκε ἁγνή,
ἀδίκως οἷς ἐνήδρευσαν δικαίων
πόλιν καὶ λαὸν οἱ ἐκ Περσίδος | ἐπιστάντες·
αὐτοῖς ἐπιστάντος τοῦ ὀλέθρου φρικτῶς,
καταστρατηγούσης σου, κόρη, τούτων
καὶ συστρατηγούσης | ἐκεῖ τῷ πιστῷ βασιλεῖ.

152–157: *Util. narr.*, PG, 106, 1344A12–C7. ‖ 160–162: Ps. 72:9. ‖ 163: 4 Regn. 18:17–19:37; Is. 36–37. ‖ 166: Ioseph, *can. in sabbato Acathisti* (Christ-Paranikas, 236–42), od. 1 str. 2. ‖ 167: Luc. 1:35.

---

153 tres syllabae redundant ‖ 154 προσαρράξαντα Ψ ‖ ἀλλά γε Ψ ‖ 161 αὐτοῦ Ψ ‖ 169 σου ε ‖ 170 σώζεις ε ‖ βαρβάρων om. Ψ

207

The Queen City, Mother of God, supporter of true belief, sings of your triumph in a yearly vigil and celebrates with manifest joy the festival of thanksgiving for its deliverance, Holy Virgin, praising in hymns the wondrous birth of your Son.

The ships of the godless are wrecked, crashing violently into each other in the upheaval of a dreadful hurricane, others sink, all without exception are lost and gone; the chieftain, too, laments, when he sees that the remainder has also been put to the sword.

The nations which assailed your inheritance have perished miraculously, because they set their mouth against the high heavens and their blasphemous tongue walked through the earth, boasting, O Virgin, as Rabshakeh did, whose destruction they shared.

Ode 9. *"Hōs empsychō theou"*

Wondrous is your tent, a palace of the King of the universe; for the Spirit, overshadowing you, Mother of God, made you an awesome Bridal Chamber; and now this city is your inheritance: preserve it unharmed by barbarous enemies.

The invaders from Persia were caught in a snare, Pure Mother of God, because they unjustly set snares for the city and the people of the just. Terrible disaster invaded them, for you led the army against them, Virgin, sharing command in that battle with the faithful Emperor.

Νομοθέτης τὸ πρὶν Μωϋσῆς
  τυπούμενος παλάμαις σταυροτύπως
  ῥύεται λαὸν Ἰσραηλίτην | παλαμναίας
χειρὸς Ἀμαλὴκ τοῦ πολεμήτορος·
  νῦν δὲ τῷ σταυρῷ καὶ εἰκόσι θείαις
τοὺς ἐχθροὺς ἡττῶσι | χεῖρες ἀνδρῶν ἱερῶν.

Ὡς ἐμψύχῳ θεοῦ κιβωτῷ
  λυτρούμεθα ἐν σοί, θεογεννῆτορ,
  ἄρδην κατακλύζοντος πολέμου | ἐξ ὑδάτων,
ἐθνῶν καλυπτόντων γῆς τὸ πρόσωπον
  καὶ ὑπὲρ βουνῶν ὑψουμένων,
σοῦ δὲ ἀφανιζομένων | τῇ θάλψει πρὸς τάχος, ἁγνή.

Ὑπερίπταται, θεομῆτορ, τὰ σὰ
  θαυμάσια τὴν δύναμιν τῶν λόγων·
  σθένει γὰρ σῷ ἀμάχῳ ἐρρύσω | ἀλλοφύλων
ἐπιδρομῆς, ἁγνή, κληρουχίαν σου·
  ὅθεν εὐχαρίστως βοᾷ σοι·
«Σύ μου, θεοτόκε, ῥύστις, | προστάτις καὶ καταφυγή.»

177–180: Exod. 17:8–13. ‖ 181–182: *Util. narr.*, PG, 106, 1340A2–6. ‖ 183–185: Gen. 7. ‖ 185–186: cf. *Util. narr.* PG, 106, 1341C2–8. ‖ 186: cf. Iudith 2:7;19; 7:18. ‖ 187: cf. Is. 2:2. ‖ 194: cf. Ps. 17:3.

189–194 om. Ψ

207

Long ago, Moses the lawgiver, holding his arms in the form of the cross, rescued the people of Israel from the cursed hand of warlike Amalek; now, through the cross and divine images, the hands of holy men defeat the enemies.

We take refuge with you, Mother of God, as God's living ark, now that a war from the waters is wholly overwhelming us, nations that cover the face of the earth and exalt themselves above the hills; but they are quickly dispersed by your sun-warmth, Pure One.

Your miracles, Mother of God, exceed the power of words: by your invincible strength you saved your inheritance from an invasion of Philistines, Pure One; therefore it gratefully cries out to you: "You, Mother of God, are my deliverer, protrectress, and refuge."

SUMMARIES

SUMMARIES

Opus 191. Ranklist of Episcopal Sees. Second Sunday before Christmas 901/4

A ranklist of the cities whose pastors are ordained by the patriarch [of Constantinople] was found necessary; with the sees of the East, it includes also those of the West, so as to prevent further fights over precedence. To this end the Emperor and the Patriarch, with a number of metropolitans, met in the Church of St. Irene on the feast of the illustrious Patriarchs (section A).

There follow contemporary lists of metropolitan and archiepiscopal sees (section B), preserved separately in MS *Jerusalem, Taphou 39,* a manuscript which also includes a complementary list of suffragan sees.

Lit.: Grumel, no. 598; Gelzer.

Date. There can be no doubt as to the identity of the patriarch, on which the manuscripts are unanimous (with the sole exception of l, where the name is left blank). Grumel's principal argument for the dating to 901 or 902, the fact that no archiepiscopal see of Alania is mentioned, no longer holds, since such a see was not established until 914 (*Letters,* pp. xxix and 577). There remains a *prima facie* probability that the reorganization belongs to the first years of Nicholas' patriarchate. In any case, the years 905-7 can be eliminated because of the tetragamy conflict, 912–14 because of the schism.

Note. The title and opening words of the Preface relate only to the lists of metropolitan and archiepiscopal sees; the list of suffragan sees (here omitted), while a necessary and contemporary supplement, required another meeting of the synod (see Gelzer).

Opus 192. Sermon on the Capture of Thessalonica. *Early August 904*

My sins and yours are the cause of this disaster. Let us repent so that our prayers may be worthy of being heard. We ourselves might have perished in the same way; in fact, the signs of God's wrath have already become manifest in recent catastrophes. Now men are killed, women raped, churches and relics desecrated. The martyr Demetrius has withdrawn his protection: why? Because he sees Christ smarting under our sins; thus a

soldier who sees his king wounded will forget his own nearest and dearest. Our hatred, our envy, our slander, our heartlessness are insults to Christ: because of them Thessalonica suffers this fate. Let us free ourselves from the bondage of sin lest worse things happen.

Lit.: Tsaras, 236–43.

Date: Thessalonica was taken on Tuesday, 31 July 904. The news must have taken several days to reach Constantinople. If the sermon was given on Sunday, this would be August 12 rather than 5.

Opus 193. Letter to Andronicus Ducas. *Fall/Winter 905*

Future Augustus Ducas: do not be persuaded by the Emperor's messengers, for Samonas is plotting against you. The City will soon ask for you through my efforts; do not forget me then.

Lit.: Grumel, no. 601; *idem,* "La révolte d'Andronic Doux sous Léon VI," *Echos d'Orient,* 36 (1937), 202–7. Jenkins, X. *Vita Euthymii,* 24–28, 32–34, 59–61, and 190–92.

Date: Some time after Andronicus' flight to Kavala (late Summer 905) and before the christening of Constantine (Epiphany 906), which according to the *Vita Euthymii* (71 lines 8–14) was a concession made on account of this piece of evidence.

Authenticity. The letter is either incredibly imprudent or deliberately incriminating. The alleged similarity in style (*Vita Euthymii,* 69 lines 20–22) is not evident.

Opus 194. First Act of Abdication. *Ca. 6 Feb. 907*

Since adverse circumstances prevent me from granting dispensation, I resign my see, though not the [arch]priesthood [and its functions; for the holy canon inexorably deposes anyone who, for whatever reason, renounces the sacred ministry].

Lit.: Grumel, no. 613.

Date: "Before five days of the Patriarch's exile had passed" (i.e., on Feb. 5 or 6), Leo demands his resignation, but Nicholas pretends to be ill (*Vita Euthymii,* 91 lines 4–15); "after this" the Emperor sends Samonas, who receives the present document (*ibid.,* 91 line 17–93 line 20).

Note. Version I is that of the *Vita Euthymii*; version II, with the preamble, is found in some canonical manuscripts, and, without it, in the *Act of Deposition* (*Op. 197*) of the year 912. The author of the *Vita* may have abridged, but it is at least as likely that II is the official version circulated in

912 with a view to proving the resignation void; in that case the original shorter text has been amplified by the essential point of the *Second Act of Abdication*, the emphasis on retaining also the functions of the archpriesthood. If the *First Act* already included this stipulation, it is difficult to see why the *Second Act* was written at all.

Opus 195. Second Act of Abdication. *Second week of Feb. 907*

Since, owing to the prevailing discord, I am unable to grant the promised dispensation, I yield my see to one who can restore unity, without, however, giving up the archpriesthood and its functions.

Lit.: Grumel, no. 613.

Date: "Not long after" opus 194 (*Vita Euthymii*, 93 line 21).

Opus 196. Third Act of Abdication. *Second week of Feb. 907*

Since unanimity has now been achieved, I leave it to you to grant dispensation, resigning my see, first, because I am weary of your quarreling, second, because this conflict has embittered my relations with the Emperor.

Lit.: Grumel, no. 614.

Date: The metropolitans are already in possession of a third abdication when they visit Euthymius for the first time at Psamathia to offer him the patriarchate (*Vita Euthymii*, 95 lines 33–35).

Opus 197. Deposition of the Metropolitans. *Second half of May 912*

Well may the Church call you rebellious sons, who have betrayed and insulted your Mother so outrageously as to make it manifest that you do not believe in justice either here or in the world to come (lines 1–22). You conspired against your Archpriest and Head; when the Emperor bade you choose between him and me, you sided unanimously with him, not once, but twice (Jan. 6 and Feb. 1). You broke your solemn promise not to grant dispensation, except by common consent, and you ignored my injunction to the same effect, when on the day of our deportation we took leave of each other (lines 23–50). Upon this, you drove us away from our flock: the Emperor was no more than your tool. Indeed, when he repented and intended to reinstate us, you answered by an ultimatum (lines 51–65). Finally, you demanded an abdication, though what you received was a snare. What validity, indeed, could an abdication signed under such duress possess (lines 66–83)? Text of the First Act of Abdication (lines

84–96). In accepting it you granted me spiritual rule over the entire world, though you imagined it authorized you to become the lawgivers and dispensers of fornication (lines 97–112). I will pass over your further misdeeds in silence and only cite the verdict of the holy canons (lines 113–27). List of applicable canons (lines 128–39). On these grounds this Holy Synod deposes you and divests you of all your archpriestly functions (lines 140–46).

Lit.: Grumel, no. 632. Karlin-Hayter, "Le synode," 71. Konstantinides, 123. *Letters*, pp. xix–xx.

Date: As far as the lacuna in the *Vita Euthymii* allows us to discern, the second half of May 912, soon after Alexander's accession and Nicholas' reinstatement.

Note. This is not a letter (Grumel; Konstantinides), but the document prepared by Nicholas and read out by his orders in a synod held in the gallery of St. Sophia to condemn the four metropolitans arrested (*Vita Euthymii*, 115 line 25–117 line 6: the words κατ' ἰδίαν προκαθεσθείς [*ibid.*, 117 line 4], must refer to Alexander's refusal to be personally involved). Immediately afterwards, Nicholas refers to the four metropolitans as "these men who have been deposed."

Opus 198. Letter to John the Catholicus. *June 913/Feb. 914*

The persecution inflicted on your flock (Armenians, Iberians, Albanians) by the Saracens grieves us deeply, in spite of the distance that separates us from you. What can be done (lines 9–38)? In the first place, pray; in the second, use your spiritual authority to stop the leaders' hostilities among themselves (lines 36–39). We wrote to the same effect to the Curopalate [of Iberia] and the Prince of Abasgia, advising them to unite with all the Armenian princes against the children of the ungodly Aposatai. If by your admonitions you can put an end to the animosity among the princes, the Emperor will send large forces to your aid so that together you will be able to defeat the enemy (lines 70–116). Only then will you forgive them and confirm their rights (lines 117–132).

Lit.: Grumel, no. 649; Konstantinides, 103–4 and 123. Maksoudian, 54–56 and 362.

Date: Grumel dates the letter to the period of Nicholas' personal government. Maksoudian arrives at the same date (*ca.* 913) on the following grounds: John is still in Gugar; Smbat's death was not yet known at Constantinople but his imprisonment was, else he would have been the addressee.

199, 200 A

Opus 199. Tract on the Tetragamy. *914 (after Feb.)*

Arguments from Scripture to prove that only the first marriage has been instituted by God, while any further marriages, even the second, are acts of human indulgence: from the Old Testament (chaps. I–III), the Gospels (chaps. V–VIII), St. Paul (chaps. X–XII). Explanation of canons 4 and 80 of St. Basil (chaps. XIII–XIV). The ruler's example (chap. XV). Purpose of dispensation (chap. XVI). The requirement of separation (chap. XVII). The words "more than fornication" in Basil, canon 80 (chap. XVIII). Who is competent to grant dispensation (chap. XIX)? What is unanimity worth (chap. XX)? The plea of compassion (chap. XXI). The appointed end of human life (chap. XXII). Once more the words "more than fornication" (chap. XXIII). The true sense of "It is better to marry than to burn" (chap. XXIV). The emperor cannot be exempted from his own law (chaps. XXV–XXVI). The case is not negligible because it stands by itself (chaps. XXVII–XXVIII). Final appeal (chap. XXIX).

Date: Arethas (*Arethae scripta minora,* I, 127 line 22–128 line 2) says that Nicholas did not venture to publish his treatise: this must have been after his political downfall in February 914.

Opus 200. The Tome of Union.

Lit.: Grumel, no. 669; *Vita Euthymii,* 53–56. *Letters,* p. xxv.

Date. The original document, as read on the Sunday of the Union (9 July, 920), consisted of the Text (section B), acclamations addressed to the Emperor Constantine VII, the Basileopator Romanus and the Patriarch Nicholas (section D; lost in this form) and the anathemas and final prayer (section E). The Argument (section A) and the Appendix (section C) are later additions, while the Acclamations (section D I–XII) have been updated at various times. The year 6428 (A.D. 919/20) is mentioned in the text, the month of July in the chronicles; the liturgical date, according to *Laurentianus 9,8,* is in the month of July (on the Sunday after the feast of St. Procopius [July 8]) and according to *Vaticanus gr. 2198,* τῇ κυριακῇ τῶν προαλλάκτων.

A. The Argument. *945/959*

The four marriages of Leo the Wise (lines 3–11). His excommunication by the Patriarch and the metropolitans, controversy over its duration; the Patriarch Nicholas is deposed because of his false promises and delaying tactics and replaced by Euthymius, who grants dispensation (lines

12–25). Widespread dissent; after Leo's death, Alexander deposes Euthymius and reinstates Nicholas with a schism as the result (lines 26–33). After Alexander's death, Constantine restores unity, obtaining a pardon for his father, while a ban is pronounced on fourth marriages (lines 34–40).

Date: The Argument is proved a product of Constantine's personal reign by its anti-Nicholaän bias and by the fact that it makes Constantine the sole author of the union, though at the time he was only fifteen years old.

B. The Text. *9 July 920*

The greatest gift that our Lord Jesus Christ has left us is peace (lines 5–17). Whenever the peace of His Church was disturbed by Satan's wiles, He has restored unity (lines 18–34). In each case a remedy was found appropriate to the trouble: this time, since the cause is a marriage, we have gathered together, archpriests and priests (except those who, driven by pride, prefer strife to peace) to eradicate the evil by preventing any such marriages in the future (lines 35–59). We therefore decree that from this year 6428 onward no one shall contract a fourth marriage under penalty of excommunication, as long as the marriage lasts (lines 60–68).

It has also become necessary to regulate third marriages, since they are no longer rare exceptions that can be tolerated as such, but have become an accepted practice (lines 69–81). For those over forty who contract a third marriage there will be a five year's penance, after completion of which communion will be permitted only at Easter; if there are already children, a third marriage is forbidden (lines 82–105). Those in their thirties, if there are children, will be excommunicated for four years and then admitted to communion three times a year only (Easter, Dormition, Christmas); if there are no children, only the traditional penance [three years] will be imposed (lines 106–19).

Second and first marriages should not be a sequel to rape or seduction, which are subject to the penalty for fornication, i.e., seven years; any priest who admits a person guilty of these to communion will be liable to deprivation (lines 120–35).

C. Appendix. *Ca. 996*

After ninety years, in the reign of Basil and Constantine, the priests and monks separated from the Church by the aforesaid cause were reunited with it. Let us proclaim and celebrate those who achieved this great work.

200 C, D

Lit.: Grumel, no. 803.

Date: In the editions the Appendix is followed by Acclamations section D III, dating from the patriarchate of Nicholas II Chrysoberges (979–91). This conflation (the work of Leunclavius; no manuscript combines C with D III) has led to the erroneous assumption of a connection between the two. The only historical information we have on the subject is found in *Ioannis Scylitzae synopsis historiarum,* ed. H. Thurn (Berlin, 1973), 340 line 4–341 line 12, according to whom it was Sisinnius who ended the tetragamy schism in 6503 (994/95; Grumel's dates for Sisinnius are 12 April 996–24 August 998). Though an allusion in a letter of Leo of Synada (*Ep.* 54 lines 22–23, Darrouzès, 209) seems to indicate that the union had already been arranged before Sisinnius' election, the formal proclamation probably took place soon after his ordination, a time which tallies well with the lapse of ninety years after the beginning of the schism. The immediate object of his appointment may have been precisely this.

D. The Acclamations. *Various dates*

I. *Date*: 14 December 928–August 931 (patriarchate of Tryphon).

II. *Date*: 5 February 970–10 January 976. After the death of the Patriarch Polyeuctus, 5 February 970; his immediate successor, Basil I Scamandrenus, deposed in March (?) 974, does not appear in the diptychs. Reign of John I Tzimisces (11 Dec. 969–10 Jan. 976).

III. *Date*: April 979–16 December 991 (patriarchate of Nicholas II Chrysoberges).

IV. *Date*: 16 December 1025–11 November 1028 (reign of Constantine VIII).

V. *Date*: Antioch, 25 March 1043–1050. Patriarchate of Michael Cerularius (25 March 1043–2 Nov. 1058); before death of Zoe (1050).

VI. *Date*: Antioch, 1050 to Spring 1052. Reign of Constantine IX and Theodora (1050–11 Jan. 1055). Patriarchate (at Antioch) of Sophronius, before accession of Peter III, Spring 1052.

VII. *Date*: 1050–11 January 1055 (reign of Constantine IX and Theodora). Updated in the margin of Q to 16 August 1118–end of April 1134 (reign of John II Comnenus, 16 August 1118–8 April 1143; patriarchate of John IX Agapitus, 24 May 1111–end of April 1134).

VIII. *Date*: after 24 October 1071 –2 August 1075. Reign of Michael VII (24 Oct. 1071–7 Jan. 1078), after the death of Eudocia (date unknown); patriarchate of John VIII Xiphilinus (1 Jan. 1064–2 Aug. 1075).

IX. *Date*: January 1078–1104. After the death of Michael VII (deposed 7 Jan. 1078), before the death of Isaac the Sebastocrator (d. 1102/4). It is not clear why there is no commemoration of John VIII Xiphilinus, who died 2 August 1075 (textual error?); Cosmas, who abdicated in May 1081, may still have been alive.

X. *Date*: 1102–before 24 May 1111. After death of Isaac the Sebastocrator (d. 1102/4); during patriarchate of Nicholas III Grammaticus (Aug. 1084–before 24 May 1111).

XI. *Date*: Antioch, *ca.* 1111. During patriarchate of Nicholas III Grammaticus (d. before 24 May 1111), after death of John V Oxites, Patriarch of Antioch (d. *ca.* 1111?).–Only a few lines of the acclamations survive; the rest has been supplied from the *Synod. Orthod.* in the same manuscript.

XII. *Date*: May 1134–Jan. 1143 (patriarchate of Leo Stypes). The second Irene is Irene of Hungary, wife of John II (d. 1134).

E. Anathemas. *9 July, 920*

Three anathemas protecting the memory of the orthodox patriarchs of the iconoclast period, of those of the Ignatian-Photian era down to Nicholas, and the ecclesiastical tradition generally (these three are also in the *Synod. Orthod.*). Three anathemas against opponents of the union (two against extreme rigorists, one against those of excessive permissiveness). Concluding prayer.

Date: This section is part of the original document, though Nicholas' name (followed by that of Stephen II in J) may have been added between 920 and 928/31.

Opus 201. Decree on Patriarchal Letters. *Date?*

Though it is difficult to discard an inveterate custom, we have decided to do so (lines 4–10). The *ostiarius* of this sacred place used to demand a fee for copies of patriarchal letters; we have replaced this by an annual salary. We instruct the *chartophylax* and his notaries not to tolerate any infringement (lines 11–24). Divine retribution, here and in the world to come, will overtake those who ignore our ruling (lines 25–32).

Lit.: Grumel, no. 733.

Date: No information; the first year or so of the patriarchate seems the most likely time.

Opus 202. Decree on the Great Habit. *Date?*

The grace of the Great Habit can never disqualify a man for the priesthood, even if some canon should say so.

Lit.: Grumel, no. 731; Konstantinides, 125.

Opus 203. Canon on the Lament of the Mother of God. *Liturgical date: Holy Saturday*

Alphabetical acrostic; in the *theotokia* the poet signs "Nikolaou", which according to the title in the manuscript refers to the Patriarch. *Heirmos*: *Octoechus* (Venice, 1881), 119–28. The canon follows the sequence of the events, which, however, are mostly touched upon only in passing and not necessarily connected with the motifs of the lament: ode 1–Christ on the cross; ode 3–flight of the disciples; ode 4–Joseph of Arimathea's appeal to Pilate; ode 5–the descent from the cross; ode 6–the Virgin addressing her dead Son; ode 7–Christ is carried to the grave; ode 8–the sepulture; ode 9–Christ answers his Mother. The last ode was obviously inspired by Cosmas' canon for Holy Saturday, ode 9 *(Triodion,* 408; Christ-Paranikas, 196–201).

Opus 204. Canon to St. Gregory the Illuminator and Rhipsimia *Liturgical date: Sept. 30*

The Patriarch Nicholas is named as the author only in the margin of the Laura manuscript. There is no acrostic; the *theotokia,* however, have been taken from an alphabetical canon to the Theotokos, which follows the same *heirmos* (*Paracleticus* [Rome, 1885], 625–32). In the first, third, sixth, and seventh ode the first strophe of each ode is used, and in the fourth, fifth, eighth, and ninth, the last, resulting in the acrostic ΑΔΙΜΝΠΦΩ. This was pointed out to me by Dr. Enrica Follieri, who lists a dozen more canons in which some of the *theotokia* derive from the same source; the canon to St. Gregory, however, is unique in that *all* its *theotokia* come from the same alphabetical canon, which is possible because it is the only known canon that has the same sequence of melodies throughout. From this Dr. Follieri infers (tentatively) that the poet of the canon to Gregory either modeled his poem on the alphabetical canon, or wrote both.

In each ode one strophe (the second in ode 5, otherwise the third) addresses itself to Rhipsimia, with the exception of odes 1 and 4; the rest describes the sufferings of Gregory on the basis of the *martyrium.*

Opus 205. Stichera to Peter and Paul. *Liturgical date: June 29*

No *heirmos* is indicated: perhaps the melody was original (*idiomela*). The first strophe, though the dominating theme is that of the catcher caught, condenses in a pregnant form everything that is said about Peter in the Gospels; in the second, Paul is celebrated as the great theologian, the chosen vessel, the fountain of love, and the bearer of the stigmata.

Opus 206. Canon to St. Nicholas. *Liturgical date: Dec. 6*

In the *theotokia* the acrostic "Nikolaou." The melody is that of Cosmas' canon for Holy Saturday (*Triodion,* 408; Christ-Paranikas 196–201). The themes of the poem are: the poet's sins, his misery, and his need of help; the saving miracles of Christ and the Apostles (odes 3 and 5); and a few episodes from the legend of St. Nicholas (odes 5 and 6 – the three army commanders; ode 7 – the poor man's daughters; ode 9 – the council of Nicaea and Nicholas' ordination).

Opus 207. Canon of Thanksgiving to the Mother of God.
Liturgical date: third Saturday before Easter

Iambic acrostic, and in the *theotokia* "Nikolaou." The *heirmos* is St. John Damascene's canon on the Dormition (Christ-Paranikas, 229–32) except for ode 9, which follows ode 9 of Theophanes' canon on the Annunciation (Christ-Paranikas, 236–42). Written to be sung on Akathistos Saturday to celebrate the victories over the Persians and Avars (siege of 626) and over the Arabs (sieges of 674–78 and 717). The historical details (dispersed over the poem without any visible method) are derived from the account in the *synaxaria* (copied in the *Utilis narratio,* PG, 106, cols. 1335–54). It is worth noting that Joseph's canon for Akathistos Saturday (IX cent.) contains hardly any allusions to military menaces. Some phrases have been borrowed from this poem (lines 7–8; 166); and one from Theophanes' canon on the Annunciation (cf. lines 13–14 in *Op. 207*).

INDICES

I: PROPER NAMES

II: TERMS

φήμη, acclamation **200D VIII**.1.
φθορά, seduction **200B**.123.
φιλόχριστος **207**.114; (emperor) **191A**.16; **194 I**.3; **II**.8; **195**.2; **196**.3, 9; **197**.86.
φύλαρχος (of Arabs) **207**.156.

χαρτοφυλάκειον (of patriarchate) **191A**.3; **191B**.5 (ιερόν); **201**.3.
χαρτοφύλαξ (patriarchal) **201**.20.
χειροθεσία, ordination **197**.98.
χειροτονία **199 X**.1, 5.

ψῆφος **197**.142; **199 XX**.2; **200A**.38, 39; **206**.148.

ᾠδή (of canon) **203**.5, etc.

III: VOCABULARY

ἁγιστεία **200E**.13.
ἀγωνοθέτης **204**.121.
ἄδυτος, "never-setting" **203**.44.
αἱρετίζειν, "choose" **207**.5.
ἀκαπήλευτος **201**.9.
ἀκατάλυτος **199 XX**.23.
ἀκαταπόντιστος **207**.12.
ἀκμήν, "still" **193**.5.
ἀλαλάζειν, "wail" **203**.74.
ἀλογεῖν **192**.72.
ἀμειώτως **204**.90.
ἀμέτοχος **199 XX**.6; **200B**.89, 108; **200E**.22.
ἀμισθί **201**.2.
ἀμφέπειν **207**.113.
ἀνάγωγος **199 XXVI**.10.
ἀναίδην (= ἀνέδην) **197**.28.
ἀναισθησία **199 XXIII**.16.
ἀνακάθαρσις **200B**.98.
ἀνάκτορον **207**.111.
ἀναστροφή **194 II**.10; **197**.88.
ἀναχωρεῖν: ἀνακεχωρημένη ζωή **194 I**.4; **II**.9; **197**.87.
ἀναχώρησις (τοῦ βίου) **200B**.130.
ἀνευφημεῖν **205**.15.
ἀνήνυτος **192**.8.
ἀνθρώπιον **192**.34.
ἀντεισάγειν **200A**.30, 33.
ἀντιρρητικός (λόγος) **200B**.113 (var.).
ἀντωθεῖν **191A**.14.
ἀνύμφευτος **204**.67.
ἀνωμαλία **196**.11.
ἀξιέπαινος **201**.27.
ἀπαραιτήτως **194 II**.16; **197**.46, 94.
ἀπείρανδρος **203**.71.
ἀπειρόγαμος **203**.49; **206**.58.
ἀπηρυθριασμένως **200B**.74.
ἀπόβλητος **200B**.62.
ἀπόλεκτος **207**.142.
ἀπόρθητος **207**.96.
ἀποστασία **197**.26.
ἀποσχίζειν **201A**.1–2 (var.).
ἀστατεῖν **194 I**.5; **II**.10; **197**.88.
ἀσυγχώρητος **200B**.101; -ως **200B**.107.
ἀταλαιπώρως **191A**.7.
ἄτεγκτος **200A**.17.
αὐτεξούσιος **199 XXII**.9.

θεόνυμφος **207**.99.
θεοτόκος **200B**.113 (var.), 114; **203**.1; **204**.15, 66, 86, 109, 138; **206**.40, 85, 121, 166; **207**.1, 146, 167, 171, 194.
θεόφρων **204**.134.
θεοχαρίτωτος **206**.190.
θεσπίζειν **199 XIX**.7 (bis).
θρηνητικός **203**.1.

ἱκετικῶς **207**.69.

καθυπομένειν **207**.47.
καταιγίς **200B**.51; **206**.133; **207**.41, 153.
κατασεμνύνειν **204**.82.
καταστίζειν **203**.59, 111.
καταυγάζειν **206**.96.
καταφωτίζειν **206**.92.
κατευοδοῦν (pass.) **193**.8.
κατορχεῖσθαι **192**.59.
κῆρυξ (τῆς μυσαρᾶς τελετῆς), muezzin **207**.130.
κιβωτός (of Virgin) **204**.83; **207**.183.
κόριον **206**.127.
κρημνίζεσθαι **206**.73.
κυριοτόκος **206**.58.
κωφεύειν **192**.97.

λῆξις (ἡ κάτω) **207**.63.

ματαιοῦν **204**.68.
μεθαρμόζειν **201**.7.
μελλοαύγουστος **193**.1.
μεταστοιχειοῦν **201**.6.
μισόχριστος **207**.18.
μνηστεία **199 V**.2.
μνηστεύεσθαι **199 V**.3; **201**.10.

μόνωσις **199 II**.3.
μυροφόροι (αἱ) **203**.117, 123.

ναὸς θεοῦ (of Virgin) **204**.83.
νυμφαγωγεῖν **199 I**.4.
νυμφαγωγία **199 I**.5.
νυμφαγωγός **199 V**.3.
νυμφοστόλος **199 XXIX**.4.

ὁλολαμπής **206**.46.
ὁλοψύχως **206**.86.
ὁμογνωμοσύνη **195**.5; **196**.2.
ὁμόζυγος **192**.47.
ὁμοταγής **191A**.14.
οὐρανοῦν **205**.2.
οὐρανοφάντωρ **206**.79.

παλάτιον **207**.166.
παλίμφημος **207**.129.
πανάγιος **206**.35, 52; παναγία **206**.19, 168, 186.
πάναγνος **200B**.26; **200C**.3; **203**.89; **204**.33; **206**.120; **207**.9.
πανάμωμος **203**.122; **207**.66.
παναοίδιμος **206**.76.
πανάχραντος **203**.100; **204**.28.
πανίερος **200E**.27.
πανοικτίρμων **203**.92.
πανύμνητος **206**.85.
παρενοχλεῖν **199 XXIV**.6.
παρόπτης **201**.25.
παστάς: ἐν τῇ μυστικῇ π. **197**.8; π. ἔμψυχος (of Virgin) **204**.84.
πέλειν **206**.44.
περίβολος: οἱ ἱεροὶ π. **199 XVII**.3.
περιποίησις **207**.37.
περίπυστος **207**.111.

IV: CITATIONS

Bible

V: INCIPITS

CORPUS FONTIUM HISTORIAE BYZANTINAE

SERIES WASHINGTONIENSIS, EDITOR JOHN M. DUFFY

DUMBARTON OAKS TEXTS

De Administrando Imperio
Constantine VII Porphyrogenitus
Gyula Moravcsik | R. J. H. Jenkins
CFHB 1 • DOT 1

Nicholas I, Patriarch of Constantinople: Letters
R. J. H. Jenkins | L. G. Westerink
CFHB 6 • DOT 2

Nicholas I, Patriarch of Constantinople: Miscellaneous Writings
L. G. Westerink
CFHB 20 • DOT 6

The Correspondence of Athanasius I, Patriarch of Constantinople
Alice-Mary Talbot
CFHB 7 • DOT 3

The Letters of Manuel II Palaeologus
George T. Dennis
CFHB 8 • DOT 4

The Synodicon Vetus
John Duffy | Thomas S. Parker
CFHB 15 • DOT 5

Letters of Gregory Akindynos
Angela Constantinides Hero
CFHB 21 • DOT 7

The Correspondence of Leo, Metropolitan of Synada and Syncellus
M. P. Vinson
CFHB 23 • DOT 8

Three Byzantine Military Treatises
George T. Dennis
CFHB 25 • DOT 9

Nikephoros, Patriarch of Constantinople: Short History
Cyril Mango
CFHB 13 • DOT 10

The Correspondence of Ignatios the Deacon
Cyril Mango | Stephanos Efthymiadis
CFHB 39 • DOT 11

The Taktika *of Leo VI*
George T. Dennis
CFHB 49 • DOT 12

The Life of Patriarch Ignatius
Nicetas David
Andrew Smithies | John M. Duffy
CFHB 51 • DOT 13

COMMENTARIES

De Administrando Imperio*: A Commentary*
R. J. H. Jenkins

A Critical Commentary on the Taktika *of Leo VI*
John F. Haldon

Please visit www.doaks.org/publications
for other books in this series and many other books about Byzantium.